Library of
Davidson College

Approaches to Democracy
Philosophy of Government at the Close of the Twentieth Century

Approaches to Democracy

Philosophy of Government at the Close of the Twentieth Century

W. J. Stankiewicz

St. Martin's Press
New York

© 1980 S. J. Stankiewicz

All rights reserved. For information, write:
St. Martin's Press, Inc., 175 Fifth Avenue, New York, NY 10010
Printed in Great Britain
First published in the United States of America in 1981

Library of Congress Cataloging in Publication Data

Stankiewicz, Wladyslaw Jozef
   Approaches to democracy.
   Bibliography: p.
   Includes index.
   1. Democracy.   I. Title.
JC423.S825   1981   320.5′1   80–21737
ISBN 0–312–04668–5

To Marketa

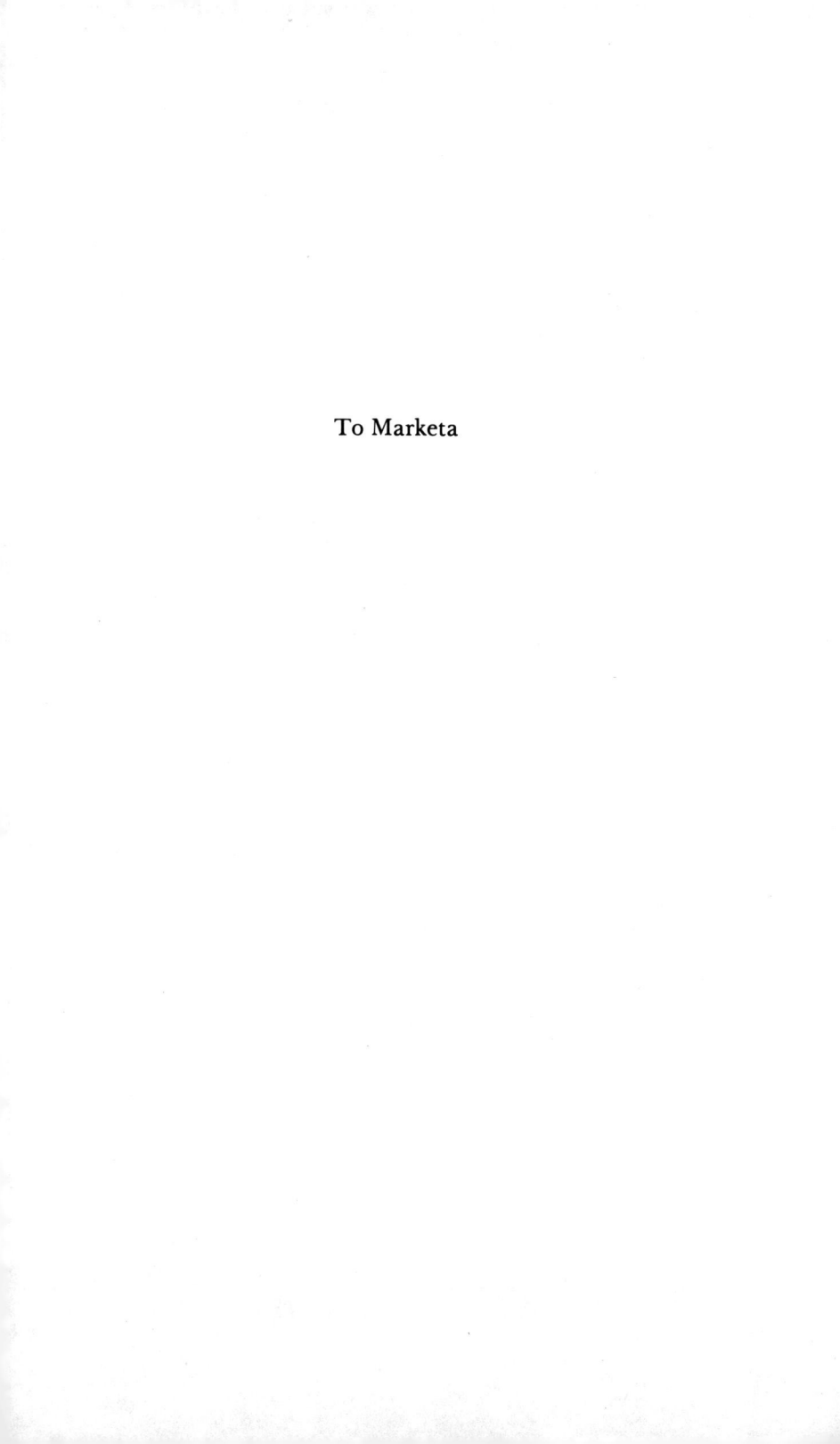

Books by W. J. Stankiewicz

Institutional Changes in the Postwar Economy of Poland (with J. M. Montias) (1955)
Politics & Religion in Seventeenth-Century France (1960)
Canada-US Relations & Canadian Foreign Policy (1973)
Aspects of Political Theory: Classical Concepts in an Age of Relativism (1976)
Approaches to Democracy: Philosophy of Government at the Close of the Twentieth Century (1980)

Anthologies and Symposia

Political Thought Since World War II: Critical & Interpretive Essays (1964)
The Living Name (1964)
Crisis in British Government: the Need for Reform (1967)
In Defense of Sovereignty (1969)
British Government in an Era of Reform (1976)

Essays and Aphorisms

What is Behavioralism? Thoughts on the Crisis in the Social Sciences (1971)
Relativism: Thoughts & Aphorisms (1972)
A Guide to Democratic Jargon (1976)

Contents

Preface

I Introductory: Reason, Relativism And Democracy   1

Anti-Rationalism   5
Reason and Non-rational Behaviour   7
Democratic Theory and Current Norms of
    Democracy   9
Democratic Theory is Not Served by
    Arguing 'From the Actual to the Possible'   12
Relativism, Egalitarianism and the
    Justification of Democracy   14

II The Relevance Of Democratic Theory To Democracy   18

Violence, Coercion and Relativism   27
Violence, Social Change and Normativism   31
Political Obligation, Obedience and Coercion   33
The Normative Position of Violence in
    Theories of Obligation   36
Can Violence be Justified?   39
Violence, Historical Studies and Functional
    Analysis   46
Violence and Political Decision-making   49
Comparative Political Violence   52
Violence, Human Nature and Behaviouralist
    Determinism   54
Violence and Democratic Theory   61

III Pitfalls In Democratic Theorizing 64

The Problem of Unconscious Relativism in
   Political Theory 64
Schumpeter's Hidden Relativism 65
Niebuhr's Unwitting Relativism 71
Tingsten's Sociological Relativism 77
Macpherson's Deterministic Relativism 82
Braybrooke's Relativistic-Normative Analysis 87

IV The Lesson Of Anti-Democratic Thinking 94

Anarchism and the Concept of Democratic
   Authority 94
Anarchism and Participation 97
Tolerance Under a Democratic System of
   Values 98
Can Democratic Tolerance be Absolute? 100
'Repressive Tolerance' 103
Can Tolerance be Subversive? 106
Erosion of the Rule of Law 108
Instrumentalist Revolution 113

V The Insufficiency Of Apologetics 117

Electoral Systems and H.B. Mayo's Justification
   of Democracy 118
Electoral System as a Norm 121
Theory as a Justification of Practice 126
Democratic Apologetics and the Democratic
   Ideology 129
Beyond Justification: Thorson's Challenge to
   Epistemological Assumptions 133

VI The Insufficiency Of Empirical Theory 138

Partial Theories 138
Systems Theories 141
Structural Functionalism and Input-Output
   Analysis 144

Behaviouralist Images of Democracy	150
The Camera Artists	155
Limitations of Empirical Democratic Theory	157

VII 'Participation' In Democratic Theory — 160

Participation and Democratization	161
The Illusion of Participation	163
Participation and Radicalization	164
Participatory Democracy and Citizenship	166
Participation and Human Nature	170
Social Contract and Participation	172
Participation and Relativism	176

VIII Whither Democratic Theory? — 179

The Insufficiency of 'Realism'	179
The Insufficiency of the 'Pure Politics' Approach to Democratic Theory	181
Group Theory and Neo-pluralism	183
Group Theory and Human Rights	183
Neo-pluralism as a Theory of Power	186
Neo-pluralism and Relativism	188
Kelso's Three Types of Pluralism	191
Democracy as a Formal Machinery of Rights, Obligations and Procedures	195
Property, Equality and Freedom	200
Macpherson's Protective Model of Democracy	200
Macpherson's Participatory Model of Democracy	203
Is Property a Norm?	205
Rawls and His Critics	212
Freedom, Equality and Reason Under Deterministic and Non-deterministic Analysis	212
Prudentialism and the Social Contract	216
Justice and Power: Democratic Violence	218
Totalitarianism and the Redistribution of Property	222

Rawls's Norm of Justice and Theory of
  Justice 225
In Defence of Yves R. Simon 228
  The Common Good and Relativism 228
  Simon's Theory in Our Time 231
Behaviouralism, Biosociology and the Perils of
  Biobehaviouralism 234
Postscript 242
  Political Theory and Political Freedom:
    The Problem of Prediction 242
  'Frontiers' of Democratic Theory 247
  Can Democratic Theory Reorder Society? 251
  The Impact of Relativism 254

Bibliography 258
Index 262

Preface

The present volume is a continuation of a longer work on political theory planned under the general heading of RELATIVISM IN POLITICS. The earlier volume, *Aspects of Political Theory* (Collier Macmillan, London, 1976), dealt with basic 'classical' concepts. While the present book is concerned with the theory of modern liberal democracy, it is a commentary on current ways of thinking about the democratic system and its values, in particular the questions of (a) the relevance of democratic theory to democracy (b) the insufficiency of the existing 'justifications' of democracy, and (c) the limitations of empirical democratic theory (seen against the background of all-pervading relativism). Each book may be read as an independent work.

I am grateful to my friends: Professors D.C. Corbett, Maurice Cranston, F.H. Hinsley and Anthony Parel and the late Roy Daniells for their interest and encouragement; and to Mr R.C. Cooke and Mr I.W. Peyman for their most valuable help. I am indebted to the Canada Council and the I.W. Killam Memorial Fund for the grant of a Leave Fellowship and a Senior Killam Fellowship respectively.

The work on this book proceeded partly in conjunction with the previous volume. Similar acknowledgements therefore apply in both cases. Some of the ideas developed here were aired before responsive audiences during my lecture tours in New Zealand, Australia and Southern Africa.

Part of Chapter IV appeared in *Contemporary Review* (September 1977); and parts of Chapters V and VIII in *Politikon* (December 1978 and December 1979 respectively).

University of British Columbia   W.J. Stankiewicz
October 1979

I
Introductory: Reason, Relativism And Democracy

Democracy is sometimes advanced as evidence of a force of reason in society. It supposedly requires the electorate to cultivate the capacity for making rational decisions about their representatives and to vote accordingly. One does not pretend that in fact men are as informed and rational in their choices as they should be. The argument is that because members of a democracy have a choice of a kind no other political order allows and that the choice does affect the laws under which men live, it is in the latter's interest to cultivate a capacity for rational decision-making. A choice between two men of similar ability and similar views may seem trivial, yet it is said to require the type of weighing of issues that occurs in any kind of moral decision-making. Thus — the argument runs — democratic man is trained in rational decision-making and in being responsible in an ethical sense.

If this is the case, it appears surprising that relativism should characterize the ethical outlook of so many. It focuses so steadfastly on intrinsic norms originating in the 'self' that the concept of ethical responsibility no longer has any clear meaning. What I want to do or get done is the normative standard and what I actually do is the evidence of what I want. An 'ought' does not exist in relativist ethical situations, except as a matter of personal regret, when an action does not lead to the expected result: 'I ought to have voted for the other man' or 'I ought to have taken the road to the right.' This 'ought' has no bearing on the 'ought' implied when we talk of 'responsibility.' It leads, at most, to a largely indifferent regret, not a sense of guilt or a desire to reform. There is nothing one can feel guilty about. The 'error' was accidental and unpredictable and relates primarily to the desires of the self.

The pervasive influence of relativism can hardly lie in any rational appeal. There are other elements at work. Where the Church of an earlier period directed men's thought toward notions of absolute natural law, modern democracy promotes relativism. It does it so successfully that many intellectuals believe that they are relativists because they have reasoned out the nature of norms. But their assumption is wrong. Like the common man they have accepted relativism in order to be — in their own eyes — 'good' citizens. It appears that most men want to believe in relativism and are ready to overlook its obvious deficiencies for the sake of a rational consistency imposed by some other factor at play in our society. They say in effect that the norms of a private citizen in his private relations reflect his own normative judgement, but that the norms of his society — such as the legal code — also have a claim on him: they reflect the collective normative judgement of the majority, whose private judgement has determined that this shall be so. In this view, it is impossible for anyone to assert that his private judgement prevents him from observing the law. If he does that, he is asserting that he is anti-social, or criminal. All that the individual can say is that his private judgement compels him to influence others to adopt his position, so that eventually the collective judgement of the majority will change the disputed part of the legal code.

What is implied in such a view is a statement about the democratic process of voting which takes no notice of any of the normative assumptions on which democracy is based. The old problems of rights and natural law, liberty and equality, and so forth are ignored. There is no attempt to analyse the norms that are used in making private judgements. It is clearly immaterial to the decision-making process whether these norms are, or are not, absolute and rational. Once we accept that private judgement is the standard, there is no point in analysing the nature of norms any further.

It is the relativists' view of reason which in their case gives such a restricted sense to 'norms'. Under relativism the application of reason means 'action consistent with the system'; 'norms' refer to the result of such an action. This view of norms is inadequate as a description. They emerge here as Hobbes's desires and aversions without any of the 'dictate of right reason' which converted them into 'natural laws'. We could have no objection to the relativist simplification of the Hobbesian scheme if it supplied anything close to the Hobbesian system — a set of principles that look like norms by which men abide. This is the minimum requirement of any ethical system which bases its conclusions on a supposed connection between man's nature and his norms. The norms found there must resemble the norms known to us by empirical observation. Relativist 'norms' are so utterly unlike those we usually have in mind that we easily overlook the fact that modern relativism is a variation of the theory of natural law, in which 'law' reflects the shifting, ephemeral desires of men. It is prepared to include a sort of 'reason' as a norm, but its analysis of norms does not allow us to incorporate a rational element into normative behaviour in the way required by empirical observation.

It is the rational element in normative behaviour which allows us to refer to the latter as a 'law'. Reason supplies the obligation to obey, a measure of codification and a degree of permanence that enable us to see a parallel between moral norms and positive law. The concept of natural law, however, has no appeal today for anyone, even for the advocates of law and order.[1]

Relativists claim that all natural law advocates are utterly mistaken: man is not a rational being. Reason may or may not be present in any particular society. It is not universally present in democratic societies today and therefore, they say, it is useless to talk about natural law or 'public philosophy', a phrase that shifts the emphasis even more onto reason.

An interesting case is provided by the reception given to Walter Lippmann's concept of 'public philosophy'. Apart from the reviews written immediately after the appearance of the book *Essays in the Public Philosophy* (1955), there has been no significant debate. One looks in vain for seminal commentaries.[2]

---

[1] One suspects that many advocate 'law and order' because they see positive law as the maximum set of restrictions on their 'freedom': once they have accommodated themselves to it, they are free do to as they choose. This may explain why so many both advocate strict legalism and protest further extensions of the law into new areas. Such individuals do not want to think of a normative code as an internal supplement to positive law: it strikes at the root of their conception of man in society.

[2] Thus, in the end, one must play devil's advocate and invent an objection to Lippmann. Does not the concept of a 'public philosophy', one may well argue, attempt to solve the problems of society by demanding an attitude which does not exist in order to counter one that does? Relativists might be quite prepared to concede that if it did exist, it would work in the way that Lippmann postulates, but as realists they must insist

Our society has moved far from an interest in ideas, which development might seem to the relativist proof of our increasing 'realism', our insistence that facts are everything. What one must recognize is that this indifference to ideas is in a way normative. Someone must be teaching that ideas 'ought not' to have the consequences they obviously have — that it is not valid, for instance, to argue that Christianity and communism have profoundly affected the course of human history. In truth, ideas are the most important 'facts' relating to human behaviour. When a society stops believing this, we must look for something that rationally compels its members to disregard the evidence.

Precisely what is it in our society that causes many persons to employ reason to deny the operation of reason in human affairs? The problem is of primary concern to anyone advocating rational normative behaviour. Lippmann and other advocates of some form of natural law (like A.P.d'Entrèves) obviously put their faith in man. Several thousand years of recorded evidence show that man everywhere, under all conceivable social orders, either holds fast to reason or uses reason to advocate unreason and then returns to a rational order again. (But this kind of faith gives comfort only if you look back in a society which has some respect for the past. When we look ahead in a society which denies that history has any relevance, it is difficult to remain optimistic.) For obvious reasons, we have no record of societies that consistently taught unreason, but we suspect that they did not flourish. So long as we hold that a denial of the validity of ideas and norms is socially induced and that the solution to our problems requires a return to a 'public philosophy', our immediate problem is to search out the factors in our society that lead to the counter view.

Relativism is convincing and acceptable to many because it stops its analysis at the point where popular thought begins, and it does so for social rather than philosophic reasons: academic theorists want to believe in democracy just as much as the common man. The only basis for democracy becomes the purely

---

that there is no public philosophy. Hence, if it is to be proffered as a solution, the main emphasis should not be on its value as a solution — as in Lippmann — but on the method of introducing it. And here is the crux of an imaginary relativist criticism: Lippmann presupposes the very rationality he is advocating.

relativist view that democracy is a normative system expressing non-normative feelings — the 'I know where the shoe pinches' theory of democracy. If you begin with this assumption, the evidence of a rational element in norms becomes evidence against 'democracy', for it makes it impossible to believe in the traditional wisdom of the electorate — however educated, rational, right-thinking and selfless the latter may be. In these conditions, any answer to relativism must be accompanied by an analysis of democracy capable of establishing that we do not need to throw aside our political system merely because the common man does not have any of the personal attributes necessary to convert the will of all into the General Will. The task of political theory is to counter the powerful negative force which influences current social philosophy. Until this is done and relativist-induced concepts are replaced (e.g. relativist 'sovereignty' by neo-classical sovereignty), socio-political theorizing will probably continue to be based on a demonstrably false description of norms.[3]

Anti-rationalism

Many defences of the modern suspicion of reason have been offered: man is not a rational being; reason demands a completely impossible 'objectivity'; the objective world can hardly be rationally ordered unless one assumes a rational orderer, whose existence is thrown in doubt by reason; reason conflicts with such principles as the quantum theory for which there is irrefutable evidence; reason has a well-known history of pure invention, etc. But the widespread acceptance of anti-rationalism not only among philosophers and scientists but also among laymen, despite the fact that the subtlest understanding and the most intricate analysis would seem necessary before a position could be taken, strongly suggests that modern anti-rationalism is not based on Hume, Freud and St Francis of

[3]A neo-classical definition of sovereignty is given in my *Aspects of Political Theory* (London, 1976): *'sovereignty refers to the necessary presence in any political order incorporating heterogeneous elements, themselves capable of exercising power, of an ultimate decision-maker whose decisions relating to his function are recognized as binding and/or can be enforced.'* (p. 76) The importance of the concept is also discussed in my symposium *In Defense of Sovereignty* (New York, 1969) and in the article 'Sovereignty', *Encyclopaedia Britannica* (15th edition, 1974).

Assisi. More probably it is forced upon us whether we like it or not, no matter how inconvenient it is for us to be left without any method of analysing our goals and society except empiricism, which by its nature can tell us nothing about what we do except that we do it.

Anti-rationalism is forced on us by our method of — allegedly — making decisions by counting heads. This is a rational method only when used as a final resort to break a deadlock when reason can go no further, as in its use of the Supreme Court. Originally, that is what voting was supposed to do. It was the condition that made the majority rule compatible with minority rights. The assumption was that when the issue had been debated and reason showed no clear path, a deadlock could be avoided if the principle of majority rule were applied. It was a principle that recognized that inaction is a kind of action that is seldom acceptable to either party to a disagreement. When made the primary principle of political action, however, it raises serious difficulties in respect of minority rights: the latter, under the primacy of majority rule principle, are reduced to a set of restrictions of dubious power and uncertain extent. What power they have depends upon the degree of tolerance within the society. In other words, if the principle of majority rule is shifted from a position of last resort to that of first resort, 'tolerance,' not reason, becomes the primary value of the society, the one without which the system will not work.

There is no real incompatibility between reason and tolerance, of course. Indeed, many argue that reason reveals the necessity of tolerance. But when decisions about goals and methods are theoretically based on the primacy of the majority principle, reason has in effect been rejected as a method of decision-making. To advocate reason is to deny that the majority principle should be accepted as a method of selecting representatives, unless one is willing to argue that all those who have the franchise are equally capable of making a rational choice. This has not, however, been a tenable view for some time past. We know too much about biological inheritance to suppose ever again that the 'right' environment will produce the equality that the original democratic theory required. By endorsing a particular method of obtaining an orderly succession of governments, then, our society unconsciously demands the rejection of reason. But the matter is so important to continuance of the political order in its present form, however, that society must also consciously reject it. The emphasis placed by social scientists and other servants of the political order on the irrationality of man, on the power of the subconscious and the importance of early experience in determining behaviour, on the hold of custom and the primacy of the biological drives over the secondary drives imposed by society, and their general tendency to interpret all reason as a form of rationalization, are not supported by unequivocal evidence. To say the least, the evidence for or against reason is ambiguous, and if we find democratic societies emphasizing one over the other the explanation is to be found in the norms of the society rather than in the 'facts' that are ostensibly the sole consideration.

Reason and Non-rational Behaviour

In what sense is the modern man 'rational'? He is not rational in the eighteenth-century sense of being always guided by reason. We assume rather that man is rational in Hobbes's sense: if the social conditions for rational behaviour are not present, man may be compelled to go against rational self-interest. In the hypothetic state of nature, rational self-interest (immediate circumstances) compels him to violate rational self-interest (long-range). As a result, democratic societies have devoted a good deal of attention to the analysis of conditions promoting non-rational behaviour.

Most 'welfare' schemes in fact can be better understood in terms of their promoting conditions necessary to 'rational' behaviour than as manifestations of democratic norms. Thus the limitations placed on economic welfare schemes — following the slogan 'No one shall starve', rather than 'All shall have equal resources' — suggest that the State is interested primarily in eliminating desperation and the irrational behaviour that follows it. Such would also seem to be the basis for the inclusion of 'mental health' in welfare programs (even though it has no obvious connection with any democratic norm) and why the State is prepared to violate democratic norms, as in legislation dealing with alcohol and drugs. Thus drugs are a 'clear and present danger', not because they result in anti-social behaviour in the usual sense but because their use is based on a preference for non-rational experience. Such a preference is not acceptable to our society.

So strong is the demand for rational behaviour that since the rise of modern democracy even the forms of pastime and entertainment have been affected. Governments have legislated against pastimes based on non-rational chance. Card games, even when money stakes are not involved, are considered a 'low' form of entertainment, rising in rank only as the amount of skill involved rises — bridge has more prestige than poker, and poker more than craps.

Whether such social attitudes to non-rational types of behaviour affect the incidence of the latter and, more important, reinforce 'reason' as a methodology is by no means certain. The essential point for political theory is that democratic societies have evidently long recognized two things: first, that reason is essential to our society; secondly, that whatever its basis in human nature, it functions as a norm: we can choose to behave rationally or not. Reason seems to be considered essential to our society because it mediates between norms.

(It may turn out that 'reason' is a technique of communication. Even if it is no more than a pure cultural invention or, like language, predominantly cultural but having an obscure basis in our biology, it would seem as indispensable as language to the learning and teaching of most human culture. Although one feels that 'reason' permits us to communicate everything we deem essential, it has never been able to say much about the arts, religion and love. Thus 'aesthetics' has not been able to convey anything an artist or aesthete finds interesting. Art and 'reason' use different languages and that of 'reason' is not, as the eighteenth century supposed, a universal language.)

There is no denying that democracy was advanced by the philosophically inclined as a rational system of government — it was meant to provide a structure for decision-making which is rational — and that there is nothing inherent in democracy that compels us to suspect the claims of reason. But democracy as popularly conceived is the culprit: it has induced a reaction to reason. Popular democracy and the Romantic movement — which developed together — repudiated the Age of

Reason that supplied their foundations. For two centuries now the literature of democratic society has been Romantic, opposing 'feeling' and 'imagination' to 'reason', 'freedom' to 'form', 'sensibility' to 'sense', the 'private' to the 'public'. As an expression of individual experience it has value; it has also helped to promote democratic social reform movements. But for all its emphasis on 'realism', its representation of man's relation to society is unrealistic. Characteristically, man and society are placed in opposition: man is represented as the victim of his society rather than a beneficiary. Reason would suggest that this does not make sense as a general statement about man's condition.

Thus the real problem for the theorist is to alter certain popular conceptions of democracy. There will be no 'public philosophy' until man can feel safe with reason.

Can political theory supply an understandable account of democracy which, like the relativist conception, gives each man the sense that as an individual he has an assured right (not just a legal right) to vote? (Or, alternatively, an argument which is so convincing, even in an age of popular relativism, that we can move from universal franchise, open-public-office-form of democracy to some other form that can equally be called democracy.) Problems of democracy arise from the elective system, not in the sense that the latter allows uninformed, weak government, but that it promotes relativism and a hostility to reason which undermines government by removing rational restraints and rational goals.

In present conditions the advocate of reason in human affairs has a twofold problem: he must establish that relativism is not a necessary condition for democracy or for the sense of individuality; and he must simultaneously deal with the relativists' claims that they make the only 'reasonable' assumption about human behaviour. He must consequently confront the question whether democratic theory is possible.

Democratic Theory and Current Norms of Democracy

The question whether democratic theory is possible can initially be reformulated as follows: Can political theory bridge the gap between its traditional normative assumptions and current democratic norms? This cannot be answered without inquiring into: first, the nature of the relationship between political theory and the democratic framework; secondly, the way in which norms influence socio-political behaviour. If the former reveals the difficulties inherent in the part played by political theory, the latter discloses the theory's crucial role vis-à-vis democracy. One should be clear, however, that all that reformulations of this type can achieve is to unveil the complexities of the problems. The initial question — Is democratic theory possible? — remains open.

Political theory should be of major concern in a democracy which advances the proposition that all normative questions raised within society can be fitted into the conceptual framework expressed by the terms 'freedom' and 'equality', the former representing the individual's normative claims, the latter those of society.[4] This is not, however, how political theory views these concepts. In the early days of modern democracy, they were in themselves norms with an ascribed content: it was natural to talk about 'freedom of speech', 'freedom of assembly', 'equality before the law', etc. when men were supposed to be by nature 'free' and 'equal'. But discussions of these concepts as norms nowadays either become unduly formal — 'freedom' means what the constitution says, etc. — or else they rise to levels of abstraction which can be of interest only to linguistic philosophers. Who among those involved in a debate about the busing of school children in the USA — which everyone recognizes as a debate about the respective claims of 'freedom' and 'equality' — would dream of asking for the opinion of a political theorist? In any case, few theorists would care to become involved in such controversies or would know how to handle them.

But what is even more significant, many theorists today put forward the proposition that such controversies 'ought not' to occur and that the participants misunderstand the nature of normative issues in a democracy. 'Democracy', they say, involves

---

[4]In modern democratic theory the term 'fraternity' has never quite achieved the status or importance of either 'freedom' or 'equality'. In the words of Ferdinand Mount: 'The ideas of Freedom and Equality are far more rewarding topics...[they] are rhetorically intensifiable. The orator can promise *more* of them'. ('The Dilution of Fraternity', *Encounter*, Vol. XLVII, No. 4 [October 1976], p. 31).

a commitment to a certain method of resolving normative conflict: 'tolerance', 'majority rule', 'adherence to the constitution' or some variant or combination of these norms. What they mean by this is that in their eyes the democratic system is essentially relativistic and cannot tolerate non-relativistic attitudes. Anyone who professes to believe this is simply admitting that his normative set is being served by 'democracy'.

Thus 'freedom' and 'equality' have ceased to be norms having an understandable content and have become a conceptual framework into which all norms within the society must fit if they are to be recognized as anything more than private sets of values. It is no longer possible to analyse the concepts of 'freedom' and 'equality' and arrive at an understanding of any of the problems put forward as issues of 'freedom' and 'equality'. By doing this we are approaching the issues from the wrong direction. When they occur in a democracy, the arguments put forward are necessarily couched in these terms, but they have their normative base in the much larger set of norms within society itself. As a result, one cannot arrive at the controversy about school busing, or any other democratic problem, from either the premise of 'freedom' or 'equality', although these are the norms one cannot avoid applying. The trouble is that theorists want to keep on doing what made good sense in the eighteenth century but is no longer valid.[5]

Understandably, the democratic theorist is reluctant to plunge into debates on controversial issues of the type mentioned and he has shown this reluctance by representing such debates as issues in relativism unperceived as such by the contestants. In effect, he promotes relativism in order to preserve his ivory tower. On the other hand, there has been a reaction by some theorists against the ivory tower syndrome and an insistence that the theorist be an activist. But neither position is really tenable. We do not know enough about norms to be able

---

[5] As Herbert Marcuse quite justly points out: 'Contemporary industrial civilization demonstrates that it has reached the stage at which "the free society" can no longer be adequately defined in the traditional terms of economic, political, and intellectual liberties, not because these liberties have become insignificant, but because they are too significant to be confined within the traditional forms.' (*One-Dimensional Man* [Boston, 1966], pp. 3-4). One does not need to make the assumptions about democratic societies and democratic norms that Marcuse makes, in order to recognize the truth of this assertion.

to describe all normative conflict as relativistic, nor do we know enough to become activists and take sides. What we do know is that if the controversy is to be settled democratically, the framework of 'freedom' and 'equality' must be applied by those who realize how agonizingly complex and delicate the balance between the two is and that a relativist stance is excluded by the very fact that a controversy exists.

Another difficulty is how to cope with such men as Marcuse, who are not relativists but dogmatists. Let us take, for instance, a single norm of our society rejected by Marcuse and by a large number of young people — the so-called 'protestant work ethic'. It is an important norm in our society — the economy could not operate without it — and in some systems of political ethics, such as the United Nations Declaration of Human Rights, it has been put forward as an aspect of 'freedom' — the right to work. Traditional democratic theory has virtually ignored it, for it cannot be derived from the abstract concept of freedom without a good deal of mental conjuring. One has to believe in the norm before one can represent it as an aspect of 'freedom', and it never struck the eighteenth-century theorists, who as a rule came from the leisured class, that anyone would actually want to work.[6] Not everyone does, of course, and that is why it is so foolish to represent it as a fundamental 'right'.

Theorists who try to convert their norms into 'rights' misconstrue their role. They pretend that you *can* derive the norm from the democratic framework and that the process of derivation makes it a right. Many of the outrageous demands made on democratic governments today stem from this absurd illogicality. It also does a serious disservice to democratic theory.

Democratic Theory Is Not Served by Arguing 'From the Actual to the Possible'

What does Carl Cohen achieve in his book *Democracy* by arguing that 'what is actual must be possible'? He continues:

[6] For them, time to reflect and cultivate the self was the obvious normative good, not 'work'. To the puritan, however, 'leisure' was 'idleness'. The devil finds work for idle hands, they said, by which they meant in part that leisure permitted cultivation of the sensuous appetites and/or cultivation of the critical mind. They were suspicious of both as being incompatible with 'faith'.

'The clearest proof of the practicality of full democracy is the actual existence and success of such government in some of the communities in which many of us participate every day.'[7] Does he show that democracy is possible?

The assertion 'what is actual must be possible' seems a self-evident truth until one realizes it is an argument, not a statement about the meaning of actual and possible. As an argument designed to promote the 'possible' it is obviously fallacious, for what is declared to be possible is evidently not the same as what is declared to be actual. The argument makes sense only if the two differ, but if so, the 'possible' receives no support from what is actual. A parallel argument would be that since water in fact freezes at $0°$ centigrade, it is possible for it to freeze at boiling point.

Cohen implicitly acknowledges the difference in situation when he notes two objections to the argument: firstly, that while participatory democracy is possible in small communities, it may not be possible in large ones; secondly, that even if possible, it may not be of the same kind ('depth'). To my mind, such objections are merely opinions. In their present form, they can be neither proved nor disproved.

There is a much more telling objection to Cohen's position which arises from the nature of his argument: the 'actual' he has in mind consists of small interacting groups in which the evidence for participatory democracy is limited to the decisions they make in terms of their common interest and knowledge. It is evident that the groups — which represent a selection of the public — can engage in participatory democracy only so long as they do not have the characteristics of the public. The same committee members who are capable of making policy decisions through participation are liable to disintegrate into quarreling factions when discussing matters outside their committee's frame of reference. The reason is plain: the committee can function as a committee because it has been selected on the basis of the qualities necessary — common interest, knowledge, ability. The farther we move from that situation, the smaller is the possibility of genuine participation.[8]

[7]Carl Cohen, *Democracy* (New York, 1971), p. 19.
[8]Let us take, for example, the case of large labour unions in the Western world, all of which theoretically practice participatory democracy by means of union meetings that

Do Cohen's arguments answer our question as to whether democratic *theory* is possible? Cohen assumes that democracy is a working — and workable — system; he believes that by describing how it works and by theorizing about it one can write democratic theory. He does not seem to believe that a theory needs to look beyond what is.[9] Furthermore, to him theory is a comparison of hypothetical descriptions showing some aspects of democracy visible in a varying degree in different societies. Or, it is a speculatively constructed framework for analysis in which the structure rests on the elements of function and behaviour rather than on interlocking ideas and clashing values. It is clear that a theory so conceived — a theory of 'abstracted quantification' — can at best be only a partial theory.

Relativism, Egalitarianism and the Justification of Democracy

It has been said that if God did not exist it would be necessary to invent Him. In order to make sense the mechanistic (as opposed to teleological) world view — which was behind the argument — needed a Designer of the mechanism. Today relativism serves a similar function with regard to political orders. It can be said that if philosophers had not invented relativism, egalitarians would have had to do so. If egalitarianism is to be accepted as a norm in a world which in fact consists of unequals, a relativistic attitude to ideas, goals, norms and policies is necessary so that the resulting differences of opinion are of no real significance. It is precisely relativism that serves this function. In fact relativism can be regarded as the ethics of egalitarianism.

---

set policy and elect officials to implement it. In fact, most unions are compulsory organizations in which the members have much less control over their officials than the public has over its politicians. The reason is that no union has evolved the complex system of organized opposition and checks and balances characteristic of democratic government. The myth of participatory democracy seems to have prevented it. As a result, governments have repeatedly had to step in to correct abuses in the unions' power struggles. The real danger in the notion of participatory democracy is that it is an indirect attack on the controls we have evolved to prevent the abuse of power.

[9]His ironic footnote about the academic man commenting on an intricate machine seems to reaffirm this position: 'Yes, I see that it works in practice. But does it work in theory?' Cohen brushes aside the academic's obsession with pure theory as ridiculous: 'The clearest proof of the practicality of full democracy is the actual existence and success of such government.' Cohen, *op. cit.*, p. 19.

The Justification of Democracy

(Consequently, we can define relativism as that attitude to norms which enables us to act as if egalitarianism and only egalitarianism were the fundamental norm of the 'good' society.) This in turn leads to the obliteration of distinctions between totally different political orders such as democracy and communism: since egalitarianism is an essential element of both forms of government, it can be supposed that they are both 'good' societies and in essence the same. In other words, both are 'democratic'.[10]

One can assume that in the social sciences relativism does not derive from any philosophic attitude but from the 'self-evident truth' of literal equality. The latter, in the absence of natural law norms, requires us to suppose that decisions about right and wrong are ultimately personal decisions and that one decision is as good as another, so that if a policy is to be made, a show of hands will establish what the 'good' for the society is. (The policy, of course, is not unalterable but depends on the current feeling of the majority.) There are unanswerable theoretical objections to this populist view of democracy but, for the peculiar kind of relativism which rejects all absolutes except egalitarianism, this is a congenial view. Unlike political theorists, who recognize that 'democracy' in any meaningful sense involves a tension between egalitarianism and freedom (or individualism), behaviouralists can focus on one single aspect of democracy — egalitarianism — and (ignoring the theoretical problems that beset the theorist) pretend that data derived from the way people behave can serve as a basis for theory. This, in turn, establishes in their minds the conviction that much of the 'traditional' theory is false or idle speculation. The latter would be true if in fact democracy were what behaviouralists claim it is — a method of proving relativism. But such a view is incompatible with democracy as we know it and as it has revealed itself historically. In effect, relativism has been used to re-define democracy.

In what sense does relativism imply democracy and how can

---

[10]Lately, the views of C.B. Macpherson on the basic 'sameness' of all political orders have achieved wide currency (See Chapter III below). The absurdity of these views needs no further stress. The point is that the 'originality' of their author consisted mainly in his falling headlong into the trap sprung by the egalitarians and giving wide publicity to their mode of thought.

democracy be seen as the justification of relativism? All systems of government require and presuppose a set of norms or an attitude to norms over and above the normative set that justifies the particular political order. Thus, in classical political theory, aristocracy or rule by the best means little unless there is a 'good' and a 'better'. So, too, monarchy and oligarchy — even though the concept of quality is not inherent in their concept of quantity — require a defence in terms of norms: it may or may not be true that the governed cannot govern themselves, but it is not true that a principle of government opposed to that supposed truth is justified by this. It is one thing to prove that government is necessary, but quite different arguments are required to justify specific forms. (This is a major objection to those theories which fail to clarify what the real principles of government are; we know only that government is necessary, but that is not enough.) Even democracy is confronted by the problem. One can no more say *vox populi vox dei* than one can speak of the divine right of kings. A set of principles is needed and it is this set which forms the real basis of arguments for particular forms of government.

Historically, the arguments for democracy were based on the contention that men had the capacity to govern themselves — that the principles necessary to government were in some way inherent in all men. Modern arguments based on the idea that the wearer knows best where the shoe pinches were unthinkable in the past. The reason is that this kind of argument is relativistic and a relativistic argument was for long unable to make headway against an argument for the divine right of kings or against aristocracy. Only when as a result of the historical advance of democracy such alternative forms of government ceased to be genuine alternatives, could the logic of egalitarianism find full expression in relativism. Now relativism can show that only democracy fulfils its necessary presuppositions and conversely it may seem now that only relativism is suited to democracy. In effect, relativism and democracy prove each other.[11]

---

[11]Can political science support such a proposition? As has been said, historically the assumption was made that the people have the knowledge and virtues necessary for government. But analysis of actual voting behaviour shows the facts to be different. There are several possible responses: (a) educate the public in the necessary qualities;

The Justification of Democracy

The assertion that relativism implies democracy has served as a justification of the democratic system. No justification of this type, however, can be satisfactory. It is true that relativism precludes any kind of value order but the democratic:[12] its rejection of moral standards makes it imperative to adopt democratic procedures as the only way by which the right action can be determined. But the argument glosses over the question whether relativism is desirable and that we in fact may require a different system of value order; it ignores other possible alternatives which may be more acceptable at some future time. If relativism leads to democracy, democracy on the other hand need not be based solely and exclusively on the relativistic set of values. Furthermore, as Holden has pointed out, the argument is self-contradictory,[13] for it derives a judgement regarding the moral basis of democracy ('that democracy ought to emerge') from an assertion which denies the possibility of making such judgements.

(b) make such changes in the system that in effect only those with the qualities required can vote or stand for office; (c) accept the reality of voting behaviour and defend it as the good. The latter approach is necessarily relativistic. It takes no great acumen to realize that political 'realists' are relativists. Now the facts of democracy, not just democratic theory, promote relativism.

[12] See my *Aspects of Political Theory* (London, 1976), p. 125.

[13] Barry Holden, *The Nature of Democracy* (London, 1974), p. 213.

II
The Relevance Of Democratic Theory To Democracy

Traditionally there have been two basic approaches to democratic theory: the analysis of, and attempts to remedy, conflicts between its normative requirements; and analysis of and, efforts to resolve, conflicts between the theory and its institutional expression. Any other type of 'problem' that has arisen in democracies has been regarded as the province of other disciplines. It is not indifference to the practicalities of everyday life that has promoted this attitude, but democratic theory itself. Liberal democratic theory has traditionally claimed superiority over other egalitarian-based systems on the ground that it is the one system that is pre-eminently tolerant and pluralistic. Any norms, beliefs or interests may be pursued by its members, individually or collectively, provided they do not conflict with the particular balance between individualism and equality that is currently accepted as just. The conflicts and misdirection that arise within a liberal democracy as a result of this view may become problems for government if the people choose to regard them as such, but they are not problems for theoreticians. The fundamental assumption about the relation between government and society excludes them.

Virtually all books on the theory and mechanics of democratic government have been coloured by this view, if not directed by it. Consequently, if the problem of (say) 'violence' within the society is debated, it is discussed only in terms of the techniques of control and limitations on the exercise of control within a democratic framework. Analysis of the nature and origin of violence is left to other disciplines, even though the very existence of rioting and mass demonstrations throws considerable doubt on fundamental assumptions about democracy.

This rejection of all social problems, except as regards their direct relation to the fundamental norms, would be understandable only if it could validly be argued that the norms express themselves solely through institutional forms and attitudes about them, as with a belief in public education, equal voting rights, the universal franchise, an attitude of tolerance towards one's fellow men, and so forth. But if it can be plausibly argued, and demonstrated by an appeal to the facts of democratic society, that the norms and their institutionalized forms cause very marked changes in other beliefs and norms and that these changes give rise to situations that society itself regards as problems, the neglect by theorists of what have hitherto been considered sociological and government problems can hardly be justified. It is by no means difficult to find issues that have been treated as lying outside theory, but which are in fact of as much concern as the balancing act between 'equality' and 'liberty' that has characterized democratic theory from its inception. Among them are relativism and violence.[1]

Relativism is one of the important characteristics of democratic societies that is neglected by analysts of the system. In a sense, of course, such a statement is rather misleading, since one of the principal defences of the democratic system today is that it is relativist. One could say that all studies today, even the pious works which speak of the moral superiority granted liberal democracy by its Christian roots, are unmistakably coloured by relativism. When I say the relation between democracy and relativism is neglected, I refer to the refusal to analyse the possibility that relativism derives from the system rather than

[1]In the last decade there appeared a sudden spate of writings on violence referring specifically to 'political' or even 'democratic' violence. Their object was to redefine the concept; to collect substantial empirical evidence for violence; and to find out whether it is avoidable. The results have been disappointing. Thus attempts at redefinitions such as those of H.L. Nieburg (*Political Violence* [New York, 1969]), Robert Paul Wolff ('On Violence', *Journal of Philosophy*, Vol. LXVI [1969]), or Christian Bay ('Violence as a Negation of Freedom', *The American Scholar*, Vol. XL [1971]) have as a rule been too broad to be of value. Some writers have been led to the absurd notion of identifying violence with any enforcement of legal and social rules. 'Violence' as we know it disappeared in a continuum which embodies a spectrum of related and unrelated concepts and actions, all lumped together. The most comprehensive earlier treatments have either been empirical studies or reviews of empirical literature on the subject (Henry Bienen, *Violence and Social Change* [Chicago, 1968]; H.D. Graham and T.R. Gurr, *Violence in America* [New York, 1969]; H.Hirsch and D.C. Perry, eds., *Violence as Politics* [New York, 1973]); their chief failings are their inability to relate analysis to the body of political theory and to find an answer to the question whether violence can be avoided.

supports it. We can see this from the peculiar way that relativism is put forward as a defence for the system. If analysts really began with relativism as a premise, they would have to hold to the view that any political order is acceptable. This, of course, would make relativism useless to the theorist, who would have to give up theory and shift to behaviouralist analysis. Only behaviouralism is consistent with the fundamental relativist view that norms are abstractions from something which is much better studied as actual behaviour. All theorists who attempt to incorporate relativism into theory are necessarily forced into some kind of deception: to juggle with different schools of relativism that are mutually incompatible. Thus if relativism is to be used as an argument for democracy, it is necessary to adopt the view of 'customary' relativism: that which is, is right. But since this does not give an accurate description of democratic processes, it is necessary to include a different kind of relativism, emanating from the 'desire' school: that which people desire or — behaviouralistically speaking — choose, is right. But the two simply do not go together. The attempt to make them fit raises in an acute form the problem of what society can do when the people choose to alter the system in the belief that what is, is no longer right. The agonizing over legal and constitutional limits and over the problem posed by the totalitarian party in a free society, which is characteristic of so much modern analysis of democratic 'problems', is due as much to the difficulties created by a confused relativism as to any new threats posed by modern conditions. This agonizing results from the purely intellectual dilemma in which the relativist places himself, when he tries to use relativism in order to make absolute what he considers to be a relativist order. It is impossible to view a society as both relativist and absolute at one and the same time.

It is essential, if democratic theory is to serve any useful function, to recognize frankly the relation between the institutionalized forms and relativism: just as majority rule entails antirationalism, so it entails relativism. It is not possible to believe in the system unless one adopts relativism and anti-rationalism. The problem is that, having done so, one can no longer feel any strong loyalty to the system. Not only does loyalty to the system seem unfounded, but efforts to defend it become special pleading. However, once the theorist recognizes the relation

The Relevance of Democratic Theory to Democracy 21

between institutionalized egalitarianism and relativism, he does two things. In the first place, he strikes a major blow at relativism by exposing it as being itself a normative attitude to norms, and also as being an inadequate description of norms in that it neglects the element of system in normative sets. Indeed, relativism so markedly fails to account for the latter element that even the philosophers, in adopting relativism, seem to have been more influenced by the requirements of their political order than by purely intellectual considerations.

The second consequence of recognizing the relation between democracy and relativism is that relativism in society now becomes a 'problem' for the theorist, rather than a 'fact' on which he can base his position. It is the theorist's problem rather than the sociologist's, precisely because relativism and its concomitant anti-rationalism have exceedingly serious consequences within society. Thus if a fundamental hostility to law and order is inherent in a system of law and order, we cannot suppose that any of the sociologists' and psychologists' proposed manipulations of the socialization process will change matters. Let us take, for instance, the problem of violence, which theorists used to regard as lying outside their field, apart from the general proposition that a theory of government is a theory of maintaining law and order. The generally held position of democratic theorists has always been that theory supplies an adequate method of coping with it and that if in certain periods there are startling outbreaks of social disorder, they are a matter for sociological investigation not theoretical analysis. Perhaps the family, church, education system and technology have changed in such a way that the old order has to be adjusted. In the meantime, theory and practice supply methods of preventing society from disintegrating. This attitude would be entirely legitimate if the relativists were correct in their assumption that normative sets are entirely fortuitous: a simple conjuncture of disparate norms deriving their authority from tradition, desire, social custom and so forth. If it can be convincingly argued, however, that the very assumptions on which the system of order is based necessarily require the acceptance of violence as a norm, the theorist must incorporate violence in his normative system. It can no longer be merely a particular condition which he professes to have remedied.

Can violence, then, be regarded as part of the democratic normative order? The very idea seems fantastic. Based on a system whose chief merit is said to be that it is the *only* system which provides a rational method of ensuring an orderly succession of governments and of ensuring that the government retains a concern for the problems of society as seen by members of that society, Western liberal democracy appears to come closer to an inherently stable system than any other. Perhaps one day the Communist States will incorporate into their system a stable method of transferring power and will then rival the Western democracies in this respect. But the stability that comes when the problems a government deals with and the methods it uses to do so are those which the society itself recognizes and regards as legitimate, would seem to be excluded by the nature of Communist assumptions. To maintain stability, Communist governments need to keep a much closer watch on the way the members of their society interpret problems than is necessary under our system. Both systems, of course, socialize their members into acceptance of their particular way of life. However, the system which requires that the government adjust to the society, rather than vice versa, would certainly seem to require a less elaborate method of socialization and hence should prove more stable; it should be characterized by a more willing acceptance of the way of life it represents. Most defences of democracy, in fact, have clearly been written with some such thought in mind: understand the system and you will willingly accept it. But there is so little evidence that violence and disorder have any relation whatsoever to misapprehensions about theory and so much evidence that Western democracies are among the least law-abiding of societies that we are led to suspect that something within our political order fosters violence and disorder.

Some, of course, have seen the cause in the liberty and individualism of our ideology: we are not termites in a termite nest but free individualists with clashing opinions and interests; because we live in a non-police state, we are freer to take issue with the law. True freedom, it is said, entails less supervision of the mind and behaviour and hence allows greater scope for violating the conventions. The opportunity for such violation in

The Relevance of Democratic Theory to Democracy

our system has increased, sociologists say, as a result of the loss of social controls consequent upon urbanization and the decline of the family as a socializing unit. But the resultant sociological problem becomes a political problem only if one sees the maintenance of law and order by the State as a fundamentally coercive process. Since democratic theory does not so regard it, violence is allegedly not its concern.

Although this view is certainly plausible, the notion that freedom entitles us to violate the concept of law and order is certainly not a part of democratic belief. Theoretically, at least, democratic systems provide a mechanism for not only enforcing the law but also avoiding majority opposition to it by incorporating methods for changing the law in accordance with rational objections. No matter what sociological changes occur, democratic theory, like any theory of government, should be capable of coping with them. If it cannot, if it presupposes only known and predictable social conditions, it is not an adequate theory of government. The 'defence' that social change and the concept of freedom induce violence is thus an attack on the fundamental proposition about the nature of government which, if it can be proved true, requires us to reject democratic theory. Furthermore, there is no evidence that the freedom and individualism which violence is supposed to represent manifest themselves to a noticeable extent in any other way. Indeed, conformity is the most obvious characteristic of democratic society, as one would expect under the principle of majority rule: when the majority is 'right', to agree with the majority is also right. Therefore, if we find that violence is both widespread and 'justified' in terms of the system, we have to conclude that it is the product of the political system itself rather than of particular social conditions, and consequently that it is a democratic norm which theorists must take into account in their analysis of democracy.

But how can violence be a norm of democracy, which — like any other system of government — is a system for minimizing violence by setting forth rules for human relations including the settlement of disputes, and which in addition has strong affinities with a moral and religious order that is opposed to violence? Part of the answer in regard to the USA and those nations which have been strongly influenced by American interpretations of man and society, lies in the Madisonian tradition of democracy. The latter, as analysed by Robert Dahl, has the following as its initial premise: 'If unrestrained by external checks, any given individual or group of individuals will tyrannize over others.'[2] This hypothesis has been structured into American society in the form of checks and balances and of legal rights for the minority which are supposed (erroneously, Dahl shows) to remove or minimize the scope for tyranny. An American who accepts his governmental system is therefore predisposed towards the assumption of power-hunger as an element in the nature of man. This belief is necessary to his whole-hearted acceptance of the system and also, of course, expresses a view of man's nature which makes the preservation of law and order purely coercive: something which man imposes on himself, or has imposed on him, in order to escape the anarchism that would be the natural consequence of his power-drive. The belief would be completely implausible, since it ignores or at least fails to analyse the social, cooperative and sympathetic elements in man, if it were not for the reinforcement it receives from institutionalized egalitarianism. The latter, by declassing man, forces each of us into a competitive struggle for position and self-identification. The result is that aggressiveness, rather than open violence, which is characteristic of Americans. No civilization could long exist if it compelled most of its members to commit unrestrained aggression upon one another. Yet aggressiveness of the American type is undoubtedly a sublimated form of violence, as psychologists have repeatedly observed; moreover it is the kind of sublimation that can be achieved only by those whose ends it will serve— men with sufficient education and intelligence to use it for the purpose of advancing themselves in a competitive society.

In certain respects there is much to be said for aggressiveness. It largely accounts for the extraordinary growth of the US economy, and for the country's position as a major power. Given the choice, most Americans would unhesitatingly prefer their system to any other, on the ground that it supplies 'opportunity', even if they could be convinced that the concomitant social

[2]Robert A. Dahl. *A Preface to Democratic Theory* (Chicago, 1956), p. 6.

attitude entails a permanent state of rebelliousness. The qualities that are lost by the materialistic value order forced upon them are not recognized. Indeed, one finds it almost too embarrassing nowadays to speak of 'materialism' and to point out that a society which compels a struggle for status necessarily commits itself to the proposition that the primary goal of the individual must be the security and esteem yielded by material possessions. The non-material goals which have marked all advanced civilizations are ruled out for most Americans because their system has institutionalized forms of egalitarianism (for example, tax laws, which make the struggle for possessions a never-ending process which does not permit one to retire and enjoy the fruits of one's labours); also, because the inherent relativism of the system discourages the acceptance of any other values, even though other values are part of the inherited tradition and are given lip-service. Since, then, all that seems good is related to aggressiveness, most Americans can easily convince themselves that the presence of social disorder is a small price to pay, and a problem that social scientists will one day solve.

It is very doubtful whether they will be able to do so. The supposition that some manipulation of the laws and social conditions can solve the problem of violence rests, it would seem on the erroneous supposition that all societies have been faced with similar problems and that since some have managed to settle them, advanced civilizations with their greater resources can do so too. Those who hold this view argue from the characteristic qualities of American society to man in general. They suppose that man is by nature an American, as it were, and that the problem of maintaining social order is synonymous with the problem of sublimating and controlling aggression. So common is this view that it is tempting to regard it as a proposition of universal validity. But it is not. And even if it were valid, it would make the origins of society and government inexplicable and would force us to regard all civilization as fundamentally coercive — the imposition on the weak of the goals and interests of the most powerful — so that the democratic order would be rank deception. Too many 'realists' already think this way, unaware of the source of their views, and are ready to rationalize their society by ridding it of its traditional freedoms. They are true only to the aggressive element in their system: to a derived, rather than a primary, value. However, it is not possible to convince them of their error by advocating a return to democratic principles, as so many analysts of democratic theory suppose. It is the principles that have begotten the attitude.

The difficulty of solving the problem of violence in a democratic society is compounded not only by the assumptions we are compelled to make about man and about what is 'good' in the society, but also by the reinforcement which the attitude towards violence receives from the strong anti-rational strain previously discussed. On the assumption that man is irrational and reason nothing more than rationalization,[3] there can be only two forms of response to any kind of disagreement or divergence of interests: retreat, or attack and suppression. Only one is open to society. Whereas the individual can either turn his back on a man who opposes him or strike him if he feels able, society can follow only the second course. Preserving law and order becomes a purely coercive process. It is for this reason that we have the astounding phenomenon of advocates of 'law and order' in the USA coupling their demands with virulent attacks on the legislature, the judiciary, the church and the educational system, those elements of society which anyone else would regard as the primary representatives of law and order. To the anti-rationalist, however, representatives of the higher levels of social organization and those responsible for continuance of the norms as a part of social organization are completely misguided mollycoddlers of criminal and subversive elements. Fire must by fought with fire; the eruption of violence demands repressive measures. This attitude has to some extent been present in all societies. The known effectiveness of coercion in socializing children leads the simple-minded to assume that the same basic techniques can be used to control those who have not been socialized in the way that society desires. It is a problem for an egalitarian society that this naïve view is not limited to those who

---

[3] On this assumption, 'rationality' becomes a value-free concept. It is therefore not surprising that H.L. Nieburg, who starts with this premise, bases his book on the theme that 'Violence in all its forms...is a natural form of political behavior.' (H.L. Nieburg, *Political Violence*, [New York, 1969], p. 5). This view has become current among many political sociologists. In a more recent study, violence is seen as 'an integral factor in the internal politics of nation-states.' (H. Hirsch & D.C. Perry [eds.], *Violence as Politics* [New York], 1973).

are naturally simple-minded. The more complex view which demands rational analysis of the choices (norms) open to the individual and society, has been excluded by the normative attitudes resulting from the fundamental assumptions made by society. Indeed, the naïve thinker had good cause for being suspicious of many of the proposals of the 'experts' he rejects. The solutions offered by psychologists, sociologists, criminologists and educators are for the most part nothing more than attempts to manipulate the socialization process so that the egalitarian norms will in fact operate: improved housing for the 'underprivileged', more intensive education in the form of 'head-start' programs, guaranteed wages and so forth. The total failure to recognize that they are attempting to cope with a normative problem without analysing their norms, and without reference to man's long history of normative experience, is significant. Whether they realize it or not, experts and authorities who express such a strong dislike for simple coercive solutions to social disorder are indulging in a process of analysis that is at bottom no more complex than the thought-processes of advocates of more police power, and that is as coercive in intent as the others.

Violence, Coercion and Relativism

An official report on violence such as that of the National Commission on the Causes and Prevention of Violence established in June, 1968,[4] which focuses entirely on sociological patterns, naturally raises questions about the kind of society which can view so lop-sided a study as comprehensive and objective. How can we explain society's accepting the report as more or less objective? It is not many years since a study would have been considered less than definitive, to say the least, if it did not contain the opinions of a philosopher, a psychologist, a clergyman and a policeman. Amazingly enough, what has made this set of papers appear objective, and even convincing, is its main contention that much of the seeming outburst of violence is an illusion: violence such as now disturbs the USA (we are told) has characterized societies throughout history! A few years

[4]Hugh Davis Graham and Ted Robert Gurr, *Violence in America* (New York, 1969).

earlier, a report making such an assertion would have been considered a whitewashing of the law-enforcement agencies.

That there has not been a loud outcry from those whose disciplines were not represented suggests that there is a general acceptance among the educated of the Commission's implicit assumptions about violence. But what can be the nature of assumptions that make it possible for rivalry between disciplines to disappear? One can never be sure in such cases, of course, but one possible explanation is relativism, whose assumptions represent one of the few factors which unify diverse scientific disciplines.

Whatever the particular form which relativism takes, one fundamental proposition it must contain is that norms are fundamentally non-rational and hence lack a predictable pattern: to kill people may be considered wrong, but not to kill (as well as exceptions to the norm that killing people is wrong) will be completely outside the terms of reference. The norm says nothing about whether war, infanticide, capital punishment and so forth are allowable. Given this non-rational quality of norms, it follows that they cannot be rationally taught: people cannot be educated to believe in them in the sense of genuine education; that is, the process of inculcating the norms, while it obviously exists, is itself unpredictable. The non-rationality of the norms excludes them from rational control. This means that whatever can be said to fall under the heading of normative behaviour can also be said to fall in the category of uncontrolled behaviour.

At one time such a view would have been considered self-contradictory: normative behaviour by its nature was controlled behaviour. But the loss of a controller — the law of nature or of God — has made it entirely possible to see normative behaviour in this new light. Limiting ourselves to the question of violence, we can see that a relativist must find it difficult to regard violence as especially characteristic of a given period of time or a particular society. Thus, if it cannot be taught or learned, it should be randomly distributed throughout history. There would seem to be no real reason why our society should have more violence than others. Indeed, there are very good reasons why we could expect it to have much less: the widely accepted frustration-aggression theory and the very common defence of democracy as a 'free' society (presumably less frustrating than others) would lead the relativist to suppose that there should be less violence in America today than there was in the earlier periods of man's history. Certainly, a case can be made for such a view. There can be no agreement on what constitutes evidence of violence, especially when there seems to be some correlation between the extent of its manifestation and the degree of coercion exercised by society. Violence could even be considered evidence of 'freedom' and non-violence as proof of coercion.

That this 'random' view of violence and freedom has not been given theoretical formulation may be due to the fact that it runs counter to the argument for sovereignty. One reason for the enduring appeal of the sovereignty concept seems to be its assertion of the simple truth that the one thing the State cannot tolerate is internal disorder. The moment we assert this, however, we are confronted with a serious intellectual difficulty: violence demands coercion, which is itself a form of violence. Why should coercion be more acceptable than violence? If violence is wrong, what possible difference does it make that the agent is the State rather than the individual? Indeed, has not the democrat's objection always been that given a choice, violence suffered at the hands of one's fellow men is preferable to coercion by the State because individuals are more or less evenly matched, whereas the State and the individual are not? Hobbes's argument about the state of nature supplies an answer to this, but it has never been entirely clear why conservatives of an individualistic bent should use something like Hobbes's argument when denouncing violence in the streets. To the conservative, perhaps, it is the alternatives that seem dangerous. Coercion of some kind is obviously a necessary response to violence. One kind of coercion, which includes 'educating' people into accepting — or eliminating — differences of (say) status and income, might well be possible. The former could be achieved without obvious State interference, but the cost would be loss of individuality, which for many conservatives is the central value. Hence many, while disapproving of government interference, prefer coercion by the law.

Coercion is, or should be, no more than an expedient. The police are a 'stop-force', a device for preventing or terminating specific types of behaviour to which society objects. What happens after the police have fulfilled this function depends on other factors. Every society needs a force of this kind, especially to counter violence or the threat of it, for violence is by definition a threat to social order. Such a threat arises not from the acceptance of coercion as a response to violence, but from indifference to the nature of government, specifically from failure to appreciate that no matter what method is used to establish a government, whether democratic or otherwise, that government will have a bureaucratic structure. Within this system coercion is not simply an expedient, but a final solution; unless the political system contains some modifying factor — for example, democratic elections — the government will be satisfied it is governing well if it simply maintains order by suppressing disorder. Indeed, history shows that governments have to be coerced into being non-coercive: that is, into treating their coercive force as an expedient to be followed by a study of the factors which made coercion necessary. Democracy does this in part through elections, which threaten heads of State with dismissal if a seething dissatisfaction continues in the body politic.

No matter how well the government has maintained the appearance of order by rigorously suppressing riots and other evidence of hostility, if the root causes of dissatisfaction are untouched, the government is likely to fall. A democracy, however, like any other system of government, must employ coercion, even if it seems clear that the majority favour something the government does not support. Because democratic governments use coercion freely, some people believe that they are not in fact democratic and must therefore be opposed by all true democrats. Since coercion seems to these people evidence that the democratic system is not working, they use non-democratic methods — violence — to oppose the system. The violence itself, curiously enough, often seems not to be deliberately coercive: that is, it is not necessarily designed to force the government to change its policy; it appears to be aimless.

In a democracy, however, a great many of the most destructive riots do not begin as acts of violence. They begin as non-violent. acts of coercion — peaceful demonstrations designed to influence the government. No matter how peaceful their origin, however, such demonstrations — if they are on a large scale — are evidence of a dangerous breakdown in democratic processes and faith in democracy. Owing to the size of modern cities and the difficulties of communication between members of the public, these demonstrations are always the work of minority activists, and the nature of crowd psychology is such that when a group comes together for a purpose that cannot be immediately satisfied, it is very likely to lead to violence. That is why riot acts exist and why the penalties are so severe. Even when no violence occurs, a peaceful demonstration is an attempt at coercion which, although justified by historical forms of democracy, is none the less dangerous because it implies the persistence of primitive democratic concepts under conditions that disallow them.

Violence, Social Change and Normativism

Democratic political theory has always maintained that all viable political orders must exclude violence; that violence within society — including violence directed against the State itself — is always an 'aberration'; and that a social order must define it as such.

Violence is considered an aberration because it is antinormative, whereas the State as a rule becomes identified with a normative order. Violence is anti-normative because it violates the premise — essential with regard to human relations — that men are open to reason and can usually be induced to behave accordingly. This is not to say they always behave rationally or that violence is never justified. Under certain circumstances, we justify violence as a response to violence. But the circumstances under which this is done are not incorporated in our normative order. When judging the decision of anyone who claims that 'circumstances' warranted violence, society accepts but one plea — that violence was not justifiable in itself but was dictated by normative considerations. The modern State is so constructed that in theory this plea cannot be raised against the State itself. This is not so because the State insists its normative order to be supreme or uniquely valid, but because (in theory) it provides devices through which normative objections to its practices can be raised without recourse to violence.

Obviously, something has gone wrong with the theory. The

State's pleas that citizens register dissent at the ballot box fall on deaf ears, and it is clear that those who march and riot are specifically rejecting the very alternative suggested by the authorities. Explanations of this rejection in terms of the rapidity of social change, breakdowns in socialization, human nature, etc. all founder on the assumption that the dissidents do not know that the traditional democratic way of coping with change has worked in the past. One is prone to suspect the opposite: thus, an often-raised claim of those who have resorted to violence is that they *are* acting in accordance with democratic principles, whereas other people are not.

The dissidents' claim reveals an assumption — present from the beginning of modern democracy — not about violence but about the nature of democracy; this normative assumption relates to the claims of private conscience as opposed to those of majority rule. The principle of majority rule is disputed when the regular process of influencing decision-makers is rejected. Those who oppose the dissident elements — by suggesting that they register dissent with their ballot — are pleading the majority rule principle; they reinforce the latter by talk about law and order. Thus today's violence is a confrontation of two relativisms: the relativism of majority rule and that of private conscience. The source is to be found in normative considerations, not in sociological changes.

The clash between private conscience and majority rule has been recognized from the early days of modern political theory. Rousseau's distinction between the General Will and the will of all was a way of coping with the problems posed by a system which attempts to have a government that both expresses the will of the people and allows the government to be guided by normative considerations which are wider than those arising from the elective process. As even strict relativists recognize, the mere process of acquiring a government does not supply the latter with enough guidelines for policy making: they recognize that special-interest groups must have ways and means of initiating legislation. Beyond this, however, they see no problem. Yet a major problem does exist: the method of obtaining a government does not make it democratic if its policies are not such. 'Democratic' cannot mean 'in accordance with the will of the people', for 'self-government' is strictly speaking illogical.

Nor can it mean 'in accordance with the fundamental principles of equality and individualism', for not only are these in conflict but they supply no adequate set of norms as a basis for governmental action. Trying to erect a domestic policy — let alone a foreign policy — on such principles would be an impossible task. The only comprehensive set of norms is to be found in the private conscience, but it cannot be exalted to the position of a supreme norm because we do not know whose private conscience must prevail. Even the theory of sovereignty does not answer the question democracies are facing: What do we mean by 'democratic policy'?

This question has now acquired a new urgency. Democracy is such a recent development and has been faced with such problems of gross inequality inherited from the past that the mere business of eroding various inequalities has until recently given many individuals the satisfying feeling that governments have been 'democratic' because of their egalitarian efforts. This feeling has now given way to an overt dissatisfaction and it is evident from the nature of many objections that the question is not merely one of increasing the pace of change. Indeed, there are regular methods of influencing government as regards this pace. The objections include other normative considerations in addition to traditional egalitarian issues: for example, protests about the 'morality' of war. Some insist that the concept of 'democratic policy' should embrace as many norms as are in private conscience. The more difficult it is to define democracy in terms of majority rule — and this has never been so hard as now — the more obvious it is that we must see disorders and violence as the opposition of private conscience to majority rule.

Political Obligation, Obedience and Coercion

Political obligation is a term very remote from the popular way of thinking: even sovereignty is being mentioned more often. The very remoteness of the concept from the community's modes of thought lends support to the behaviouralist views that much political theorizing has no real bearing on actual issues of the community. It seems pointless to supply an argument 'proving' that we have a duty to obey the law of the State if the concepts of duty and obligation in general are not part of the average man's world view. If political obligation cannot be related to some commonly held attitude about 'obligation', the argument is bound to become an assertion that members of the State are legally subject to its laws. Some resist this fact and defend their position normatively. To take account of this normative resistance to the State's coercive powers is the object of discussions of political obligation. In this respect we must be clear how the concept has been used. (The question of 'how used' relates to the apparent purpose of discussions of the concept, not to the assumptions of theorists who argued for political obligations. All these theorists were bound to make normative assumptions which did not reflect those of the 'people' to whom they related the concept.)

The most obvious purpose of traditional discussions of political obligation — as reflected by the Anglo-American democratic tradition — has been to provide a normative defence of State coercion to enforce its laws. The concept of government by consent is difficult to reconcile with the fact of coercion, unless there is something called political obligation with a normative content which implies that the citizen 'consents' to the act of coercion.

The difficulty with such arguments is that while democratic in intent, they label the non-consenting citizen as at least 'misguided', so that he is not only subject to the coercion of the law but the coercive disapproval of his fellow citizens as well. Thus arguments whose purpose is to make coercion acceptable in terms of one aspect of democratic norms, make others — such as the right of acting and judging by the dictates of individual conscience — anti-social. Since government by consent rests on the assumption that private conscience is not anti-social, an awkward dilemma results.

Another obvious purpose behind discussions of political obligation is to reduce the amount of coercion by making the acceptance of coercion a moral principle which is meant to override all others. The result is the same as before: the 'good' citizen — being a moral man — submits. The rest — being immoral — do not, but may legitimately be compelled to. Arguments of this type invite the extension of coercion into an area which does not belong in a democratic State — the area of thought control, euphemistically called 'education' by educators and 'socialization' by social scientists. The object becomes the inculcation of habitual obedience — a far cry from the democratic tradition.

Theorists who deal with the problem of political obligation usually say little about those who do not habitually obey and whose behaviour demonstrates their denial that obligation has the nature attributed to it by the theorists. As a result, traditional analyses of political obligation are usually not relevant to modern issues, despite the fact that political obligation — as a concept — is growing in importance.

The weakness of such traditional analyses is that they have not begun with the fact that all States are coercive. Rather, they have begun with an assumption about a normative order which is (or seems to be) incompatible with the fact of coercion. The outcome has been detrimental to analysis of the concept under discussion, because it is impossible to make this concept valid unless we base it squarely on coercion — not on some normative position that may or may not be taken. It is misleading to begin with a normative position which cannot be reconciled with the fact of coercion and then somehow insert this fact as a norm into the system.

The right of the State to coerce arises from our normative assumption that we want to live in a society; having that desire, we recognize the fact of coercion as a right which needs no further defence. Only doctrinaire egalitarians question the State's right to be coercive. It is they who create the circumstances in which the right needs to be defended: by advocates of law and order. The latter's attempt to derive the right of the State to coerce from the duty of the citizen to submit brings out the incompatibility of this duty with the requirements of democratic principles. It is imprudent to bring the State's right to coerce into conflict with other normative principles, as must happen if we attempt to derive it from a duty. There is only one case where the State's right to coerce is *not* incompatible with other norms: when we all agree that State law is the source of all legitimate norms.

The concept of political obligation can be best seen as the concession to a State of the unqualified right to coerce its citizens, a concession which is equivalent to admitting a desire to live within the State. As regards this right one must be careful to avoid two mistakes: firstly, using it to demolish all other norms; secondly, bringing it into irreconcilable conflict with normative schemes which regard coercion as inherently wrong. The first occurs only if we wish to derive the right from a duty rather than from its more obvious source. The second occurs when we insist on the 'consent' norm, irrespective of the requirements of social life.

Traditional democratic theory has bred unnecessary hostility to the State's coercive power. 'Idealistic' youths regard coercion as evidence that democratic governments have become tyrannical. Theorists have expounded the concept of political obligation — arguing from contract, legitimacy and so forth — sometimes ingeniously but never satisfyingly: it is not possible to begin with consent and end with submission. It should be made clear there is no need for any conflict between recognition of the State's right to coerce and one's own right to private judgement. Those members of democracies who think about these matters know quite well that they have no duty to subordinate their private conscience to State decisions. What they need to be told is that although the State has an unqualified right to coerce, the nature and extent of that coercion depend on the ideological foundations of the State. The task of theorists is to examine the effect of ideology on the State's coercive nature, not to 'prove' that it is not really coercive, or that it is one's duty — whatever the ideology — to submit. Such arguments may please legalists but they have little effect on those who question legalistic interpretations.

The Normative Position of Violence in Theories of Obligation

In discussing political obligation, we must consider the fact neglected by virtually all recent discussions: the argument must address itself to two quite different groups — the government and the governed. The utter incompatibility between the positions of Howard Zinn and Abe Fortas conveniently reflects the difference between the relation of those very groups to the law. Fortas gives the government's (any government's) viewpoint:[5] the primary law of government is that the law must be

[5] See Abe Fortas, *Concerning Dissent and Civil Disobedience* (New York, 1968).

obeyed and dissent expressed within the framework of the law. Zinn expresses the viewpoint of the governed:[6] dissent, to be meaningful, must be as free to choose its mode of expression as it is to choose its content. Neither, however, really touches on the problem of obligation, which is that the two opposing views exist and must somehow be reconciled in a way satisfactory to both parties.

The nature of the problem is obscured for us by the strong vein of relativism within our society. Each author when challenged would no doubt admit that he is implying a form of relativism as an absolute: the sanctity of law and private conscience respectively. Neither of these can be defended as absolutes, though each can be upheld as the essence of democracy, the kind of political order to which each author seems to limit his discussion. Because each author is likely to be aware of his relativism, he can suppose he has supplied an answer to the problem of political obligation: even though each discussion expresses the view of only one element in a political order, one can assume that the other side can adopt it because our (relativistic) society is not committed to any one view. In other words, if we are to see either the Fortas or Zinn position as a discussion of political obligation, we have to assume that the implicit position they hold in common is that the problem of political obligation can be solved in a relativist society by the common agreement of government and governed on a single normative system. Logically, no fault can be found in such a view, since the problem of political obligation arises because the law commands what conscience and private interest may resist. A difficulty does arise, however, in respect of Zinn's view when we ask what being governed can mean if the source of the norms lies with those being governed: law is not truly law if it may be legitimately resisted and applies only to the type of behaviour to which people would resort if it did not exist. And without true law, of course, there is no government to govern, so that the problem of political obligation is 'solved' by disposing of one of the facts of life in society. It is for this reason that some form of legalistic view expressed by Fortas has appeared the only possible solution to the problem of political obligation: it appeals even to

[6]See Howard Zinn, *Disobedience and Democracy: Nine Fallacies on Law and Order* (New York, 1968).

those who are not legalists and are indeed troubled by a requirement that makes positive law supreme in society.

Thus this argument for solving the problem of political obligation presupposes the acceptance of relativism as a philosophic position: it will not work if those whom Zinn addresses insist that the norms they oppose to the legal norms are absolutes. No process of 'socialization' not based on the inculcation of relativism would enable the problem of political obligation to be solved in this way. This is what many sociologists forget. They recognize the importance of socialization in terms of maintaining a social order, but think of it primarily as a process, a technique of social manipulation whose 'content' does not matter. However, as long as some men suppose that some norms are absolutes and so long as some of these norms differ from those of positive law, the problem of political obligation is left untouched if we simply argue that above all else the law must be obeyed. The *facts* are that the strong relativist elements in our society are not based on philosophic relativism but on what are felt to be absolutes — majority rule, the supremacy of private conscience, the rule of law and so forth. No doubt the problem of political obligation could be solved if only one absolute or one supreme source of norms — the rule of law — were recognized, but this is not a fact of modern democratic society and we cannot base an argument for political obligation on it unless we suppose it can become a fact, as through 'socialization'. Fortas's argument and those like it are in effect attempts at such 'socialization'. They strive to convince the whole of society that we all 'ought to' — above all else — adhere to the law and seek change only within prescribed legal forms for doing so. Such an argument cannot overcome the fact that men like Zinn are equally convinced that the society they believe in would change to something else if the legalist view were made universal.

Some accommodation is obviously necessary: the problem of obligation must be faced. The Fortas argument exacerbates the problem by convincing the authorities that utter indifference to other norms is the only possible response to dissent; this invites hostility to authority from dissenters by making 'authority' the expression of an alien power. Against such 'authority' the dissenter can bring to bear the entire body of democratic principles. Zinn's argument, by making violence a legitimate expression of a normative position, invites an equally resolute opposition from the government. Theoretically, neither party wants violence since it is at odds with their normative viewpoint, but each in effect makes it the next in importance to the supreme norm of their normative system by making it the ultimate response to opposition from the conflicting system. It should be the task of political theory to make clear that coercion can be at most a technique of socialization and of maintaining order among members of a community where socialization has been imperfect and that as such it has no normative standing whatsoever. Certainly it cannot be exalted as the penultimate principle of society. Viewed as a technique of socialization, of course, it cannot be used against authority. Zinn's view is indefensible unless violence is something more than a technique; but if we accept it as a legitimate coercive technique allowable to anyone who wishes to influence another's behaviour, we convert it into at least the second most important norm in the system. Fortas defends the law against all other systems of norms and places coercion in defence of the law above all other norms in any other system. As statements about normative systems, neither view is satisfactory.

Can Violence be Justified?

Courtroom practice establishes two types of justification. In one, an attempt is made to transfer responsibility to someone or something other than the one who seems responsible. For this reason we can say that any study of violence which attributes it to environmental factors, historical forces or human nature can be called a 'justification' of violence. (It is precisely this type which is 'scientifically acceptable'.) If we accept the view, we are not, of course, compelled to tolerate the behaviour in question, but our response to it must be different from what it would otherwise be. Coercive measures, while sometimes necessary as a stop-gap device, will — under the hypothesis — not prove effective in controlling violent behaviour. Hence, instead of attempting direct control, society is required to eliminate, redirect or mitigate the factor or factors which are supposedly responsible.

The second type of justification, which takes the form of fitting disapproved behaviour into a normative scheme so that it can be approved of under certain circumstances — the violation of one norm is then shown to include observance of another — confronts society with some awkward problems when the object of justification is violence. If coercive measures are adopted to control violence, the State will (paradoxically) define itself as not 'free' or 'just', since the justification establishes the violent behaviour as 'right'. If they are not adopted, the State itself is not acting responsibly, nor is the government true to one of the purposes for which it was founded — the maintenance of law and order. What can we make of a book which in effect poses this problem? Can ideologies of violence be justified?

There are now very many studies purporting to 'explain' violence and, it would seem, many that attempt to 'justify' it. The novelty of Grundy and Weinstein's *The Ideologies of Violence* consists in bringing together and commenting on the various justifications that have been offered. Can we justify a compendium of justifications when the latter are commonly defined as 'rationalizations'?

The authors' own justification is rather weak. Their preface contains the following statement: 'Knowledge of how ideologies of violence are used to maintain and expand political power and to affirm or undermine normative orders, decreases naïveté about politics and thereby allows human beings to exert greater independence of judgment in their political choices.'[7] This seems to be saying only that knowledge increases knowledge (decreases naïveté) and hence promotes free choice. This is much too vague a justification of an endeavour like *The Ideologies of Violence*. Can there be a better justification for this kind of book?

First we should keep in mind that a justification, no matter what form it takes, must accept as one of the basic facts about human behaviour that there are usually normative objections to it. Any justification that professes to establish that the behaviour is always normatively acceptable is by nature false, for it denies this fact.

The justifications in Grundy and Weinstein's book attempt to establish exceptions to the rule that violence is normatively

[7] Kenneth W. Grundy and Michael A. Weinstein, *The Ideologies of Violence* (Columbus, Ohio, 1974), p. V.

objectionable. Unlike the 'scientifically acceptable' type of justification, they accept the fact of the totality of a society's norms and not just the one immediately under consideration.[8] The norms of a society are facts about society, says the scientifically *unacceptable* approach and consequently the only valid justification entails a demonstration of the relationship of the unacceptable behaviour to the totality of norms. If it is possible to show that certain kinds of violence are in accord with certain norms, one has justified the behaviour. In other words, justification does not take only the one form of *non mea culpa*. You can also argue that you are following a higher principle. It may be true that norms are not verifiable by the methods of science, but the fact remains that they are facts about society which cannot be ignored, or analysed in isolation from each other.

To illustrate this point, let us compare behaviouralist approaches to violence with the quite different type of justifications presented in Grundy and Weinstein's book. Since one type discusses 'responsibility' and the other normative aspects of society, our task would be relatively simple if it were not for one difficulty: behaviouralist views are mutually incompatible. Inasmuch as one behaviouralist is successful in attributing violence to, say, human nature, he reduces the credibility of arguments attributing it to environmental factors. This is something other than the difference of opinion found in *The Ideologies of Violence*. Although 'legitimist' arguments in that book are not likely to be acceptable to those holding an 'intrinsic' view and vice versa, the views are not mutually exclusive. The arguments are held together by the overall normative order of society and it is essential that any personal stance one may take should be based on a knowledge of all the arguments and not just of the particular one reflecting personal interest or predilection. 'Justification' in the behaviouralist sense requires only a

[8]In the 'scientifically acceptable' type of justification, responsibility for the behaviour is assigned to something other than conscious choice — environmental factors, historical forces, unconscious drives and so forth. The reason that only this type of justification is 'scientific' is not based on the fact that other types cannot be supported by induction or deduction — they can be and are — but that simply assigning responsibility to something other than choice enables the investigator to fit human behaviour securely into the cause-effect pattern that has proved so successful in explaining the world of physics and chemistry. This is not the place to expose the fallacies of scientism, which is the underlying philosophy involved. The point is mentioned only because the justifications in *The Ideologies of Violence* are mostly not of this type.

knowledge of one's own field of interest and is increasingly unsuccessful as one moves away from it (or as someone with another interest is successful). 'Justification' in the normative area is unsuccessful inasmuch as it so limits itself.

Let us now take from the field of the social sciences the 'justification' of violence based on human nature and see to what extent it is the pure science it professes to be, and to what extent it is a submerged type of what Grundy and Weinstein call 'Intrinsic Justification'.

In recent years there has been a considerable popular interest in this type of argument. Robert Ardrey, Konrad Lorenz and Desmond Morris, among others, have written best-sellers presenting this view.[9] Counter-arguments, such as Robert Claiborne's *God or Beast: Evolution and Human Nature*,[10] have not done nearly so well. Now we can argue that the evidence is all on the side of the beast, but in fact the arguments violate the only perhaps acceptable theory of biological nature we have — that deriving from evolution. If the behaviour cannot be shown to be biologically advantageous to the species, then it must be false. In other words, if we treat Hobbes's argument in favour of the social contract as a statement about evolution, we have an irrefutable case against Ardrey's original position. Significantly enough, Ardrey has written a more recent book, *The Social Contract* (1970), in which for the most part he retreats from his earlier position. But he does not wholly abandon it even though the theory of evolution establishes 'natural' violence as inimical from the point of view of 'biological advantage'; also, the known facts about our closest relatives, the Primates, are clearly against it. Is there some other factor that can explain why a large number of social scientists — perhaps most — are open to theories of 'natural violence' when the only generally accepted theory of life — and natural behaviour — disallows it? I think there is and that its nature is established by the fact that the arguments for 'natural violence' receive their principal support in the United States, which is by

---

[9] See Robert Ardrey, *The Territorial Imperative* (New York, 1966); Konrad Lorenz, *On Aggression* (London, 1966); Desmond Morris, *The Naked Ape* (London, 1967).

[10] Robert Claiborne, *God or Beast: Evolution and Human Nature* (New York, 1974).

long odds the most violent state with a stable government.[11]

If you define violence as in some way 'natural', you can explain the lower incidence of violence in other states as evidence that they are in some way less 'free' — that their system of education and social controls is presumably such that the individual has less opportunity to follow his 'real' nature. Violence, in other words, is the price of 'freedom'. It is still objectionable, but it is not unjustifiable. This argument — it should be noted — is not based on an analysis of the meaning of 'freedom' but on a justification of one's acceptance of a particular society and the conditions prevailing there. No one who accepts freedom has to accept violence, even if he sees violence as part of human nature: we can argue that the existence of other norms so modifies the concept of freedom that it cannot be said to include the expression of violent impulses. It is in the nature of norms to interact with each other. For this reason, the Grundy and Weinstein compendium has merit, despite its weaknesses. The 'justifications' are in fact statements about norms in our society related to the issue of violence. Bringing them together enables us to be clearer about just what the problem is and what kind of decisions we should make.

Justifications of this type have a special function in a democratic society. Because they present violence as an allowable response to certain conditions, they convert what would otherwise be regarded as an abstract question of justice into a social problem that cannot be dismissed as purely theoretical. The apathy about social questions and politics — a characteristic feature of democratic publics — is presented as a threat to democracy as we know it. We are offered the choice of answering the arguments, remedying the conditions or being faced with civil disorder. This type of argument demands an attention and response that no abstract appeal to justice can command. It may easily be the only realistic argument possible in the times when abstract values are not of much interest even to philosophers.

In answering the question whether ideologies of violence can be justified we must keep in mind that an argument for anything so socially disruptive as violence need not be taken as a call to

---

[11] Note that the murder rate in the USA is at least five times as great as in Canada, which is itself not among the most peaceable States.

arms. Implicit in any argument for violence is an assertion that certain conditions are so intolerable that either the government remedies them or it loses its claim to sovereignty. Although this is not an unreasonable position to take, the formulation is dangerously misleading. It is addressed to the public rather than the government, and hence is capable of encouraging those inclined to violence — for reasons unrelated to the justification — to do what they are inclined to do, using the justification as an excuse. There is good reason to believe that this is precisely the issue when we talk of 'rabble rousing'. All of the arguments in Grundy and Weinstein need to be seen in this light. Are there *any* that cannot be reformulated as advice to the government? If not, one should be aware of the book's major weakness. If, on the one hand, its strength is that it brings together material important to any government intent on maintaining law and order, its weakness, on the other hand, is that much of the material is misleadingly formulated.

There is a passage in *The Ideologies of Violence* which illustrates an important problem facing political theory. Consider in particular the following assertion: 'The Hobbesian position is the most impressive of the blanket condemnations of violence. However, in the light of the functions of violence described by such theorists as Coser, Nieburg, and Roucek, its scientific standing is in question.'[12]

This sounds as if the authors' analysis of the theories of Coser, Nieburg and Roucek will have a direct bearing on Hobbes's argument. Yet when we turn to the relevant pages, we find the Hobbesian argument is not mentioned. Since my point does not require support or refutation of either Hobbes or those who have reputedly thrown his position in doubt, I shall take a brief passage from the discussion of Nieburg to set alongside the above statement about Hobbes: 'For Nieburg violence is neither a residual base of power nor a last resort after the onset of a long train of abuses.... At the heart of Nieburg's theory is the notion of bargaining. Nieburg holds that bargaining is a process of adjusting conflict.'[13]

Confronted by the assertion about Hobbes after reading the

[12]Grundy and Weinstein, *op. cit.*, p. 32.
[13]*Ibid.*, p. 22.

passage on Nieburg, one is likely to feel a sense of bewilderment, for the violence that Nieburg talks about does not remotely resemble the violence Hobbes had in mind. To Nieburg violence includes or perhaps even consists exclusively of bargaining, with an implicit threat of non-cooperation if demands are not met. Hobbes of course would not have regarded such a political process as 'violence'. Now the problem here is not that the authors have failed to define their terms or to notice that Hobbes and Nieburg are using two different senses of 'violence', but that the narrower Hobbesian definition has been dismissed on the implicit grounds that our modern, much broader definition is the true one. The point I would like to make is that this is not arrogance or ignorance on the authors' part, but an inescapable consequence of modern relativism.

To be sure, Hobbes himself was a relativist of sorts and he believed we are inclined to violence by nature — 'Seek power after power' — but both his relativism and his ideas of man's nature differ markedly from current views. His evolutionary theory of man's nature and ethics was essentially prudential and rational, whereas modern evolutionary theory is not directed by goal-seeking but by unwilled biological processes. For Hobbes, violence was a part of man's nature only in the sense that if it was to his advantage, he would use it. If it was not, there was no need for him to suppress any urge within him in order to be peaceable. Man's behaviour was always essentially rational and hence even a government instituted to maintain peace in the State never needed to be oppressive or tyrannical to achieve its goals, because there was nothing in man that needed to be suppressed — that is, nothing that he could not suppress himself. The modern view is quite different. If man is aggressive by nature (as a result of evolutionary processes) several consequences follow: firstly, aggression cannot be wholly 'bad', since it serves a biological function; secondly, it cannot be really suppressed, since it is a part of our nature and not under rational control. A further consequence is that social institutions will reflect this; society will not be a cooperative endeavour in the interests of the members but will consist essentially of interest groups in conflict.

It is within this context of thought that the authors of *The Ideologies of Violence* write, and it is this that explains their curious willingness to see a seemingly irrelevant statement about violence as a serious criticism of Hobbes. They have made an assumption about the meaning of the term 'violence' which they know receives general support from the social sciences and have allowed it to guide a discussion about the term in an area that has always given violence a much narrower definition. The question political theory must face is whether classical theory is being unrealistic in using its narrower definition of violence.

Violence, Historical Studies and Functional Analysis

The new preoccupation with violence also extends to historical studies. When reading E. V. Walter's *Terror and Resistance* [14] one cannot avoid asking how relevant to political theory are historical studies of violence in areas outside the Western tradition and what lessons can be drawn from them. Those who are hostile to the study of history sometimes point out that what we call history is almost entirely limited to developments in Europe and its colonial offshoots. But there is a good reason why historians have traditionally been ethnocentric. The moment we shift to cultures with non-European norms and traditions, we lose the basis that validates historical studies — we have no real way of knowing what a sequence of events 'means'.

Before considering Walker's thesis — that the violence of the Zulu king Shaka was functional in terms of social conditions and Shaka's own goals — let us consider the implications of two non-European cultural elements which may have significantly affected the course of events. First, we already know from J. G. Frazer's classic *The Golden Bough* (1890) that there was in Shaka's domain a strong tradition of the god-king and that although the combination of arbitrariness, unpredictability and ruthlessness found in his rule seems to us worse than no government at all, it would in the eyes of his subjects have seemed proof of his god-like attributes. Behaviour which to us appears insane might well have been 'functional' — the function being to increase the awe in which he was held.[15]

---

[14]Eugene Victor Walter, *Terror and Resistance: A Study of Political Violence* (New York, 1969).

[15]It may be significant that within the Western tradition both Caligula and Nero not only behaved in many respects in the same way as Shaka but declared themselves 'gods'.

A second major difference between European and many non-European cultures concerns the concept of justice. Traditionally, throughout Africa — and certainly in Shaka's region — no event has as a rule been considered 'uncaused'. If a crocodile ate a man, the assumption was that someone has arranged matters so that the path of man and crocodile will cross. Men knowledgeable in such matters are then called in to detect the culprit, who becomes guilty (he himself accepts the fact) *because* he is charged. It is such an attitude that helps to explain the acceptance without protest of Shaka's arbitrary selection of victims for execution: they were guilty because he selected them and they died praising his discernment. When the differences between notions of justice are so profound, we must be very cautious in speaking of the functions of Shaka's *Schrecklichkeit*.

With the foregoing caveats in mind, let us look from the viewpoint of political theory at the problems posed by Walker's studies of political violence and his functional analysis.

The functions Walter mentions — such as the breaking up of tribal loyalties and reducing the surplus of young warriors — are understandable from the point of view of the State as sovereign, but this does not make them acceptable to the individual members of the communities involved. From their point of view, the ruler is failing to fulfil the functions of the sovereign and their own lives and property are much less secure than they were before. Evidence that this was indeed the case is supplied by the fact that Shaka and his successor had to isolate the newly-founded State by creating an uninhabitable buffer zone and by threatening any outside community that harboured refugees. The situation then, in terms of classical sovereignty, is that the sovereign power, though not fulfilling the requirements of theory, was able to maintain its power by eliminating one of the alternatives to living under such a system.

The regime was clearly unstable, but the historical evidence that Walker supplies does not enable us to decide the extent to which it was so. Classical theory would lead us to expect that Shaka would be assassinated and that the assassin would not

---

Consequently, we may well have to reconsider the view that their self-deification proves that the rest of their behaviour was evidence of insanity.

need to conspire, organize resistance or fear opposition from adherents of the old regime. Shaka's policy was such that neither true loyalty nor power base — or true 'sovereignty' — existed. The evidence comes from the fact that he was assassinated and power transferred without any upheaval or major incident — despite an apparent lack of previous planning or organization. (Recourse to Machiavelli's precepts was unnecessary since Shaka's tyranny had destroyed his sovereignty.) The evidence, then, lends strong support to the classical theory of Hobbes and throws doubt on Walker's analysis of the 'functions' of Shaka's behaviour. In conclusion, the following points should be noted: sovereignty in the strict sense is not applicable to Shaka's rule; Walter talks of the Zulu State, while disregarding the theory of sovereignty; the history of Shaka's regime suggests that we can talk of primitive, undeveloped 'States' only outside the context of sovereignty.

There are several aspects of Walter's account that are by no means clear. We do not know, for instance, to what extent community life was threatened by Shaka's behaviour. True government seems to have remained in the hands of tribal chiefs; it is not obvious, however, what influence Shaka's conquest had on its effectiveness. Nor do we know whether the 'State' Shaka sought to establish was viable even under the most benevolent ruler. Its essentially pastoral economy does not seem to have needed larger political units and the tribal basis of the economy was — as Walker suggests — incompatible with a larger political union. In the end, we do not know whether in such circumstances a true 'State' was possible. All we know is that Shaka made extensive conquests, that he was in a position to exercise 'sovereign' power and that when his successor continued his policy all vestige of the 'State' disappeared from history.

In essence, Walter's theory is that Shaka's violence was functional in terms of social conditions and Shaka's own goals. Now as an analytical concept, 'function' has important advantages over 'purpose'. Firstly, it focuses on what is actually observable rather than on deductions from observation; secondly, it recognizes that outside a court of law what really matters is the observable consequences rather than motive or intention; and thirdly, if we are looking at human behaviour that continues over a period of time — policy-making and institutional behaviour —

it is certainly the function that matters, not the original intention. (It would, for instance, be pointless to attempt to understand a legislative body purely in terms of the constitution which set it up.) But when talking about 'function', we are adopting a pragmatic view — we ask: 'Does it work?' — and since we are not testing but observing, our answer will always be 'yes'. All actions have effects and the concept of 'function' does not provide us with a method of deciding whether they were desired or desirable. It merely relates consequences and conditions. Thus we will always be able to supply a pragmatic justification of violence — 'It works'. How do we know? Because it has a function. How can we be sure? There, you can see for yourself what happened. That's the function.

The problem with pragmatism as an analytical technique — and any talk of 'function' is precisely that — is that pragmatism is essentially solipsistic: the point of view is always that of the pragmatist. Although you may think you are talking about something other than yourself, you are not in fact doing so, with the result that you do not advance the reader's understanding about anything other than yourself. By the nature of the approach you can always justify everything that happens simply because it happens.

Violence and Political Decision-making

Mackenzie's thesis that violence or the threat of violence is the motive force in decision-making[16] is an interesting variation of the Hobbesian theory of sovereignty. Instead of seeing that violence or the threat of it was the explanation of the *existence* of a decision-making power whose actual basis for decisions is left unexplained, Mackenzie argues that the decision-making itself is to be accounted for in terms of violence. We can thus see the thesis as a supplement to the theory of sovereignty and an indication that certain ideas retain their seminal vigour although they may not be directly alluded to or even put consciously before us.

Characteristically, in an age of relativism, the thesis is thoroughly relativistic. Where Hobbes made violence and the

[16] W. J. M. Mackenzie, *Power, Violence, Decision* (Harmondsworth, 1975), p. 9.

threat of it an absolute, something which the members of a community sought to avoid, Mackenzie makes it the means to attain action from the government. Without it, apparently, government would make no policy decisions.

The book does not make it clear which of the two positions Mackenzie holds, although it seems unlikely he could believe in the alternative that no decisions would be made. Some policy decisions, for instance, are based on simple economic facts or emerge as a reaction to them. Monetary and fiscal policies are largely pursued as required by economic principles and not with the impending violence in mind. This does not mean that violence or its threat has not been able to override such fundamental considerations: the disastrous policies of the Peron régime in Argentina are an example. Normally, however, governments are not so irresponsible, and Mackenzie's theory does not explain why this is so. We can hardly argue that members of most States are sufficiently conscious of economic factors as not to press for policies that may undermine the stability of both the economy and government. (Indeed, much of the hostility to particular governments can be shown to stem from a general incomprehension of the simple fact that such obvious 'goods' as subsidized employment and the extension of welfare programmes must somehow be paid for.) What Mackenzie offers is a theory of why some governments have occasionally ignored this consideration, but not why most governments do not (no matter how great the threat of violence if they do not). In sum, it would appear that the thesis is a better reflection of current popular views of government than it is of the government's own view of the nature of decision-making: the actual decision-makers appear to be acting as if the basis of their decisions ought and must be something other than violence or its threat.

Mackenzie, of course, professes to be talking of facts, not appearances. But if he is correct, it is difficult to understand why there is a point beyond which no government will tolerate violence, even when there appears to be majority support for the opposition. Under Mackenzie's thesis, it is hard to see how the British General Strike of 1926 could have been successfully resisted, let alone why it should have been. Taking this as a test of the thesis, it looks from this point in time as if members of the

State rallied to the side of government at least to help it resist the pressures engendered by the threat of violence. Yet Mackenzie's book offers no explanation of the resistance to revolution, which — as history shows — is much more typical of human behaviour than revolution itself. There seems to be widespread support for the view that a government should never allow itself to be influenced by threats of violence based on private or sectional interests.

The point has been made obscure for us by the democratic concepts of majority rule and — to a lesser extent — pluralism. In effect both imply that a democratic government ought to be open to at least a potential for violence or its threat (even if this means only a change to a more amenable government). Yet it is also clear that a democratic government defends itself against the accusation (even when it happens to be true) that its decisions have been influenced by fear of sectional interests (e.g. the power of a national minority or of labour unions): moreover, the defence sometimes offered for policies that are clearly against majority opinion (e.g. the abolition of capital punishment) is that 'justice' — something other than majority rule or the power of private interests — demanded such a policy. Mackenzie's thesis makes the latter standpoint incomprehensible and the former an obvious falsehood.

If it is true that violence or its threat are the sole motive forces in governmental decision-making, it follows that they are a 'good' if decision-making is a 'good'. If the government sees itself as the decision-maker, it must welcome violence or its threat in order to perform its function. But in this case, how are we to explain the government's tendency to monopolize the capacity for violence and force? Are we to conclude that the essence of government is negative — that it is not to make decisions?

In conclusion, Mackenzie's book leads us to expect a discussion of a possible interrelationship between the concepts 'power', 'violence' and 'decision-making', but in actual fact the study takes on the form of independent essays which make no reference to each other. This would not necessarily be a fault if there were a chapter that sought to show their interrelation. As it is, the framework described in the blurb as 'an unprecedented synthesis of the motive force behind decision making' appears to be an excuse to put the essays between two covers. Each of these essays can stand the test of criticism when judged apart from the others and their publication does not have to be justified by the exorbitant claim that they represent an 'unprecedented synthesis'. The lack of such a synthesis reflects perhaps a difficulty in relating the discussion of violence to the fashionable empirical 'frame of reference' in contemporary political science.

Comparative Political Violence

To the political theorist von der Mehden's book on comparative political violence does not make much sense as an organized analysis, for his divisions of the topic are in serious conflict. He begins by setting forth five basic types of political violence, but, he says, 'these categories are not to be considered either necessarily causal in nature or totally comprehensive'.[17] It is rather surprising to be told at the beginning of an analysis that the categories used are incomplete. One wants to know what has been left out and why. What matters even more is that the author speaks of categories as 'not necessarily causal' in a book consisting of two main divisions: 'Types and Justifications of Political Violence' and 'Select Causes of Violence'. The 'select causes' have no relation whatsoever to the 'not necessarily causal' typology. There is another puzzling feature of his analysis. What he calls 'causes' seem more suited to what one would think of as 'justification' and some instances of what von der Mehden calls 'justification' are what others would list under 'causes'. Although the concept of 'justification' is vital to his analysis, he does not define it. We have to guess the meaning.

The first 'justification' offered here is the same as his first typology — 'primordial' religious and racial conflict — but the discussion that ensues does not make it clear in what sense the incidents of such conflict are in fact a 'justification'. Thus he speaks of the Catholic-Protestant conflict in Northern Ireland being justified 'in terms of historic animosities, charges of bias on the part of the authorities...economic and social conditions which were not changing under peaceful pressure, and antipathy toward outside interference'.[18]

---

[17] Fred R. von der Mehden, *Comparative Political Violence* (Englewood Cliffs, N.J., 1973), p. 7.
[18] *Ibid.*, p. 20.

I suggest there are at least three different senses of 'justification' of conflict within this context: (a) as defended against outside criticism; (b) as explained in terms of a theory of social and historical causation; and (c) as represented to members of the society as a just and necessary course of action. Each of these senses has quite different consequences. If (b) seems sound, (a) and (c) are to some extent irrelevant. There is some evidence that such is von der Mehden's view, because two of the 'causes' he discusses in separate chapters are the 'class-communal pattern' and 'social and economic conditions'; furthermore, his chapter on 'justification' is entitled 'The Justification and Rhetoric of Violence', as if 'justifications' in his eyes were a sort of verbal froth that comes from the mouths of angry people.

Theorists as a rule do not dismiss evidence in this way. To them, justifications in the sense of (a) and (c) are as much a part of a conflict as guns and fists or the justification in the sense (b). Indeed, they can be supremely important: it is a necessary premise in political theory that men can choose their behaviour, and that in order to do so they need norms, or — if one wants to use the term — 'justifications' in the sense of (c). (Justifications in sense (a), incidentally, are also important in gaining outside support or in resisting interference.)

In one way von der Mehden acknowledges this: in discussing 'causes', he devotes a whole chapter to 'legitimacy', observing that 'low levels of violence are positively correlated with the legitimacy of institutions'.[19] But is 'legitimacy' to be regarded as being on the same level as social and economic conditions? The fact that von der Mehden includes it in the same section of the book in which he discusses the latter may perhaps suggest that he does not recognize the normative element in the concept. We cannot be sure, however, for he does not define legitimacy. Throughout the book terms are not defined. Concepts are not analysed. Consequently, the part of the book which might have proved a valuable contribution to political theory — 'The Justification and Rhetoric of Violence' — cannot even be considered a preliminary study of the subject. How, for instance, can von der Mehden possibly conclude that 'there is no necessary relationship between the degree of aggressiveness of the rhetoric

---

[19]*Ibid.*, p. 74.

of violence and the extent of conflict that accompanies or follows it'[20] if he isolates the discussion of 'legitimacy' from such 'rhetoric'? Surely the question of the legitimacy of a régime is pertinent to the 'rhetoric' that questions that legitimacy. This should virtually be a self-evident proposition.

Violence, Human Nature and Behaviouralist Determinism

Hannah Arendt's discussion of violence is marked by the flashes of insight that make her writings interesting, no matter what her basic thesis might be. Thus in her essay 'On Violence' she says, 'If we look on history in terms of a continuous chronological process, whose progress, moreover, is inevitable, violence in the shape of war and revolution may appear to constitute the only possible interruption. If this were true, if only the practice of violence would make it possible to interrupt automatic processes in the realm of human affairs, the preachers of violence would have won an important point.'[21]

This is a fascinating idea, but it has been tossed off seemingly at random. Why did she not, for instance, use it to explain the apparent contradiction in the views of professed Marxists: 'The question remains', she says, 'why so many of the new preachers of violence are unaware of their decisive disagreement with Karl Marx's teachings.'[22] If she believes what she says in the earlier quotation (p. 132) — that violence can change the course of events — she has an answer to the latter question that is far more telling than the speculations she presents. She says 'It seems to be incontestable that the disruptive student activities in the last few years are actually based on this conviction'[23] — the conviction that violence makes it possible to 'interrupt automatic processes' or change the course of events — but since she does not specifically make the point that Marx's teachings about the historical process have been amended by a new principle (which can be attacked only as a principle and not as an aberration from the master's words), her insight is likely to be

---

[20]*Ibid.*, p. 35.
[21]Hannah Arendt, *Crises of the Republic* (New York, 1972), p. 132.
[22]*Ibid.*, p. 124.
[23]*Ibid.*, p. 132.

overlooked and her analysis of modern violence neglected as an occasional piece.

The essay 'On Violence' seems to have been written as an isolated response to the civil disorders of the Sixties rather than as a permanent contribution to political theory. The essay is not inconsistent or superficial, but it is undeveloped. 'No government exclusively based on the means of violence has ever existed' says Arendt.[24] Later on she expresses the idea conceptually: 'Power is indeed of the essence of all government, but violence is not.'[25] This in essence is Arendt's position which also implies the essential difference between her views and those of most writers on the subject — a difference of which she is well aware. Although she develops the idea by means of evidence and analysis, she does not develop it *conceptually*: she does not explain the logic of her position.

One would be inclined to say that there is a corollary to the view that 'Power is of the essence of government, but violence is not' namely that violence against the State cannot 'succeed' (cannot form a government) without power. This is indeed Arendt's position, although — as has been pointed out — she does not explain it. The matter can be taken further. A still further corollary is that the State's concession to violence is an implicit admission that the apparent yielding to violence is really a concession to 'power' or the concerted action which in a democratic State would likely lead to the overthrow of the government if the concession were not made. The danger in making such concessions is that it looks as if the State is yielding to violence and hence, in effect, encouraging it. None of this is inconsistent with what Arendt says. Although the points are basically hers, the connection between her observations is not expressed. In other words, she has not presented a genuine thesis.

The same is true when she deals with the problem of human nature. Arendt, who does not analyse her own assumptions about human nature, is troubled by what she regards as a curious consensus in discussions of power: 'If we turn to discussions of the phenomenon of power, we soon find that there

[24]*Ibid.*, p. 149.
[25]*Ibid.*, p. 150.

exists a consensus among political theorists from Left to Right to the effect that violence is nothing more than the most flagrant manifestation of power....The consensus is very strange; for to equate political power with "the organization of violence" makes sense only if one follows Marx's estimate of the state as an instrument of oppression in the hands of the ruling class.'[26]

The consensus is *not* strange and most certainly does not require us to accept the Marxian analysis. We can, for instance, accept the Freudian analysis of human nature: if man is driven by his biological urges and each of us is a separate biological unit that on occasion comes into conflict with other biological units, it follows that social organizations must be coercive, but it does not follow they must be Thrasymachian in nature.

Arendt attributes the consensus to traditions of political thought, fortified by the Hebrew-Christian tradition and 'imperative conception of law' and 'recent discoveries of an inborn instinct of domination and an innate aggressiveness in the human animal'. She herself, as we would expect from her views on the nature of power, denies the importance of the 'recent discoveries', pointing out that 'If we would trust our own experiences in these matters, we should know that the instinct of submission, an ardent desire to obey and be ruled by some strong man, is at least as prominent in human psychology as the will to power, and, politically, perhaps more relevant'[27] and that there is 'another tradition and another vocabulary no less old and time-honored...[of] a concept of power and law whose essence did not rely on the command-obedience relationship and which did not identify power and rule or law and command.'[28]

Arendt draws on empirical evidence and the evidence of history to support her own position, but what she is really confronted by is a theory of human nature and a concomitant theory of the State put forward by people who do not believe in 'philosophic' theory. The Darwinian revolution — which represented man as a part of the physical world and subject to its laws — made 'will' a confused description of the biological and environmental factors that operate on man and 'reason' a

[26]*Ibid.*, pp. 134-5.
[27]*Ibid.*, p. 138.
[28]*Ibid.*, p. 139.

rationalization of them. In consequence, even though the assumptions Hobbes made about human nature were not changed — if anything, they were reinforced — the actual theory he presented about the relation of man and State became unworthy of serious analysis. 'Science' now expects us to believe in essence what Hobbes believed, but to avoid raising objections.

The fundamental issue today remains what it was in Hobbes's time: what is man's nature? If we are by nature in conflict with one another, the State itself will be essentially coercive. Hence in seeking evidence to support a particular view of man's nature, we can draw on two sources: man's relation with man when the State organization breaks down (the main source of Hobbes's evidence) and man's relations within an organized State — the evidence of history. It is curious how seldom anyone other than historians is concerned with the latter source. Arendt uses it, but unfortunately does not construct a coherent theory of human nature in opposition to those who think they are dealing with facts when they are instead putting forward uncritical assumptions about human nature and the State.

The behaviouralist analyses of violence — as well as other categories of human behaviour — are based on two assumptions: firstly, that human behaviour is part of the modernized version of the Great Chain of Being which sees it in terms of a cause-effect sequence traceable to the principles that operate in the world of inanimate objects; and secondly, that the categories used to bring together diverse phenomena must be relativist — that is descriptive rather than implicit moral judgements on the rightness or wrongness of behaviour. As a consequence of the first assumption, specific instances of violence which allow us to analyse the circumstances, possible 'causes' are regarded as scientifically more sound than speculations about patterns or tendencies. We do not have enough specific information — the argument runs — to extrapolate. From this point of view, the use of historical evidence — lying outside of modern behavioural analysis since at the time of its being recorded it was not subject to such an analysis — can be dangerously misleading. The observations of the scholar and historian are set in opposition to those of the scientist. We can see the influence of this school of thought even on Arendt, whose analysis of violence was clearly affected by the particular events of the Sixties and considerably weakened by her failure to systematize her observations.

A more serious weakness arises from the unconscious influence of behaviouralism on non-behaviouralist studies: the confusion of categories of behaviour. So long as ethical judgements were felt to be valid, discussions of violence revolved around the concept of legitimacy and this, of course, required a theory of the State. Relativism changes legitimacy into a descriptive category — permitted by law or legal — and invites us to look at violence in terms of function: what needs or drives within the individual are served by the acts of violence and what response must the State make in view of its legal position? This produces an absurd dilemma: it justifies both violence against the State and the latter's attempts to cope with the violence. In consequence students of violence divide themselves into legalists and anti-legalists. Neither camp can offer any sound reasons for its position and no solution acceptable to both is possible, for both sides have been 'justified' (shown to be 'natural' and inevitable).

Arendt shows the influence of this relativist line of thought when she refers to the dramatizing of grievances made possible by riots and demonstrations. But she differs from the determinists who see grievances as 'causes' ('if there are grievances, there will be violence'), for to her violence is 'instrumental by nature'.[29] It is furthermore neither necessarily effective nor necessary: 'Violence and disruption make sense only for short term goals' and the danger 'will be not merely defeat but the introduction of the practice of violence into the whole body politic.'[30]

This view is unintelligible to determinists, not simply because goal-seeking, though obviously characteristic of human behaviour, has no real place in their scheme, but also because their assumptions about human nature make them see violence as the essence of the body politic; it is never introduced, but is present 'by nature'. For them each individual is a biological entity necessarily in conflict with others for a limited supply of goods; hence what we call 'violence' is fundamentally a shift in power

[29] *Ibid.*, p. 176.
[30] *Ibid.*, p. 177.

relations: either the grievances of a number of individuals have become so pressing that they are ready to risk the organized opposition of the State, or the State has lost some of its 'power' or capacity to coerce. Arendt's argument that the power of the State cannot possibly be simply coercive is bound to be ignored because determinism demands that the State be seen as coercive, since it must reflect the character of its members, who are necessarily self-assertive and aggressive.

Leslie Macfarlane's dismissal of Hannah Arendt is a curious case. 'One of the most celebrated modern political theorists who has dealt with this problem [of political violence] is Hannah Arendt', he says;[31] however, after summarizing her views, he proceeds to develop his own theories without any further reference to Arendt, even though his own position is incompatible with her view that power, not force or violence, is of the essence of government and derives its legitimacy from the 'initial getting together'[32] — an essentially contractual view. Not only does he assume what Arendt specifically denies — that the State is essentially coercive — but he suggests that the consent so important to Arendt is really a form of coercion.

Why has Arendt been treated in such a high-handed fashion? Is it implied that the difference in their views is not even open to discussion? There may be a clue in Arendt's own dismissal of the evidence for innate violence brought forward by natural scientists: 'First, while I find much of the work of the zoologists fascinating, I fail to see how it can possibly apply to our problem';[33] and secondly, 'The research results of both the social and the natural sciences tend to make violent behavior even more of a "natural" reaction than we would have been prepared to grant without them.'[34] Her discussion of the issues at this point is not convincing: the tone of her remarks suggests she is not really interested in what they have to say. A writer like Erich Fromm (whom she does not mention) makes a much better case against the use of such evidence. Anyone with faith in the

[31] Leslie Macfarlane, *Violence and The State* (London, 1974), p. 42.
[32] Arendt, *op. cit.*, p. 151.
[33] *Ibid.*, p. 156.
[34] *Ibid.*, p. 157.

behavioural sciences might be discouraged by the tone of some of her observations.

Now Macfarlane's position that consent ultimately derives from coercion is not understandable outside the framework of behaviouralist science. In political theory consent and coercion are polar terms and are treated as such by Arendt. But in a deterministic behavioural theory a term like 'consent' implying free-will becomes illusory. In line with this position, Macfarlane argues that 'Men who obey out of fear of coercion come in time to obey, in part at least, out of habit';[35] further that 'Citizens who positively identify themselves with their own political system will not normally require to be coerced' and that such consent necessarily involves coercion.[36] His analysis of violence is based on assumptions about man's nature derived (consciously or not) from the behavioural sciences. He seems unaware that many of the terms used by political scientists do not fit into the behaviouralist pattern. As a theorist, he rightly condemns Graham and Gurr's analysis of force and violence on the ground that they make no attempt to relate the terms to the concepts of 'authority' and 'legitimacy'[37] — but those terms are to a behaviouralist purely social conventions that have no place in objective analysis. When Macfarlane himself attempts to relate force and violence to 'legitimacy', the latter remains a highly subjective term — now meaning 'right to act', now being defined in terms of the purpose, method and consequences, despite the 'right to act'.[38] Arendt has achieved a far more intelligible analysis by speaking of power and violence instead of force and violence and arguing that 'power' is by definition legitimate.

When behaviouralists speak of 'violence' they do not speak of what empirical evidence shows to be true of man's behaviour but assume that the fundamental unit of investigation is a biological organism with inborn drives that necessarily bring it into conflict with other members of its species and any type of social organization that has evolved under such conditions. Under these assumptions, we may each recognize that some kind of

---

[35] Macfarlane, *op. cit.*, p. 57.
[36] *Ibid.*, pp. 58-9.
[37] *Ibid.*, p. 43.
[38] See *ibid.*, pp. 48-9.

government is in our own interest, but this will not change the fact that it is still at odds with our biological impulses. According to this school of thought, 'violence' is nature's technique for enabling the individual organism to assert its needs; it is therefore inescapable.

There is a big chasm separating Macfarlane and Arendt although they share the same fundamental interests. Arendt could hardly conceive of a political theory in which opposites like 'consent' and 'coercion' become one; fundamental and necessary concepts like 'legitimacy' become purely subjective; 'violence' not 'reason' expresses man's essential nature; and the lessons of history are of less account than laboratory studies on rats. Macfarlane, on the other hand, obviously finds unworthy of consideration anyone whose treatment of concepts 'has undertones of the moral strictures attaching to the use of force and violence'.[39] The theory of political violence is in a sad state when theorists such as Macfarlane and Arendt are not on 'speaking terms'.

Violence and Democratic Theory

What has happened as a result of the inclusion of the concept of violence in political theory? In traditional democratic theory, the underlying assumption was that man is a social animal who is by nature cooperative; he becomes violent only as a result of circumstances. Violence was regarded as a device of the self to coerce others to conform to the will of the self; hence it was by nature anti-social and consequently illegitimate, except as a technique used by authority to control such anti-social egoism (the concept of punishment). The legitimate democratic state coerced only the egoist, not the individual as such.

After Darwin, however, and above all in Freudian and Freudian-derived theory, man has been represented as a biological egoist who is coerced into acting like a social animal. Aggression is shown as part of man's nature; coercion by the State not only reflects this fact but is made necessary by it. Man and the State are set in opposition: the State by nature coerces all its members.

[39] *Ibid.*, p. 42.

Democratic theory has been slow in adjusting to the altered view of man's nature, although the new view has obviously important consequences. One adjustment has been the revival of pluralism, which sees conflicting private interests as being capable of achieving some sort of order similarly to what conflicting interests achieve in the market place. However, neither the advocates nor the critics of democratic theory relate their respective defences and attacks to the changed conceptions of human nature. Even then violence is discussed as a legitimate device for the citizen in his relations with the State (as in Marcuse) or in arguments opposed to this (as in Arendt) no direct reference is made to the theory of human nature underlying the arguments and to the fact that this is a departure from classical democratic theory. The emphasis is on violence as a norm and its legitimacy as a norm, though in an age of relativism the legitimacy of a norm can hardly be discussed without reference to man's nature.

Most troubling of all is that the general trend of discussions of violence is in terms of the 'social problem' posed rather than the implications for political theory. The principal question discussed is what the responses of a democratic government should be, whereas — if violence reflects something in man's nature — the really important questions are: 'What kind of State is possible?' and 'Is democracy possible?' In other words, democratic theory, while ready to discuss violence, is not ready to examine its fundamental implications.

If the implications were understood, we would expect a much greater interest in the Hobbesian theory of sovereignty, for it is based on a theory of human nature similar to that held today. (Significantly, Rawls's revival of the social contract has been discussed more as a response to the problem of relativism than as an adjustment to a revised view of human nature.)

Let us assume that man is aggressive by nature and that altruism and cooperation — indeed all social norms — are ultimately the product of coercion (the internalized law theory that is universal today). Under such an assumption, 'freedom' is the desirable state for the psychologists, interested in curing inhibitions and guilt, but not for the political theorist. To the latter, 'freedom' would represent anarchy in the popular sense. The desire for freedom becomes anti-social, a desire to act according to one's biological drives despite the fact that one is dependent on society for one's very existence. It becomes an irrational urge. In this view, talk of democratic 'liberty' becomes just what Ayer once said all normative talk is — an expression of an attitude which apparently need not be 'about' anything in the real world. Behaviouralists may have cause to rejoice at such a turn of events, but the theorist who needs 'freedom' as a realizable description of man's relationship with the State is placed in an untenable position (unless he interprets 'freedom' as a statement about 'equality' or man's relations with others and views the State as a sort of corporate 'other' towards which he must act as equal). What becomes necessary is the introduction of staggering readjustments to traditional democratic theory. There is a suspicion that if this is indeed what 'freedom' means, then there cannot be much difference between the aims of totalitarianism and those of democracy. Furthermore, the theory of sovereignty and the theory of democracy come into direct conflict. Under the former, if man is aggressive by nature, it is quite impossible for the individual and the State to be on 'egalitarian' terms. Under a revised theory of democracy — that makes 'freedom' an expression of egalitarian relations with everyone, including corporate bodies — they must be. The only way out is to interpret 'freedom' as a mere attitude and to regard traditional democratic theory as a discussion of unrealistic and illusory goals.

Such seems to be the tenor of contemporary democratic theory. Equality of power is becoming the main concern and 'freedoms' an obstacle — but how 'democratic' is such democratic theory? Do we have to break with the classical tradition? The nature of 'human nature', for instance, is not a self-evident truth. The facts of violence by themselves prove nothing; they were quite familiar to classical theorists. They were viewed, however, as aberrant. This is the important question still facing democratic theory: Is violence aberrant or normal, and — if normal — can we still have a democratic theory?

III
Pitfalls In Democratic Theorizing

The Problem of Unconscious Relativism in Political Theory

Anyone familiar with democratic society but not the literature describing it might well imagine that studies of democracy would emphasize the link between relativism and democracy: not only are democracies the mainstay of philosophic relativism and its related linguistic theory, but also of the supportive theories, such as Freudian theory and scientism. Though the advocates of these and other philosophic and scientific stances have never admitted it, theories of this kind have an unmistakable political distribution; they seem more convincing in the context of liberal democracies. Even those who may disagree about the obviousness of the link would certainly accept the statement that democratic societies attempt to inculcate relativist views: tolerance of individual views and submission to the majority on public decisions — both practised relativist attitudes — are essential to the working of democratic societies.

The meaning of democratic norms has been eroded. In theory, 'tolerance' and 'majority rule' could have remained norms, but the complex mental attitude required to be truly tolerant and to see majority rule as a technical device — valuable principally for what it avoids — is probably beyond the capacity of the average mind. Perhaps it is precisely the denial that the attitude is beyond the average man's capacity that accounts for the fact that relativism and democracy are seldom linked. Given relativism, the popular interpretation of tolerance is given respectability. Far from representing the inadequacies of popular thought, it proves that the majority have always been able to rise above the shortcomings and blindness of abstract reason. The legal qualification of the majority to decide issues becomes a moral qualification; tolerance becomes indifferentism.

The absence of any recent extended discussion of a link between relativism and democracy is difficult to explain. It is true that many defences of democracy employ some appeal to relativism, usually in the guise of a discussion of tolerance, individualism and majority rule. It is also true that virtually all theorists lapse into relativist assumptions, even when they hold essentially anti-relativist views, as does for instance Reinhold Niebuhr.

The reason for any particular theorist's unconscious relativism can only be found through a study of his particular use of it, for there are too many possible sources of relativism for any general observation to hold true. But when we find unconscious relativism in a political theorist's work, we may well ask whether the work has not been invalidated by it. Can one be both a relativist and a political theorist? If we find theorists who reveal marked relativist attitudes, we have to conclude that these derive from their society rather than intellectual commitment and that they have not been analysed by the man who holds them. If the consequences of relativism were of no great moment, such a lack of self-awareness would not matter much. However, the consequences of relativism are as far-reaching for both the individual and society as the acceptance of an ideology. Indeed, relativism can in many respects be considered to play the role of an ideology. Thus for many people today it is relativism rather than the norms of democracy which accounts for their adherence to the democratic system.

Schumpeter's Hidden Relativism

In regard to the classical theory of democracy, Schumpeter maintains, 'the selection of the representatives is made secondary to the primary purpose of the democratic arrangement, which is to vest the power of deciding political issues in the electorate.'[1] He proposes to 'greatly improve the theory' by reversing the roles of the two elements, making the deciding of issues by the electorate secondary to the election of the men who are to

---

[1] Joseph A. Schumpeter, *Capitalism, Socialism and Democracy* [1942] (New York, 1962), p. 269.

take the decisions: 'the democratic method is that institutional arrangement for arriving at political decisions in which individuals acquire the power to decide by means of a competitive struggle for the people's vote.'[2]

Anyone familiar with democratic processes will recognize that Schumpeter's definition is much more realistic than the one it is designed to replace, but one doubts that it can solve the major problems that the classical theory poses and still remain a democratic theory. The gist of Schumpeter's criticism of the classical theory is that the 'people' lack, and cannot acquire, the qualities necessary to make the classical theory work. If this is so, it is hard to see how a mere shift in the order of importance of elements can solve the problem. The shift is intended to eliminate the faulty element as a factor in government; but once it has been eliminated, our definition of democracy is of course changed beyond all recognition. The fact that Schumpeter evidently feels that he can shift the importance of the elements and still retain a democratic form of government suggests that his analysis contains assumptions or lines of thought which require more scrutiny.

Schumpeter gives the following as the eighteenth-century philosophy of democracy: 'the democratic method is that institutional arrangement for arriving at political decisions which realizes the common good by making the people itself decide issues through the election of individuals who are to assemble in order to carry out its will.'[3] The implications are, he says, that 'there exists a Common Good...which is always simple to define and which every normal person can be made to see by means of rational argument.'[4]

Now I cannot agree that these are 'implications' of the classical definition as Schumpeter represents it. We cannot deduce the nature of the common good, or the way it is apprehended, from the definition. We can, however, deduce that if the common good is to differ from the 'will of the people' or 'will of the representatives' or 'will of the majority', some further postulates about men and the common good are necessary (such as the rationality of man and the 'reasonableness' of the common

[2]*Ibid.*
[3]*Ibid.*, p. 250.
[4]*Ibid.*

good). But these postulates are not implied in, or derivable from, the definition. They can be accepted or rejected independently of the definition, as in fact they have been: the classical definition of democracy remains for most people what it was, while the assumptions about reason and equality which made it plausible have been eroded. The distinction between the 'common good' and the 'will of the majority' or 'will of the representatives' has also been eroded. A convincing case for a distinction can no longer be made and is no longer really intelligible to those who have accepted the logic of institutional practices.

Schumpeter's belief that the classical definition implies an inescapable identification of the common will with the common good induces him to analyse the common good in an unsatisfactory way. He says, first, that 'there is no such thing as a uniquely determined common good...[not only because] some people may want things other than the common good but [because] to different individuals and groups the common good is bound to mean different things.'[5] Schumpeter calls this assertion a 'fact'. It is of course not a 'fact', but a relativist argument which contains some highly dubious propositions.

First, there is the proposition that the presence of other 'goods' prevents agreement about the nature of the common good. Why should they? We may well be inclined to feel that the existence of private goods could override the desire to pursue the public good under certain circumstances, but that is not the same as saying that private goods inevitably prevent agreement about the existence of a recognizable public good.

Secondly, there is the proposition that 'to different individuals the common good is bound to mean different things...because ultimate values...are beyond the range of mere logic'.[6] Is Schumpeter asserting the relativist position in opposition to the classical view of norms? The following statement shows that this is so: ultimate values — our conceptions of what life and society should be — 'may be bridged by compromise in some cases but not in others.'[7] No doubt this is true, but the impossibility of compromise poses a problem only if the 'common good' is identified with the 'will of the people'. If it is

[5] *Ibid.*, p. 251.
[6] *Ibid.*
[7] *Ibid.*

identified with the 'will of the majority' or 'will of the representatives' no democratic problem arises, for under such circumstances no compromise is necessary. The modern shift in the interpretation of the common good, now sanctioned by relativism, makes Schumpeter's views rather irrelevant to the classical definition. On the other hand, to a relativist society, which has grave doubts about 'reason', the classical definition of democracy given by Schumpeter is acceptable as it stands.

Nor is Schumpeter correct when he says that 'a common will or public opinion...lacks...rational sanction...[so] that in order to claim ethical dignity for the result it will now be necessary to fall back upon an unqualified confidence in democratic forms of government as such — a belief that in principle would have to be independent of the desirability of results.'[8] If it is true that the 'good' is an expression of taste or attitude, then a form of government which recognizes this will be on one of the 'goods' and the will of the majority will generally be recognized as the most feasible way of implementing it. The belief in democracy, then, is not necessarily 'independent of the desirability of results.' Rather it is an institutionalization of the relativist statements about the 'good'.

Schumpeter's analysis of the classical theory of democracy is weakest when he discusses the reasons for its survival in the face of the fact that it is 'a doctrine so patently contrary to fact.'[9] He suggests then that the classical doctrine is powerfully supported by association with religious belief.[10]

We can certainly agree that protestantism and democracy are still very closely related and help to reinforce each other to such an extent that many Catholics in strongly democratic countries unconsciously become protestant in outlook, as is shown by their attitude to both dogma and doctrine. Yet if the relation were particularly close, we would expect to find the decline in religious convictions which is charateristic of modern times to be paralleled by a decline in democratic faith. Since there is no

---

[8]*Ibid.*, p. 253.
[9]*Ibid.*, p. 264.
[10]The decision to follow democratic rather than religious norms would not, however, as Schumpeter believes, parallel the faith of the true believer. The faith which permits willing martyrdom and blind obedience to Church authority has its secular parallel in patriotism rather than in democratic principles.

insurmountable intellectual obstacle to accepting theological premises (all that is needed is to go beyond the available facts rather than resist them), one may even argue that the decline in religious belief has been brought about by the rise of democratic piety: democratic relativism makes the moral structure of religious orthodoxy seem misguided. In other words, the objection to religion today is normative, not intellectual or rational.

Relativism creates some very difficult problems in respect of Schumpeter's requirement that the effective range of political decision be limited.[11] Schumpeter feels that 'almost any type of human affairs may conceivably be made to enter the sphere of the State without becoming part of the material of the competitive struggle for political leadership beyond what is implied in passing the measure that grants the power and sets up the agency to wield it and the contact that is implied in the government's role of general supervisor.'[12] He mentions the independence of judges, the position of the Bank of England until 1914, the Interstate Commerce Commission and State-supported universities. He tries to eliminate the objection that a sovereign power arrived at by a 'competitive struggle for leadership' would reinforce the tendency of democratic governments to allow their decisions to be influenced by the desire to return to office: in other words, the objection that his redefinition of the classical theory would not remove his own objections to the classical theory. In supposing that the existence of semi-autonomous agencies in some way counters the objection,

---

[11] One of the limits that Schumpeter proposes is that Parliament should rely on the advice of experts. All governments have, of course, done so in modern times. The decisions are never made on the basis of mere opinion only. But a difficulty arises when one supposes that the expert can give advice not only about possible consequences but also on actual policy. If the relativist position is true, if there is no relation between norms and facts, how could a man with special factual information do anything more than he does at present — give facts? A very odd consequence of relativism has been this shift to a faith in experts who, by the nature of relativist assumptions, cannot possibly serve as policy-makers. In part this has been concealed from us by the readiness of 'experts' to give advice on matters where the facts have nothing to say. Any recommendation by 'experts' involves normative assumptions which cannot be derived from the particular field studied. Indeed, a disastrous consequence of relativism is the tendency to rely on the advice of men who are in no position to give advice until they analyse their normative assumptions and make it clear to others just what the latter are.

[12] *Ibid.*, p. 293.

Schumpeter shows himself unaware of the importance of the qualification 'beyond what is implied in....' He seems to feel that the sovereign power is 'limited' by the existence of agencies which it has itself limited, a piece of illogic that is oddly common in discussions of sovereignty.

In a sense, all governments are limited;[13] furthermore, any discussion of this problem must ultimately lead to the normative question — an issue which Schumpeter endeavoured to ignore. How limited can the government in a relativist society be? At what point does the government decide that the behaviour of citizens is so anti-social or so detrimental to them as individuals that it must be stopped?

The danger of relativism is as follows: when behaviour or conditions are 'abnormal' they become a cause for government action. Traditional democratic theory limited this wide scope by adding the qualification 'if it is the will of the people that action be taken'; this was further limited by the presence of other norms in the form of constitutional limits, as well as by conceptions of what a government is, that set very narrow limits to its action. So long as man thought government was merely a coercive institution that enforced a criminal code on deviants and prevented conflicts between divergent interests in society, no real problem of limitation arose. Since then, however, the pressure of the community, fostered by democratic egalitarianism, has required the government to act on the behalf of the 'unequal', who were formerly the weak, the poor and the afflicted, but are now everyone who is not 'normal'.

Relativism makes the limits of government power indefinite by defining the wrong and the bad (which have always been subject to the authority of the government) as the 'abnormal' and by removing the moral distinction between immoral behaviour, criminal behaviour and sick behaviour. They are now all one, and the real limits of government power are primarily economic: it is just not possible for it to do as much as it would like to do, or as much as the public would like. It is difficult to see how Schumpeter can talk about limited government without stating the normative limits.

Schumpeter's weakness in regard to normative considerations

---

[13] Political power depends on the capacity for independent action of a certain number of citizens.

is nowhere better shown than when he advocates 'democratic self-control' as a condition for democracy. He asks that the public shall have all the qualities that he had earlier argued they do not have. In effect, he is merely saying that if people were 'nice', democracy would work. We know that. Any government would work and any society would be utopian if everyone had the right kind of qualities. Unfortunately they do not, and the problem of government is to overcome this obstacle.

Niebuhr's Unwitting Relativism

According to Niebuhr's early (1944) statement, 'Democracy is a "bourgeois ideology" insofar as it expresses the typical viewpoints of the middle classes who have risen to power in European civilization in the past three or four centuries. Most of the democratic ideals, as we know them, were weapons of the commercial classes who engaged in stubborn, and ultimately victorious, conflict with the ecclesiastical and aristocratic rulers of the feudal-medieval world. The ideal of equality...gave the bourgeois classes a sense of self-respect in overcoming the aristocratic pretension and condescension of the feudal overlords.'[14]

This seems an odd standpoint for someone whose aim is to uphold democracy; it makes the latter's origin an expression of a class viewpoint and a mere reaction to the norms of another class. To overcome the initial bias, Niebuhr must argue that the actual source of the democratic norms is irrelevant, that what matters is their normative sets and their relation to larger principles of justice. It may be fairly easy for a (protestant) theologian to adopt this view in religious matters. But a similar attitude to the norms of one's political order may lead to serious difficulties. A modern State having an ideological basis cannot allow its members to believe anything or nothing without endangering its existence, for unlike church members, non-believers in the State cannot simply 'leave'. By the nature of the State, the dissident is virtually compelled to demand changes, so that if it becomes widely felt that democracy was originally an expression of a class position and economic conditions, and that no further justifications of the norms are possible, a serious problem results. Just

[14]Reinhold Niebuhr, *The Children of Light and the Children of Darkness* [1944] (New York, 1960), pp. 1-2.

how serious can be seen from the comparison of two different interpretations of the democratic norms.

For A.D. Lindsay, a classic student of modern liberal democracy, norms and beliefs come from other sets of norms and beliefs: for instance, there is an affinity between democratic norms and those of Christianity. For C.B. Macpherson, on the other hand, norms are related to particular social conditions and economic arrangements and he stresses the relation between liberal democracy and capitalism. Those who want their norms founded on some kind of empirically observed conditions might be tempted to side with Macpherson rather than Lindsay, who necessarily deals with norms and beliefs not themselves proved or provable.

The real difference between the two approaches is that only those who derive norms from norms and patterns of thought are in a position of justify their theorizing. The Marxist school of historical determinists are compelled to stop their analyses when they have established the relation between the historical conditions and the norms; by their own assertions norms are products of social conditions and this view excludes the possibility that these products could now affect social conditions. If they allowed the norms to acquire an existence of their own — such that they could influence behaviour — they would be forced to give up their historical determinism. By talking about the social conditions that give rise to norms as if he were uttering self-evident truths, Niebuhr has put himself in the determinist camp. If he is to get out, he must adopt a view which is not open to the determinists — that norms acquire an independent existence and can be validated or invalidated through an analysis of the type used by Lindsay. In fact Niebuhr adopts this approach. Indeed, his observations on origins seem to be only a nod in the direction of those he assumes to be authorities.[15]

How the 'ideal' of democracy comes into a system of norms relativist in origin and in practice becomes clear when we examine Niebuhr's conception of evil and man's nature. For Niebuhr,

---

[15]Consider for instance the following passage: 'Ideally democracy is a permanently valid form of social and political organization which does justice to two dimensions of human existence: to man's spiritual stature and his social character; to the uniqueness and variety of life, as well as to the common necessities of all men.' *Ibid.*, p. 3.

'evil is always the assertion of some self-interest without regard to the whole....'[16] 'Self-love, which is the root of all sin, takes two social forms. One of them is the domination of other self by the self. The second is the sin of isolationism.'[17] This self-love is, of course, inherent in the nature of man and as such forms the central problem of government. The 'children of darkness' recognize no law beyond their will and interest. 'The children of light' believe that they 'should be brought under the discipline of a higher law.'[18]

But if evil is to be controlled and yet all men are by nature inclined to evil, what system of government can establish the justice that is presumably the goal of the State? Any system which seeks 'freedom' in the sense of freedom from restraints on the individual — as traditional liberal democracy does — is wrong. So is any system which foresees the elimination of all restraints at some indefinite future date, as does communism. So, too, is any system which exalts the State and places inordinate power in the hands of the few, since their inherent capacity for evil will be unrestrained. What is left to Niebuhr is democracy modified by the insights of Hobbes and Luther: 'For certainly one perennial justification for democracy is that it arms the individual with political and constitutional power to resist the inordinate ambition of rulers, and to check the tendency of the community to achieve order at the price of liberty.'[19]

It is not our purpose to follow out Niebuhr's various arguments for democracy in his book *The Children of Light and the Children of Darkness*. Probably its chief value lies in the insight it offers about the close relations between democracy and protestantism. It shows — perhaps without intending to — why democracy has such a strong hold upon protestant-oriented societies; and also, why Niebuhr's predominantly protestant country of origin was willing to exchange its democratic forms for one of the most monstrous régimes of modern times. It is this last point that must concern us, for it introduces the relativism

---

[16]*Ibid.*, p. 9.
[17]*Ibid.*, p. 55.
[18]*Ibid.*, p. 9.
[19]*Ibid.*, pp. 46-7.

which Niebuhr is ostensibly counteracting.

Niebuhr criticizes Hobbes and Luther for advocating a repressive government: 'They assigned only the negative task of suppression to government.'[20] This criticism is rather curious: 'In their opinion the business of government is to maintain order by repression. Though it is true that government must have the power to subdue recalcitrance, it also has a more positive function. It must guide, direct, deflect and rechannel conflicting and competing forces in a community in the interest of a higher order. It must provide instruments for the expression of the individual's sense of obligation to the community as well as weapons against the individual's anti-social lusts and ambitions.'[21] It is not, then, coercion he opposes, but the kind of coercion which prohibits. Other kinds — for example, re-education — are permitted, provided they do not stem from the mere desire to strengthen the power of a State. In theory, Niebuhr believes in principles of justice transcending relativism: 'Every society needs working principles of justice, as criteria for its positive law and system of restraints.'[22] What are these? 'The profoundest of these actually transcend reason and lie rooted in religious conceptions of the meaning of existence.'[23] This does not mean, however, that he advocates theocracy: 'But every historical statement of them is subject to amendment. If it becomes fixed it will destroy some of the potentialities of a higher justice, which the mind of one generation is unable to anticipate in the life of subsequent eras.'[24] We are back, then, to democracy without its relativism. Or are we? If we examine the consequences of Niebuhr's conception of man's nature, it becomes obvious that some kind of relativism is inescapable.

Insofar as man's impulses are evil, it follows that a 'good' government is one which controls them; but the good — being unknown to evil man — can only be defined negatively — as that which counteracts the 'evil'. Conceptually, there is another good, usually called natural law, but given Niebuhr's concep-

---

[20]*Ibid.*, p. 44.
[21]*Ibid.*
[22]*Ibid.*, p. 71.
[23]*Ibid.*
[24]*Ibid.*

tion of evil and his consequent suspicion of reason and 'revelation', this absolute good cannot function. The 'good' known to man must be laws of the State passed to enforce restrictions which will serve to limit the human capacity for evil. But such laws would not resemble those now being passed in any democratic country. Some of Niebuhr's observations point in the direction of laws regulating morality passed in sixteenth-century Geneva, not the laws we have in the twentieth century: our premises about man and moral principles are different.[25]

Niebuhr is mistaken, I believe, in his supposition that the theoreticians who laid the foundations of modern democracy had a naïve faith in man's nature which disregarded his obvious capacity for evil. Rather they began with the only possible assumptions about man and morals if one were to establish an essentially non-coercive system of government: man must by nature be either good or morally neutral. The view that most men are inherently evil results in a hopeless contradiction; that he be strictly governed and that the government — since its members are not exempt from man's capacity for evil — be limited in action. Niebuhr sees an approximation to these conditions in a democracy capable of giving up its faith in man's nature. However, the working conception of the good under such conditions could only lead to coercive laws whose justification would be the degree to which they limited or redirected biological drives and other manifestations of self. Since the method of arriving at the laws has all the relativist implications of the majority rule system of democracy — and none of the restraints furnished by the democratic respect for the self-interest and private conscience of the individual — Niebuhr's interpretation of man could only lead to the unwitting relativism prevalent among fundamentalists, who hold views similar to Niebuhr's about man's nature. A belief in man's evil demands uncritical respect for the law, no matter what the law says, provided it has been passed in accordance with democratic principles.

In a more recent work, *The Democratic Experience* (1969), the essential relativism of Niebuhr's outlook is revealed by his statements about contingent factors in the history of Western

---

[25]Consider, for instance, his observations regarding sex, food, housing, and clothing. *Ibid.*, pp. 61-2.

democracies. Summarizing his own view, he says: 'If we seek to distinguish between the factors contingent to Western history and the basic norm relevant for all communities, which is that there must be a tolerable equilibrium of power for the sake of a tolerable justice, we come to the conclusion that an industrial civilization is more able to establish such an equilibrium than an agrarian culture, but that it can do so only after a strong class of organized workers is able to make a balance of power with the owners and managers of the industrial enterprise.'[26]

It is easy enough to see Niebuhr's relativism in the view that some norms at least are historically determined — that they require non-normative preconditions to be norms at all. (This kind of view has always had the defect of requiring us to believe that an 'ought' can be easily derived from an 'is'.) The mechanism in Marxian analysis seems to be self-interest, which becomes a norm of a society when there is a sufficiently large class of individuals with the same interests — and recognizing this — to impose it upon others. Niebuhr follows the Marxist view sufficiently closely to speak of the 'bourgeois sense of the individual'. Once we start along this line of thought, we encounter serious problems when we want to move to norms which are universal and absolute (as proponents of the view inevitably do). Indeed, given the self-interest basis of norms, it seems likely that members of the class *homo sapiens* have in common certain interests that can be called universal and absolute norms. The difficulty is that while it is possible that such interests exist, it is not possible by the mechanism postulated for them to become norms: the 'class' interest (as opposed to some other class) no longer exists. Furthermore, the historically determined class norms must presumably continue to preclude the development of universal norms as they did in the past. Even if one postulates a 'class' aware of the universals — an intelligentsia, a political party, etc. — the norms that arise as a result of its interests as a class must militate against the universals. The problem with seeing any norms as historically determined is that universals

[26] Reinhold Niebuhr and Paul E. Sigmund, *The Democratic Experience: Past and Prospects* (New York, 1969), p. 86. We will not quarrel with the view expressed here that there must be democracy in the sense of a particular type of power distribution before there is democracy in the sense of particular principles of justice, even though it does not seem to reflect historical developments. For our purposes, the issue is the elements of relativism.

become excluded.

It is true that Niebuhr may merely have wanted to express the idea that certain norms can be exercised only with difficulty if conditions are not propitious — the starving man is more tempted to be dishonest than the rich — but in talking about preconditions for democracy, he made a case for the historical determinism of norms; and for an obvious relativism, which is a view not devoid of absolutist tendencies.

Tingsten's Sociological Relativism

Excellent though Tingsten's book *The Problem of Democracy* is for the clarity, succinctness, objectivity and range of its discussion of democratic 'problems', his own position comes as a surprise: 'Democracy must be an ideal which can be attained by everybody, everywhere. For this form of government means that all mankind has the opportunity of reaching a certain degree of political insight, that everyone has the opportunity of making his opinion carry weight, and that this influence on the arrangements made by society is combined with the possibility of man's living in freedom and enjoying an enriched personal life.... Democracy presupposes personal independence. It cannot be fully justified except as an attempt to liberate and to develop human personality.'[27]

Tingsten is no doubt sincere when he makes his statement, but there is no indication in the book of the way in which he arrived at such a view, expressed after a section discussing the public as 'consumer rather than producer of political demands.'

He speaks of 'successful democracies' (especially the USA) as characterized by the attractive packaging of personalities and stereotypes rather than ideas.[28] Such views make it difficult to

[27]Herbert Tingsten, *The Problem of Democracy* [1945] (Totowa, New Jersey, 1965), pp. 203-04.
[28]The following passages are characteristic: 'Owing to the lack of ideas, the lack even of real arguments which can be marketed, the parties imagine that attractive pictures and slogans...will give them the two or three per cent of the voters who make the difference between resounding victory and fearful catastrophe.' *Ibid.*, p. 200. 'Discussion of ideas and issues has been replaced to a large extent by forms of propaganda.... The vitality which marks the passionate battle of ideas has no place in the atmosphere of adjustment and compromise which characterizes the successful democracies. We cannot have both.' *Ibid.*, p. 202.

understand what Tingsten means when he speaks of the 'opportunity for political insight'. Yet the conjunction of such seeming disparates appears to be deliberate. To understand him we have to look at his interpretation of the nature of norms — the relative versus absolute values.

It is evident that Tingsten's views would appear consistent only within a relativist context. Is he a relativist and, if so, of what kind? Here his discussion of Kelsen is significant. When discussing the relativist defence which Kelsen offers for democracy, Tingsten sees it as no more than 'an overly generous extension of a valid thought that is close at hand: when an individual or individuals attain a certain amount of strength or have a fanatic belief in what the state ought to do, they are inclined to regard as unimportant the means used to achieve their ends.'[29] He regards Kelsen's interpretation of relative and absolute truths as nebulous: amounting, it would seem, to a simple distinction between weak and firm conviction. Tingsten rightly suggests that such a distinction has no bearing on political theory. However, Kelsen's case seems to be much stronger than Tingsten allows.[30] It seems that Kelsen advances the proposition that democratic society is the only one compatible with philosophic relativism: if it is true that there are no absolute norms, a society whose very method of choosing a government and deciding issues embodies such a view, can be said to be compatible with that truth and hence to be 'true' or 'good' (insofar as such terms have the relativist viewpoint). The difficulty with Kelsen's view is the philosophic antinomy that results — the requirement to accept at least one absolute norm (as for instance, to be intolerant of intolerance) in a system that excludes all. There are also some practical difficulties — of which the confrontation with totalitarianism is only one — but the position can hardly be considered unclear. Why, then does Tingsten find it so? The most likely answer is that Tingsten is himself a relativist, but belonging to a different school from Kelsen's. Where Kelsen has been influenced primarily by

---

[29]*Ibid.*, p. 73. His comments are based on Hans Kelsen's *Vom Wesen und Wert der Demokratie* (1929).

[30]See, for instance, Hans Kelsen, 'Foundations of Democracy', *Ethics*, Vol. LXVI, No. 1, Part II (October 1955). Reprinted in W.J. Stankiewicz (ed.), *Political Thought Since World War II* (New York, 1964), pp. 65-115.

philosophic relativism, Tingsten has been influenced by sociological analysis. Throughout his book, *The Problem of Democracy*, Tingsten exhibits the belief that norms and ideas come from institutional practices and social conditions. Thus he says 'The political theories of the left-wing Puritans — often called "Levelers" and "Diggers" because of the democratic outlook of the former and the communist cast of mind of the latter — originated in their experiences in their own congregations, held together by a common faith and ruled in a democratic fashion.'[31] He does not ask why the congregations had such an organization of spirit; it seems that if one believes in sociological explanations of norms and ideas, on neither hopes nor needs to trace the sociological influence on political ideas by going behind the immediate situation. So, too, Tingsten traces the rise of toleration in New England to the social conditions then prevailing[32] and suggests that individualistic democracy 'was especially suited to American conditions.'[33] The reform of the franchise in England, the introduction of universal suffrage in the German Empire and the establishment of a democratic republic in France also have a sociological basis;[34] furthermore, the communist theory of revolution was 'particularly designed and appropriate to the situation in Russia during World War I.'[35]

It is needless to multiply examples: the norms and ideas which some believe to have an independent existence and to exert an independent influence on society are for Tingsten very closely dependent on particular social conditions. The view is a relativist one (with some affinities to the Marxist interpretation) but it is quite unlike Kelsen's position. Thus, where Kelsen links tolerance with relativism (he does so because of his very interpretation of relativism), Tingsten sees no such connection. To him, the mere fact that norms and beliefs are related to social conditions should in no way affect one's attitude to the norms. This is precisely why Tingsten finds Kelsen's view obscure. He assumes that when Kelsen speaks of relativism he must be

[31]Tingsten, *op. cit.*, p. 21.
[32]See *ibid.*, p. 23.
[33]*Ibid.*, p. 26.
[34]See *ibid.*, pp. 39-40.
[35]*Ibid.*, p. 177.

thinking of Tingsten's own postion, whereas in fact the two proceed from quite different premises.

Tingsten's relativistic position is also revealed in his discussion of the debate of planning initiated by Hayek. As Tingsten says, his own 'personal position coincides in [the] main with the views of non-socialist thinkers.'[36]

To consider, incidentally, the planning debate in terms of planning alone is to commit oneself to a materialist set of norms and thus to limit discussion of the real issues. The debate is only a subsection of the wider issue of relativism *versus* absolutism. Discussed independently the planning debate can be reduced to the idea that an unwilled direction is free and a willed one is not because the will behind a planned economy cannot be that of the people. This is another way of saying that we are free to the extent that the norms and desires we have are not directly traceable to another's influence. Such a position demands sociological relativism: willed norms are suspect because they may well reflect the private interests or desires of another and, as such, are of course incompatible with the concept of the equal worth of all members of society. Those who are not committed to relativism may well find this view unpalatable, for it leaves man without any genuine choices. Thus we are forced to suspect the motives of those who profess to offer long-range views and to resign ourselves to circumstances, or rather circumstances given a will through majority opinion. One would no doubt find it easier to retain some faith in reason and the critical examination of norms.

By assuming that norms derive from sociological circumstances and at the same time emphasizing the worth of the individual — which is equivalent to showing respect for the individual's norms — Tingsten is compelled to deny that democratic norms form an ideology in the sense of a system of norms which must be accepted if one is to be considered an adherent of the political system; such an ideology would be an artificial constraint upon democratic individualism. It is for this reason that Tingsten says 'people have slowly drifted into democracy without realizing it'[37] and that 'democracy may be described as a

[36] *Ibid.*, p. 168.
[37] *Ibid.*, p. 79.

sort of superideology in the sense that it is common to different political persuasions.'[38] If 'democracy' were a specific goal that could be sought or a specific ideology that could be imposed, it would not have what is an important element in Tingsten's own normative scheme — sufficient respect for private judgement.

The term 'superideology' is not particularly well chosen either in regard to definitions of political orders or for our understanding of political behaviour. First, it is not clear, given the concept of 'superideology', why Tingsten should want to distinguish the British political order of 1776, which he calls a 'privilege state' from the American order of the same period, which he is willing to call democracy. At one point,[39] he emphasizes limitation of the franchise as the criterion; at another,[40] that the 'privilege state' presupposes 'a definite social structure'. The views are not inconsistent, of course. Both are logical objections based on democratic egalitarianism. But if the egalitarian norm must find expression in a particular form of enfranchisement and a particular social structure, is it still possible to talk of democracy as a superideology?

Exactly how 'super' (= 'comprehensive', 'embracing more than one method of ordering the norms') is democracy? The term 'superideology' is not all-embracing; some ideological formulations, even of democratic norms, are excluded from it; and the term seems to have an arbitrary content. It cannot be true that democracy permits the 'coexistence of ideas' if its definition excludes certain formulations of its own norms. To be a recognizable political order, it must of course set limits to the beliefs and practices of its members: an attempt to permit the coexistence of all ideas, as being of equal worth, would result in anarchy. Democracy may be tolerant and its norms at such odds with one another that no certain statement can be made about what the norms require, but this is not the same as saying that it permits an unrestricted coexistence of ideas or that it is a superideology. The concept 'superideology' is plausible only if one assumes that ideas and ideologies, norms and normative schemes are not in themselves forces which affect human

[38] *Ibid.*, p. 49.
[39] *Ibid.*, p. 14.
[40] *Ibid.*, p. 49.

behaviour except in the way that men suppose they should. If norms and ideologies arise from social conditions and require certain circumstances in order to be accepted by free man (sociological relativism), it is the task of the theorist to show their true nature and to stand by the system that allows this — democracy, the 'superideology'. This, in short, is the main direction of Tingsten's study. The approach has the awkward consequence of forcing us to suppose that goal-seeking (normative behaviour) is a dangerous illusion which becomes more dangerous as it becomes more orderly (ideological).

Macpherson's Deterministic Relativism

An author such as C.B. Macpherson, who not only attempts to define democracy normatively but calls his book *The Real World of Democracy*, can hardly regard himself as a relativist. Yet there are aspects of his seemingly normative approach to democracy which raise doubts about his normativism.

There are three 'facts' on which Macpherson bases his analysis of democracy. They are firstly, 'that the clearly non-liberal systems which prevail in the Soviet countries, and the somewhat different non-liberal systems of most of the underdeveloped countries of Asia and Africa, have a genuine historical claim to the title democracy'; secondly, 'that liberal democracy, like any other system is a system of power'; and thirdly, 'that liberal democracy and capitalism go together'.[41] A discussion of the consequences of these 'facts' will reveal the extent to which Macpherson is compelled to be relativist in outlook.

The first proposition — that things having a common origin belong to a common class — is not a serious argument for extending application of the term 'democracy' in the way Macpherson does. This proposition is the basis of many classifications in the physical and biological sciences. Thus dogs, wolves, foxes and jackals are placed in the class 'canines' because of a common ancestry and it would be ridiculous to bring out their differences when comparing classes of animals. 'Scientistic' thinkers may insist that this principle should also be applied to ideologies and maintain that the class of believers in 'democracy' must include

[41]C.B. Macpherson, *The Real World of Democracy* (Toronto, 1965), pp. 3-4.

those who support communism. But the normativist must reject the analogy, since for him it is not the source of the norms that is at issue but the entire set. When discussing ideology we are talking about normative interrelationships, not about history. Although it is true that communist egalitarianism as a concept can be traced back to the same source as democratic egalitarianism, to conclude that — since both concepts are fundamental norms for each system — the two are therefore fundamentally the same, is to misunderstand normative sets. The egalitarianisms of communism and democracy are utterly different because they exist in utterly different contexts of norms. In our society many 'innocents', who have never come under direct communist influence, develop Marxist types of reasoning which most of them later abandon: equality is 'negated' by differences in property; slums are 'proof' of class exploitation, and so forth. They do exactly what Marx did — abstract a single norm of democracy and work out its implications without regard for other norms. A true non-relativist would not regard 'egalitarianism' — or any other norm held in common by two normative systems — as evidence of a fundamental similarity between the systems, but as evidence of the importance of considering total systems of norms. It obviously matters a great deal that individualism (or the concept of freedom) is not a part of communist ideology, for it helps to set limits on what we mean by equality and how we strive to realize it. Macpherson is not a relativist in the sense of saying that it does not matter what norms one advocates, but he has allowed relativism (derived from scientism) to muddle his thinking about norms.

The second 'fact' which stands out in Macpherson's analysis ('Liberal democracy, like any other system, is a system of power') tends to obliterate the very necessary distinction between democracy and totalitarianism, one being governed by consent and the other by coercion. Critics who are aware of this are likely to suppose that Macpherson will have no great difficulty in showing that coercive systems are also 'democratic', provided those in power profess 'democratic' principles and promote through legislation some of the conditions characteristic of democracy. Although Macpherson is quite right in maintaining that any political system is a system of power, or that all systems are in part coercive — the positive law is justified, because in certain areas of behaviour deemed important to the community, consent is impossible to attain — he nonetheless departs from the argument for the coercive nature of the State in a way that invalidates his premise. Instead of holding to the view that any State — in order to be a State — has an unqualified right to coerce, he defends coercion in terms of particular normative goals: the State is democratic if coercion is designed to promote 'democratic' norms. (This is a variation of the argument that the end justified the means, the difference being that here the end is represented as a *definition* of the democratic nature of the means.) Coercion, instead of being a fundamental aspect of government, is 'educative' and presumably temporary in nature. This view is contradictory to Macpherson's original position, for, if it is true that coercion has a specific normative goal, it cannot be plausibly held that all systems are systems of power. (Some normative systems could have reached their goal and thus no longer need to be systems of power.) Instead, if reaching a normative condition is the raison d'être of coercion, it would seem impossible for the object to be achieved by such means, since normative behaviour is defined in terms of choice, not compulsion. The circumstance that — after long coerced habituation to certain modes — direct coercion becomes unnecessary, does not mean that the behaviour is made 'moral': it means that one's normative standards have become relativistic.

Macpherson's third assumption — that our form of democracy grew up alongside capitalism — is a hostile way of expressing the link between Western democracy and the concept of property. The latter was essential to 'democracy' long before anything like modern capitalism developed. Although we may regard Locke's attempt to link the concept of property with that of the individual as unsatisfying, we would be wrong if we dismissed his theory as an aberration. The concept of property is an extension of the concept of self; thus a child develops a sense of property before it can speak and regards an assault on its property as assault on itself. The attitude is universal: all mankind seems to have a concept of property.[42]

---

[42] During the early days of communism, reports were circulated of societies which have no concept of property. It was necessary that such societies be 'discovered,' since it was

The concept, of course, need not imply the ruthless Victorian form of capitalism which so appalled Marx. This particular aberration followed from the ambition of a rising middle class. The latter took 'equality' literally — as excusing exploitation of the weak and impoverished on the ground that anyone who wanted to, could rise in the world: those who did not were quite properly penalized by the system for their lack of will-power and ambition. We retain the competitive spirit because our democratic society obliterates formal class divisions so that most people must strive to attain or retain status; but today's competition exploits to a lesser extent.

Although there have been changes in the attitude towards acquiring property, the concept itself has remained the same: property is always 'private', because of its association with the individual. Consequently, those societies which emphasize 'private property' — as ours does — emphasize the importance of the individual in the normative scheme; those societies — like the USSR — which emphasize State property, give the State a corporate identity which is incompatible even with their own definition of democracy. The result is that a property-owning State cannot wither away. It is a 'super-individual' whose 'personality' derives from its ownership, just as in the case of the Victorian capitalist. This leads to the savage penalties imposed in communist countries for damage to State property: the act is regarded as an assault on the State itself. When the State is viewed as the only legitimate property owner — which makes only a few small concessions to man's weaknesses — it is given a personality that it cannot have under the liberal system. The real issue between communism and democracy is not free-enterprise versus state capitalism, but the concept of the State created by that of property. Thus, Macpherson's classification notwithstanding, the West has very little in common with the Soviet Union, despite the historical links between the respective ideologies.

Macpherson's conclusions result from his assumptions and not from historical analysis. Like all theorists of a Marxist bent,

---

inconceivable that all mankind should fall into the same normative 'error' as the Western democracies. Modern anthropologists, however, have been unable to confirm these findings.

he raises doubts about his normative views (which, incidentally, neither he nor his critics have analysed satisfactorily). His historicism has affected his normative position. Why should this be so? The answer will explain the mutual suspicion of the various types of 'democracy' which Macpherson has lumped together under a common denominator.

Was England in the days of Hobbes a 'market society' or was it not? Are the points made by critics like Isaiah Berlin, who object to Macpherson's theory of the seventeenth-century 'market society', relevant? At times, Macpherson and his critics seem to be in doubt as to the true nature of their disagreement.

I suggest that Macpherson was not attempting to describe exactly an historical situation but to set forth examples of how economic structures and social conditions mould ideas. It is precisely that idea which is at issue, and it is neither provable nor disprovable empirically, because the sources of norms and ideas are not empirically observable.

If we are to question Macpherson's views, it must be on the grounds of the logical relation between his humanistic norms and his determinism. Given determinism, is it possible to hold a genuinely normative position? The answer is negative. The assumption that norms have a single source — a body of inspired doctrine or historical conditions — places the subject of discussion outside the concept of 'norm'. In order to talk about norms (and also hold them up as goals to be achieved, principles of action, or things which can be mentally manipulated to form significant statements) it is necessary to believe that their essential feature is not their source but their capacity to affect human behaviour. Once we believe this, it is unimportant how they originated. If we insist on the importance of their origins — and that they would not exist if it were not for some particular circumstances — we cannot believe that normative statements made outside of those circumstances are of any significance. For this reason, relativists abandon discussion of norms after having established that these norms have one particular source or 'nature'. When someone continues to manipulate them — in this case make recommendations based on a frankly normative position about freedom and equality — we have a right to question his analysis of their origins and the sincerity of his normative position.

If we assert that norms affect behaviour, we commit ourselves to the view that there is a relation between norms and other aspects of culture, such as particular historical circumstances. But the point is that historical determinists argue that the relation is one way: norms are the product of circumstances but cannot themselves produce new circumstances without violating the premise about the nature of norms. It is this that creates doubts about Macpherson's analysis: to lay the stress — as he does — on historical determinism, is to deny a function to his own normative views; to give them a function — to believe he is sincere in his talk of freedom — is to deny his determinism. Macpherson must give up one of his positions, but because we do not know which one he prefers, we cannot accept what he says.

Braybrooke's Relativistic-Normative Analysis

Braybrooke approaches democracy from a fresh point of view. Instead of wrestling with the problem of liberty versus equality, he regards the concept of freedom as suspiciously vague and treats the issues it raises under the concept of rights, which for him are not limited to the constitutional ones. Beginning with a larger conception of rights and a distinction between the possession of them and welfare, and distinguishing this in turn from preference ('collective preference'), Braybrooke's approach holds much promise. That the promise is not quite fulfilled is in part the result of Braybrooke's rather careless use of phrases, but much more of his failure to apply adequate normative analysis to an approach that is normative by nature.

It is by no means clear just what 'rights' are to Braybrooke. He speaks of them as 'devices for advancing welfare'[43] and states that, such being the case, advocates of democracy 'could perhaps dispense with the concept of rights'.[44] Yet he also says that 'one of the basic principles behind the practice of asserting and heeding rights is precisely to forestall general considerations of happiness or well-being and the like from being freely invoked to decide the particular cases embraced by rights.'[45] It is difficult

---

[43] David Braybrooke, *Three Tests for Democracy: Personal Rights, Human Welfare, Collective Preference* (New York, 1968), p. 80.
[44] *Ibid.*, p. 85.
[45] *Ibid.*, p. 39.

to see how a concept of welfare that embraces the welfare of the individual and that of the majority can be intelligible without a clear-cut concept of rights, which historically have been norms designed to counterbalance the heavier weight automatically given to majority opinion in a system of popular government. Fundamentally, rights are normative absolutes incorporated into a relativistic system in recognition of the facts that those using the system are not really relativists at heart and that the system is not relativist in intent. To deny the importance of rights is to deprive society of any possibility of self-criticism.

For Braybrooke, rights are clearly a type of norm having no necessary connection with a Constitution (constitutional 'bill of rights'), for he mentions a right to marriage and the right of a rejected friend to be heard. Some of these rights appear to be absolutes, since he speaks of inalienable rights.[46] On the other hand, one cannot be sure that he would abide by the view if challenged. The particular example he gives of an inalienable and 'inextinguishable' right is poorly analysed. He says: 'Could the alienation or extinction of the right to a fair trial be accepted under any social conditions?...it would be possible for a society not to have trials at all.... Societies are imaginable...which do not have any concept of rights. Yet it seems to be true, nevertheless, that if a society makes any use of the concept of rights to regulate its affairs, then in that society there must be a right to a fair trial...'[47]

He rests his case upon a feeling (note his 'seems to be true') and makes no attempt to relate what is 'possible' or 'imaginable' to that feeling. The feeling is sound enough, for it stems from an objection to an implicit contradiction in the use of terms: if a trial is assumed to be necessary to the concept of justice, then an unjust trial would be a contradiction of the concept. The question Braybrooke poses is a mental trick that does not move us an inch further towards an understanding of inalienable rights.

Other statements which he makes suggest that he is vague about his reasons for holding to a concept of inalienable rights and does not appreciate the true nature of the position he has

---

[46] *Ibid.*, p. 21.
[47] *Ibid.*, pp. 42-3.

taken. Thus he says: 'The justification of particular rights requires empirical evidence about effects promoting human interests in ways conducive to general welfare. This evidence is fallible; it therefore demands periodic review.'[48] He recognizes that such a position raises doubts about whether there can be inalienable rights and attempts to resolve the difficulty by saying 'a right is inalienable or inextinguishable because people understand it to be so.'[49] Since, however, their understanding of it in this way depends upon circumstances and attitudes that are not themselves permanent,[50] the rights are in no sense inalienable. They are purely relative.

One might also question Braybrooke's assertion 'the justification of particular rights requires empirical evidence.' In what way can there be empirical evidence about norms? If a man shouts 'Fire!' in a crowded theatre when there is no fire, do we have empirical evidence for limiting the 'freedom of speech' norm? Justice Holmes seemed to think so, for he used precisely this example to justify a decision which limited the right to freedom of speech. However, the example does not prove much. To suppose that the situation involves a problem demanding a solution, one must make three normative assumptions: (i) it is right to be allowed to have one's say (apart from the truth or falsehood of one's statement); (ii) it is wrong to endanger others by exercising that right; (iii) endangering is more wrong than suppressing. It was the supposition that the example involved an empirical truth — rather than two norms set into a normative hierarchy — that led Holmes and those who support his 'clear and present danger' principle to use the analogy to decide a quite different normative situation, in which the third assumption was by no means self-evident. Our society, then, because of its belief that empirical evidence is pre-eminent and has universal relevance, may lead even staunch advocates of its principles to abandon them and become in effect relativists. It happened to Holmes and in all likelihood it has happened to Braybrooke.

The frequent need to convert into relative concepts that most

---

[48] *Ibid.*, p. 41.
[49] *Ibid.*
[50] See *ibid.*, the argument on p. 42.

of us would like to feel are absolutes, is an inevitable feature of our society. Thus our courts, even though they often try to approach the legal code as if they were dealing with absolutes,[51] are compelled to make decisions about the relative importance of the whole range of society's norms. This is because the question of responsibility, which is their concern, frequently entails considerations of the plea that violation of the legal code was caused by the observance of some other norm ('I crashed the car to avoid hitting a dog,' etc.). In a relativistically oriented society the result may be to convert what were formerly 'absolute' rights into mere legal forms having no real effect, since it is the court decisions that count, not the abstract formulation.

This is certainly what has happened to the right of free assembly: if treated always as an inviolable right, it would have remained such and the large number of restrictions on it would have been disallowed by the courts. But the right so obviously fails to fulfill its original function and is so dangerous in a society that regards man as basically irrational that only the doctrinaire democrat and constitutionalist endeavours to make any case for it. Although the example is an extreme one, it demonstrates that no matter what the courts' attitude to constitutional rights is supposed to be, they are compelled slowly but surely to abandon those rights which are not recognized by membes of the society as important and to treat the remainder from the relativist viewpoint held by society as a whole. Braybrooke may have a similar idea in mind when he says 'historical processes gradually raise up new rights to fixed positions and simultaneously undermine the rigid position of old ones'[52] ... and also when he refers to a sort of life process of birth, maturity and decline among rights: 'One beholds rights ascending from championship to full recognition, moral and legal simultaneously; and then, in some cases, with the passing of time, losing their moral force while they retain a foothold in the letter of the law.'[53]

---

[51]Consider, for instance, the following observation of H.L. Mencken: 'The average American judge, as everyone knows, is a mere rabbinical automaton, with no more give and take in his mind than you will find in the mind of a terrier watching a rathole. He converts the law into a series of rubber-stamps.' Alistair Cooke (ed.), *The Vintage Mencken* (New York, 1955), p. 195.

[52]Braybrooke, *op. cit.*, pp. 40-1.

[53]See *ibid.*, p. 35.

With this idea in mind, Braybrooke analyses the support given to the right of free speech by the concept of property and argues that the right to a livelihood would under our present system be a surer safeguard of the first right, now that historical conditions have changed. His analysis is interesting and may prove of some value to those who argue for the right to a livelihood, but it seems very doubtful whether a respect for freedom of speech could induce our society to place further restrictions on its property rights; and the latter would be needed to ensure that the right to a livelihood was held generally.

One suspects that if Braybrooke were really a non-relativist, as some of his assertions imply, he would have further developed the concept of a normative natural history. Instead of doing so, he goes on to suggest that 'what presses for mentioning as rights depends partly on what sorts of dangers, obstructions, and interferences actually exist.'[54] This seems to make rights no more than defences against successive changes which vary with circumstances, a thoroughly relativist viewpoint. It is not really surprising that Braybrooke does not regard rights as one of the crucial defences of democracy and that he fails to see that when rights are given his broad definition, they become norms and as such are indispensable to the concept of 'welfare' and not, as he would have it, concepts that can be dispensed with if we introduce the concept of welfare.[55]

Braybrooke's second test for a democracy, 'welfare,' is difficult to appraise because the term as he uses it does not have any definite content. He calls it a 'convoy concept' which includes such elements as food, safety, clothing, shelter, medical care, education, congenial employment and companionship.[56] He makes it clear that these are not necessarily the only elements and asserts that 'material welfare is basic', so that some of these oddly sorted components do have some logical basis. But on what grounds does he include 'companionship' and how does he imagine a government could supply it? One would surely have to feel very lonely to put up with a friend appointed by the government. Ridiculous as the idea is, it is easy to see how Braybrooke

[54]*Ibid.*, p. 77.
[55]See *ibid.*, p. 85.
[56]See *ibid.*, p. 92.

came to entertain it. The moment we say that a government is responsible for 'welfare', either we confine ourselves to purely material considerations and thus help undermine the rights to life, liberty and the pursuit of happiness, or we make impossible — even ridiculous — demands upon the government.

Braybrooke is so intent on finding 'tests' for the government's fulfilment of its 'welfarist' role — he makes much of the notion of 'census' as opposed to Bentham's 'felicific calculus' and Pareto's 'optimum', as we would expect from someone with his sociological leanings — that he gives inadequate attention to his subject matter. When we find that individualism and marriage[57] are part of the concept of welfare, it is clear that welfare is a general term for 'norms.' But if this is the case and Braybrooke is willing to say that a failure to provide for the welfare of even one member of society is an outrage,[58] the government is confronted with the impossible task of ensuring that no one's normative expectations shall be disappointed. One is almost tempted to suppose that Braybrooke has allowed political slogans about the 'Welfare State' and the 'Great Society' to override his common sense. Aristotle could rightly talk of the good State, but a democratic State with an individualist tradition and a marked relativist inclination is in no position to use 'welfare' as anything more than a slogan. We cannot use it as an analytical tool, unless we are ready to abandon all norms except those deriving from basic animal wants. Braybrooke is apparently not ready to do so.

Braybrooke completes his analysis of the tests for democracy by asserting that neither the concern for rights nor for welfare distinguishes democrats from non-democrats.[59] In other words, the major part of his book, by his own admission, deals with non-essentials! From now on, what he regards as really important, what he describes as 'flagrantly undemocratic' is the adoption of a policy which a majority has voted against. Certainly his hypothetical case,[60] in which a community of 'sane adults' is invited to vote on which of several policies it prefers and then has its

---

[57] See *ibid.*, p. 115 and p. 95 respectively.
[58] See *ibid.*, p. 92.
[59] See *ibid.*, p. 159.
[60] See *ibid.*, 151-2.

majority preference disregarded, produces a momentary sense of the rightness of his view. But when we pause to reflect, we realize that the situation he describes arises only when a referendum is at issue. In such a case we feel that to disregard the majority preference would be unjust (or undemocratic) because it would involve repudiation by the government of the rule it had implicitly agreed to observe when offering the referendum — the rule that the majority decision shall prevail. Needless to say, the referendum is not a regular part of democratic procedures in most societies. The majority is not usually asked to vote on platforms or policies having any clear-cut content; hence, a violation of expectations or implicit rules does not occur when a democratic government acts against an expressed majority preference. Braybrooke's paradigm, as he calls it, is not relevant to everyday democratic procedure.

Braybrooke attempts to make his paradigm relevant by boldly asserting that we can infer from it that the tests which 'advocates of democracy wish to impose [in regard to] collective preference are more fundamentally concerned with relating collective preferences to policies than with relating them to the choice of representatives or rulers.'[61] There is very little evidence to support this view. We might be tempted perhaps to believe him if there were any great demand for extended use of the referendum, or for the introduction of what is now technically feasible, home voting machines for the instant communication of public preferences.

The belief that the people's preference is the key to democracy is held primarily by those who are unable to produce an adequate normative scheme to replace the one lost as a result of relativism. If we cannot establish a set of norms to guide policymakers, then we must obviously fall back on voter preference or majority preference, if democratic government is to differ in any way from other forms. Braybrooke must be quite aware of the problems involved in interpreting democratic government as rule by the people, and he is not enough of a relativist to suppose that — feasible or not — it is the goal to pursue.

[61]*Ibid.*, p. 152.

IV
The Lesson Of Anti-democratic Thinking

Democratic theory has shown itself indifferent to a recurrent problem — the resurrection of exploded alternatives to democracy, particularly the advocacy of anarchism. It is clear from the popularity of communes that the idea of anarchism has a very strong appeal to the young. Such tendencies could of course be dismissed as naive and a more widespread study of history and theory recommended. But when some writers, who have a knowledge of both history and theory, are tempted to adopt the same outlook, one feels compelled to conclude that the fault must be inherent in current presentations of democratic theory.

Anarchism and the Concept of Democratic Authority

The fundamental normative conceptions of democracy and anarchism — 'equality' and 'individualism' (or 'autonomy' or 'freedom') — are similar. Anarchism's challenge is a demand that democratic concepts of authority be justified. Unfortunately, it is being made at a time when nearly everyone, including those holding authority, seems hopelessly confused about the nature of that authority.

The principal problem is that the relativists, who are responsible for most normative analysis today, usually define authority in a purely arbitrary way. According to them, the term merely describes an observable fact of social life: that those having a certain position or role in society have 'authority'; such authority, they say, is indistinguishable from 'power' — it is part of a coercive structure. If relativists attempted any further definition, they would be forced to ascribe to norms rational attributes of 'duty' and 'obligation' which would conflict with their premises about the nature of norms.

Now such arbitrary authority conflicts seriously with the 'authority' inherent in democratic norms: the majority 'ought' to rule; private conscience 'ought not' to be violated. The relativist is unrealistic in asserting that the operating system in a democratic society defines what democracy is and that the task of society is to 'socialize' its members to the extent that they adhere to the system as a whole, including its 'arbitrary' system of social authority. If 'obedience' and 'authority' had the irrational basis ascribed to them by relativists that would certainly be true, but the very inculcation of the democratic norm, of individualism and equality entails the inculcation of grounds for rejecting any type of authority inconsistent with them, whether that 'authority' is defined as part of the democratic system or not. Relativism, in short, does not have the 'authority' to suppress those concepts of authority which it finds inconvenient. Those who have been 'socialized' or habituated to believe in equality and freedom cannot also be 'socialized' to believe in an alien concept of 'authority'.

The relativist interpretation of authority also propagates a false notion of how 'authority' operates in a democratic society. It is not as arbitrary as relativists see it. In fact, the hierarchical nature of authority makes it clear that the system is essentially normative and non-relativist. Unlike the bureaucratic structure of business and civil service organization, which is essentially a system of division of labour, the structure of social authority includes a system of normative review of the exercise of authority. When the decision of a lower court is reversed by a higher, 'reasons' must be given. Decisions cannot be justified solely by the social position of the decision-maker. This demand for reason proceeds right up through the structure of authority to the supreme power and authority, the sovereign. What is disturbing about modern democratic theory is that its advocates have allowed this rational element to be obscured by relativist attempts to 'defend' democracy, although such defences result only in breaking down all concepts of authority that are not arbitrary.

Here is the crux of the modern problem: 'pure' democratic theory is anarchistic. At one time it was possible for theorists to focus on this issue and point out that this kind of 'democracy' is not a form of political organization at all but a statement about the individual's attitude to norms and his fellow-men: that it is private. To become social and political, two problems had to be the central issue: that of not having such norms and that of the conflict between the norms of those who have. The problem of 'authority' in a democracy was to find a solution to normative conflicts; it did not require a repudiation of normative assumptions. The problem has now become more complicated. Normative assumptions no longer have the 'self-evident' quality they had when they were securely attached to religious conceptions about the nature of man and his relations with God. Unable to give a plausible (generally acceptable) definition of equality or decide what limits there are to 'freedom', democratic theory has been willing to adopt an arbitrary 'solution': since the definition of democracy's norms seems arbitrary, let us cut the Gordian Knot and let the operating system which calls itself 'democracy' define all its terms. 'Equality', 'freedom' and 'authority' are what the system says they are, and the result is 'democracy' if the members have been socialized to call it that. In other words, many democratic theorists are prone to use relativism in order to abandon theory, while occupying social (academic) positions that require them to do otherwise. Instead of promoting concepts of 'natural law' and rational behaviour, they set themselves in opposition to them: to all 'authority', in fact, except that of private taste. Such is the case of R.P. Wolff. In his book *In Defense of Anarchism*[1] he defends anarchism while — one suspects — not really wanting to. He has no doubt been profoundly influenced by the relativist society in which he lives. The terms he uses — 'obligation', 'responsibility', 'reason' — are drawn from non-relativist ethics but he is a victim of a relativist order. This order is imbued with two kinds of relativism: juristic and individualist. Both imply that all valid norms of society have a source — a particular 'authority' which must not be questioned. They are in irreconcilable conflict: American law is set in opposition to the private conscience. They could be brought together if such a thing as non-relativist ethics were recognized, a system which would make it possible to reconcile such concepts as 'autonomy' and 'authority'. But authors like Wolff have not had enough experience of manipulating ethical

---

[1] Robert Paul Wolff, *In Defense of Anarchism* (New York, 1970).

concepts to know what they are doing. Their society does not demand such experience from its members. It is dangerously authoritarian — asserting the duty of obeying the law as well as obeying the conscience, but never the duty of examining precisely what one is doing.

Anarchism and Participation

The normative difference between democracy and anarchism is the primacy of participation in the anarchist normative order: in consequence, there is strictly speaking no such thing as an anarchist political order, whereas there are many democratic societies. The reason is that it is not logically possible — or practical — to fit anarchist norms into the hierarchical structure necessary for the existence of government. Modern democratic theory developed within the framework of a theory of government and society — the theory of sovereignty. Theories of anarchism split off from democracy by ignoring this theory. Modern advocates of 'participation' are not arguing for a return to the classical theory of democracy — as they pretend to do — but rather to classical anarchism.

In all democratic theories the concept of 'participation' has played a very minor role. Similarly, due to society's hierarchical structure, its part in the life of democratic society has been small. Significantly, theorists of democracy have not attempted to eliminate the hierarchical elements in order to make room for participation. They all accepted the fact that by its very nature social organization is a technique of limiting participation; and that norms should correspond to the theory and practice of social organization. These endeavours were reflected in theories of 'representation'. Modern advocates of 'participation' — not satisfied with these efforts — consider their task in the new light. Instead of seeing their goal in adjustment of norms to social realities, they see it in adjusting reality to norms. Theories of participation are frankly normative.

This puts the political theorist in a difficult position. He should be pleased with any evidence that relativism is proving unsatisfactory. Current interest in participation, however, is unrealistic, misbegotten normativism. Essentially, the cry for participation hopes to create conditions for a normatively desirable improvement in the individual by ignoring all man's experience with social organization and its theories. It is not good enough to argue that 'participation' will be good for man. It is necessary to demonstrate that it is compatible with social organization. The issue is not, as Pateman[2] and others pretend, its compatibility with the *present* social framework but whether the ideal of participation is equivalent to anarchism as an ideal. It seems that the argument — based on scattered sentences from classical writings — that participation was an important part of democratic theory is an attempt to evade the issue of anarchy. What advocates of change in the social order must keep in mind is that any normative scheme must fit the pattern of social organization. All 'classical' theories of democracy are defined as democratic because they recognized this fact. On the other hand, neither theories of anarchy nor modern advocates of participation have done so.

Tolerance under a Democratic System of Values

Democracy is a relatively new ethical set which, for most members of democratic societies, is replacing the 'other-world'-centred norms of religion. One of the history's many ironies is that though democracy originally derived some of its fundamental assumptions from religion and has always been associated with the preservation of private belief and religious freedom, its acceptance entails a shift in emphasis from the religious to the political sphere[3] and with this the decay of what it seeks to preserve. A democratic State may claim to be 'under God', but it is difficult for a member of such a State — who believes that questions of policy should be determined by the interests and desires of its members — to suppose that the absolute values of a Church have any absolute validity. In effect, he rejects the notion by accepting the right to vote and shifts from a belief in the authority of a moral order to a belief in the authority of the majority.

Democratic insistence that the ultimate decisions about goals

---

[2] See Carole Pateman, *Participation and Democratic Theory* (Cambridge, 1970).

[3] This shift originated in the days of post-Reformation with the first signs of the passing of the era of intense religious persecutions.

must lie with the people undermines the very foundations of the Church's moral authority and with this the significance of being religious or holding a particular set of religious beliefs. Under a democracy, as is the case in North America, religion becomes a matter of taste: 'Pray in the church of your choice', as with the other piety of modern life, voting: 'Vote for the party of your choice, but vote.' It is no longer important how one prays or votes. What is important is that one performs the ritual which symbolizes one's attachment.

Now if the 'public service' billboards which make the statements about praying and voting altered their wording only slightly to 'Support the political ideology of your choice', they would no longer be performing a public service. They would more likely be considered subversive, for as democratic society has usurped moral authority, there can only be one set of assumptions as to how society ought to be managed — those which assert the right of the majority to make decisions. All others are necessarily wrong.

Can democracy be tolerant of other political beliefs and statements? Hans Kelsen, arguing in support of democracy and tolerance from a relativist point of view, makes the following statement: 'We are sure of our political truth, to be enforced, if necessary, with blood and tears...we are sure of our truth as was, of his truth, the son of God.'[4] Naturally, this is a piece of rhetoric, a reply in kind to an absolutist, but it accurately reflects the limitation placed on tolerance by those who are convinced that the democratic system is a tolerant system. In other words, tolerance ceases to apply in the very area in which it must apply if it is to say something significant about the modern State. It is only when there are rival statements that the question of tolerance arises. It is as absurd to speak of a democratic State's tolerance of Church doctrine under its jurisdiction as it would be to speak of its intolerance of criminal behaviour. An important function of the State is the maintenance of order and this is not achieved by the State suppressing statements which in no way conflict with its own or even by 'tolerating' behaviour which does interfere with the peace and good order of the realm, as for

---

[4]Hans Kelsen, 'Absolutism and Relativism in Philosophy and Politics', *The American Political Science Review*, Vol. XLII (October 1948).

instance the anti-social behaviour of the criminal. Those who argue that tolerance is not applicable to the democratic assumptions are not talking about tolerance, but about the best method of maintaining social order in a heterogeneous society consistent with the sovereignty of the State. If the State fails to remain an impartial arbiter of disputes, if it supports one group against another, it becomes but the political arm of the group it fosters. The issue is that of the tolerance of the particular group by the State and not that of 'democratic tolerance'.

Having based its claim to superiority upon its system of values, of which tolerance is an element, the democratic State now faces the same problem that confronted the Church in the seventeenth century. If, under the principle of tolerance, one grants equal rights to a rival system of belief, one is not only recognizing the right of private conscience but also implicitly making a statement about truth. Either one is assuming that truth will prevail or one is abandoning one's exclusive claim to it. The Church — acting under pressure from the State, which recognizes the threat to civil order inherent in intolerance — has been compelled to decide upon one of these alternatives. But it is not possible for the State to do so. The assumption that truth will prevail is plausible only if the truth is self-evident — a position which can no longer be seriously maintained about democratic values. The alternative — abandoning one's claim to truth — is even worse, for allegiance in the modern State is largely determined by the set of values professed by the State. An admission that the ideology one accepts is no better than any other would play havoc with the citizen's sense of political obligation. Because belief in another ideology usually means a division in loyalty, complete political tolerance would make it impossible for the State to control the potential for subversion present among those who profess an alien system. Yet if a democratic State does not at least keep up some appearance of permitting rival statements to be made, it will only encourage disaffection, for adherence to the principle of tolerance is one of its claims to superiority and one of the proofs of its identity as a democratic State.

Can Democratic Tolerance be Absolute?

When Jaspers asserts that 'Democracy must be able to become

Can Democratic Tolerance be Absolute? 101

intolerant of intolerance itself'[5] he is arguing that adherence to a norm excludes its contradictory. This appears to be one of those 'self-evident truths' which if propagated as fundamental insights can lead to misunderstanding. The norms of democracy are not only in the hands of philosophers but in those of ordinary citizens. Taught about the absolutism of individual norms — which Jaspers is trying to counteract by his assertion about contradictories — citizens have created difficulties for democratic societies by insisting on 'pure' democracy. Their democracy is an unrealistic and illogical pretence that the normative system of democracy is not a normative system but a set of unrelated absolutes, which must remain such even while being applied. (Jaspers's assertion, it should be noted, does nothing about this absolutism. It invites the absolutist to attempt to solve the normative issues, arising from the fact that democracy is a normative set, by ignoring the norm 'freedom' and classifying behaviour that we would call a threat to the norm 'freedom' as a threat to the absolutism of 'tolerance'.) What one needs to recognize is that a viable normative system cannot consist of absolutes — this is logically impossible — and the logic of contradiction is irrelevant to the issues raised by the *system* of norms.

Any normative set serving to define a group is liable to serious aberrations when the believers themselves — members of a democracy must be 'democratic' — have to interpret the norms. Were the norms just customary ways of behaving, as some relativists say all norms are, the problem would be simple. But the norms of democracy are not patterns of behaviour but general and quite abstract requirements. The democratic man believes in 'freedom', 'equality' and 'tolerance' and to act in accordance with these he must apply them to specific conditions. While many members of democratic societies insist that they are true believers — they have no doubts about the validity of the norms and insist that they act in accordance with them — yet they are not very good in applying these norms to particular situations.

We must narrow the problem further, ignoring the normative issues raised by the failure on the part of the citizens of

---

[5] Karl Jaspers, *The Future of Mankind* (Chicago and London, 1967), p. 295.

democracy to be democratic and focus on their critics — those who insist on democratic absolutism and who believe that 'freedom', 'equality' and 'tolerance' either exist without exceptions and qualifications, or do not exist at all.

Absolutism is the bane of all normative systems but the fundamental requirement of any particular norm. It is not possible to defend 'tolerance' — or any other norm — if it is not put forward as an inviolable absolute parallel to other fundamental assumptions we make in order to organize experience. No exceptions are possible if the assumptions are to have any meaning. But to say that all the norms of democracy are traceable to one assumption, or to a set of orderly assumptions such as exist in mathematics, is another question. We could then say that 'democracy' means 'equality' or 'tolerance' or 'freedom' and establish that, logically, certain behaviour is required from the true democrat under certain conditions. There are people full of good intentions – and naïve beliefs — who attempt this. Their criticism of democratic societies goes back to the lack of 'purity' in normative behaviour: we are not 'equal' enough or 'free' enough or 'tolerant' enough. This would be right if we could assume democracy to be a norm instead of a normative set. In fact, no democratic society approaches the conditions that would exist if any single norm were applied absolutely and none shows any tendency to move towards such absolutism.

Normative absolutism is impossible when there is a normative set. It is also illogical to demand absolute tolerance when 'tolerance' is not the sole norm. The reason is that while each norm is an absolute by itself, it inevitably interacts with other norms to produce something less than absolutism. Thus, those who argue that democracy must be absolutely tolerant are really arguing that 'tolerance' *is* democracy and that no other norms matter. But clearly, tolerance is not the sole democratic norm. No assertion about the requirements of 'tolerance' in a particular situation can be made until one examines the statements made by other norms such as 'freedom' and 'equality'. Being true to the norm 'freedom', for instance, is an integral part of being democratic and no statement made by the norm 'tolerance' can be followed through until the requirements of the norm 'freedom' have been allowed to make their claim. Being 'democratic' requires a more or less even balance between them, not absolutism.

'Repressive Tolerance'

Oxymorons such as 'cruel kindness' or 'repressive tolerance' have been traditionally avoided in scientific and philosophic writing because to make sense conceptually, at least one of the component terms has to be redefined: if either of these phrases meant what it appears to mean, it would be self-contradictory. Those, however, who are working within the Hegelian-Marxian tradition, do not have such scruples, for to them such phrases can express the synthesis of thesis (tolerance) and antithesis (repression). In their eyes the synthesis is not a contradiction but a new insight, and the difficulty non-Marxists have to face when trying to guess its meaning can be ignored.

Marcuse is unaware that to make a case in a non-Marxist society he must redefine tolerance in order to remove the contradiction inherent in his concept of 'repressive tolerance'. For him, 'tolerance' is a conditional norm resting on the uncertainty principle — our consciousness that we do not know the truth but desire to attain it: 'The uncertainty of chance...necessitates freedom of thought and expression as preconditions of finding the way to freedom — it necessitates *tolerance*.[6] If this is indeed the basis of tolerance, it follows with deadly certainty that when the truth is known, tolerance merely allows error to flourish. Some errors can have such dangerous consequences that the just society must repress them: 'But society cannot be indiscriminate where the pacification of existence, where freedom and happiness themselves are at stake: here, certain things cannot be said, certain ideas cannot be expressed, certain policies cannot be proposed, certain behaviour cannot be permitted without making tolerance an instrument for the continuation of servitude.'[7]

With a little manipulation of concepts Marcuse makes his view resemble a logical extension of current democratic practice. Thus he observes that democratic society does not tolerate any of the behaviour proscribed by the criminal code. Though hardly a conservative himself, he advocates what is basically a 'conservative' view that in the extension of law lies the answer to social

---

[6]Herbert Marcuse, 'Repressive Tolerance' in Robert Paul Wolff, Barrington Moore, Jr. and Herbert Marcuse, *A Critique of Pure Tolerance* (Boston, 1965), p.88.
[7]*Ibid.*

problems and that this extension is not really repressive: behind it there are ethical principles on which democracy is founded.

According to both Marcuse and many conservatives, democratic society is *not* relativistic. It is a fact that it is 'tolerant' of criminal behaviour. Hence if one can argue that current 'tolerance' (= absence of legal sanctions) violates democratic norms, can one not argue that such 'tolerance' is undemocratic?

It is remarkable how unwilling our society has been to face the Marcusian argument. The standard response has been to invoke the principle of uncertainty or the principle of relativism, both of which have been represented as the essence of 'tolerance'. According to this view norms cannot be proved: they are tastes and attitudes. We should not be certain about anything, least of all about normative issues. Such relativism is not 'tolerance', of course, for it 'tolerates' everything, including intolerance, and no one who holds the norm 'tolerance' can also accept its contradictory.

Apart from the fact that the usual (relativistic) argument against repression is not based on 'tolerance', it is not relevant either. It demands from the advocate of intolerance an attitude to norms he does not have; indeed, it demands an attitude that hardly anyone has. By nature, norms express convictions about what we regard as universals. It may be quite true that none of us can 'prove' the validity of the norms we hold, but it is quite true that no one can disprove them either; nor can anyone prove that we would be better off without them. Norms are necessary to human behaviour and almost all members of democratic society — as of all societies — have deep convictions about what is right and wrong. It is unrealistic to say that we 'should not' have them.

But if each of us is convinced of the validity of his norms, are we required to adopt Marcuse's intolerance? At one time, it should be remembered, his position was universally accepted. It is not long ago that the Catholic Church officially abandoned it. Throughout its history the Church has held — like Marcuse — that error should not have the same rights as truth. Only when ideologically-based political orders developed did this view show signs of being transferred to the political sphere: totalitarian societies have endeavoured to suppress alien ideologies. What has prevented democratic societies from undertaking the kind of behaviour advocated by Marcuse is the norm 'tolerance'.

'Tolerance' does not allow combination with its contradictory, and conviction about the truth of one's position has nothing to do with the issue, as the Catholic Church has at last realized. Despite its claim to being a normatively-based institution, the Catholic Church was slower in accepting the norms of tolerance than secular institutions, mainly because this required the Church to surrender all claim to secular power. As a result, the Church abandoned its age-old claims to a sovereignty opposed to that of the State. The issue of tolerance is now transferred to the State. (This has had the curious result that there is now no way of knowing whether the Church is showing true 'tolerance' or mere 'toleration'.)

What brought this situation about? At a time when a man like Marcuse is arguing that the State should take over the position formerly held by the Church, the Church has adopted a norm that the State has observed for some time and which according to Marcuse should now be abandoned. Will roles be completely reversed and will the ideologically-based State of the future adopt the policies of the pre-Reformation Church? Did not the Church adopt tolerance in order to counter just such a development? To answer this question in the affirmative would be to explain the Church's current policies towards tolerance solely as a manoeuvre in its power relations; to assert that it is adopting the only position possible when its claim to authority is threatened. But there are other quite different reasons why the Church has incorporated tolerance as a norm and why the democratic State should not abandon it.

To the Catholic Church it must be abundantly clear that the prohibition of error and the inculcation of right-thinking does not lead to right conduct, as Marcuse imagines, but rather to self-righteousness and hypocrisy. In his *Canterbury Tales* Chaucer drew a striking portrait of the Church at the height of its power: a group of pilgrims ostensibly meets in pious duty, but all except the humblest — the poor Parson, who represents the ideal Church — are corrupt in varying degrees. Hypocrisy, as we see from the portrait of the Pardoner, has become a skill, a sort of virtue to boast about in the expectation that fellow hypocrites will acknowledge one's mastery of the art. Such a portrait cannot be dismissed as an attack on the Church: the presence of the ideal Parson makes that clear. It was certainly not an unfair portrait of the true state of morality at the time, as we know from other sources. Somehow, the regulation of human behaviour had not prevented a moral breakdown.

The lesson for democracy is clear. When moral action ceases to be voluntary and an expression of the self — the way we choose to behave because we think it is right — and becomes instead the kind of behaviour imposed on the self by society, the biological being with inherited impulses acquires an importance which it cannot have in a genuinely free society.

It is true that we can legislate and educate a society into certain types of habitual obedience. Society tries to do this, for instance, by penalizing drunken driving. The partial success achieved with this type of 'moral' improvement has fostered hope for general improvement through legislation. Those — like some fundamentalists — who believe in the general depravity of man are convinced that this is the only way man can be improved. They point to the laws on murder and theft as evidence that society not only has the right to be intolerant of some types of behaviour, but must be. Marcuse himself uses this argument. Yet it is impossible to proceed from these particular instances[8] of 'intolerance' in a democratic State to the general conclusion that legal prohibitions advance the cause of morality. Thus the lack of success attained in changing sexual habits through legislation shows that morals cannot be enforced. Ethical behaviour, which requires debate and reasoning about norms and the establishment of general principles of behaviour, vanishes under coercion. Tolerance is the norm necessary to norms. It stands against both relativism and repression and is closely linked with democracy, which cannot work as a purely relativist society.

Can Tolerance be Subversive?

To the philosopher, the norm 'tolerance' derives its normativeness from the theory of knowledge: given the imperfection of

---

[8]These instances represent a special case where legal penalties are superimposed on an already existing universal. Everyone, or nearly everyone, is convinced about such norms as the sanctity of life or property. By taking away from the victim the right to retaliate, the State is not so much enforcing these norms as trying to ensure that justice is done.

man's knowledge as a seemingly permanent condition, and given 'truth' as a good, it follows that the suppression of, or even marked hostility towards, opinions other than one's own is not a 'good'. If 'tolerance' as we know it required such a lofty and detached viewpoint, it could never have become an issue in political science, which can hardly predicate itself on the assumption that the good society demands philosopher-kings. But the 'tolerance' that the philosopher requires is incorporated into the theory of sovereignty not as a demand on the goodwill, moral principles and intelligence of the sovereign but as a requirement of his self-interest: the sovereign who sided with one creed or interest-group against another would in effect be sharing sovereignty.

The modern emphasis on democratic norms as the central issue in discussions of the democratic State has given the issue of tolerance a peculiar 'democratic' bias. Instead of being a necessary attribute of the sovereign, tolerance is represented as the necessary quality of a democratic society. The people of a democracy are supposed to have the attributes of a philosopher-king: calm rationality, objectivity, 'tolerance' — no matter what ideas are presented to them, or in what manner. Otherwise, they are not 'democratic'.

This attitude has had an unfortunate effect on the tolerance debate. Philosophic relativism has made most demands for 'tolerance' irrelevant. When the 'good' can no longer be rationally discussed but represents private interests, the issues in a normative dispute are necessarily personal. At best, the 'good' man sees himself as the representative of a larger class whose interests he promotes in opposition to those of his adversary, who either speaks for himself alone or for some narrower interest. Any technique then becomes acceptable. 'Reason' is excluded from debate; invective and personal insult are cultivated as ways of making a point, and tenacious adherence to one's position is admired. To be open to reason is to be uncommitted and commitment is all-important when 'truth' is out of the question. Among relativists, 'tolerance' is necessarily in disrepute. In its absence, force and violence become legitimate techniques of settling normative disputes. They become, in fact, the only possible techniques.

At this point, of course, the new attitude to 'tolerance' clashes with democratic tradition, which excludes violence as a technique of settling normative differences. Democracy attempts to solve the rising acrimony of debate and the demands for a show of force against State policy by fostering adherence to the system of 'majority rule', the submission of disputes to a vote and the like. In other words, the State itself does not demand 'tolerance' or 'reason' but — as a minimum requirement for life under a democratic order — agreement to a mere expedient for settling differences. In a relativist-oriented society this is put forward as the essence of democracy and democratic law and order.

The discussion of 'tolerance' in a modern democracy differs from earlier debates on 'tolerance', in which the limits of tolerance were set by the definition of liberty. The question then was: how 'free' can a State be; to what extent must the democratic norm of 'liberty' constrain the State in its relations with its members so that it can remain 'democratic'? Now, when the democratic State is (self) defined as a system, no such question arises. The norms of democracy are replaced by an arbitrary method of settling disputes and taking action. It is clear that, on the assumption that the system is democratic, the State cannot tolerate rejection of its method. 'Tolerance' becomes subversive of law and order and at least an indirect invitation to violence.

Those who find this new attitude to 'tolerance' unpalatable must be quite clear about what lies behind it. It is not an emotional response to disorder in society, the view of 'conservatives' or the result of the rise of the 'systems' view in political science. Behind the so-called 'conservativism' and the new systems analysis lies the relativist view of norms. Only when this is shown to be philosophically unsound will ideological tolerance become part of democratic order.

Erosion of the Rule of Law

What do we mean by 'erosion of the rule of law' in liberal democracies? Some people tend to think in terms of a rising crime rate,[9] but then one should realize that what is involved is only a minute percentage of the population. Crime rates are still

---

[9] Much depends upon changes in the definition of a 'crime'. In the past there have been 'crime waves' which were solely the (artificial) result of changes in the definition itself: the waves were not real, but only apparent.

expressed relative to tens or hundreds of thousands of members of the public. If crime rates are our criterion, the law is still in good shape. The overwhelming majority of people have not committed a crime and could not imagine themselves doing so, and the majority can still expect to get through life without being robbed at gunpoint, raped or murdered. There is nothing more comforting than crime statistics when you begin to worry about the rule of law.[10]

Since all States have formal legal systems and techniques for their enforcement, some observers may be tempted to think of the 'erosion of the rule of law' as a reference to a decline in the State's capacity for enforcement. This is evidently the view of some jurists and a large body of the public. But for the political theorist, who must make distinctions between different kinds of political — and legal — systems, the concept of the rule of law is more limited.

The 'rule of law' — like democracy, with which it is closely allied — is a normative concept, and as such has a strong rational element. The assumption — or perhaps goal or ideal — is that for every law under a system of the 'rule of law' the temptation to violate the rule could be countered by rational reflection: an ideally rational man with adequate knowledge of the total situation would observe the law. Since we cannot expect such behaviour from anyone (otherwise anarchism would be a plausible political system), the law simplifies decision-making by sanctions: break the law and you will get 'busted'. The penalty is a condensed expression of the self-interest in obeying a particular law.

Acceptance of this view of the law requires that the legislative process partake of the nature of just such ideal reflection. Both the law and proposed legislation must be openly debated, no matter how long the process takes and no matter how frivolous and self-interested some of the objections may seem. Democracy is the only political system that does this and that is why strictly speaking the concept of the 'rule of law' is necessarily limited to democratic states. Consequently, the 'erosion of the rule of law' can refer to two quite different things: a decline in the public

---

[10] A different problem is the unprecedented growth in recent decades of the body of legal rules and regulations which has got 'out of hand': the citizen cannot be sure whether or not he is breaking the law.

belief that the process of legislative debate is the actual basis of the democratic legal system and secondly, a decline in the belief that it 'should' be (which reflects a change in our society's normative system). There is evidence that both have taken place.

The rule of law is seriously endangered when it is seen as coercive rather than regulatory — when one thinks primarily of a policeman handing out traffic tickets rather than of the regulatory function of traffic laws — and furthermore, when one sees the offender as a victim of the system rather than violator. In other words, if we shift our attention from the central issue of law and its function to the subsidiary of enforcement and violation — aspects of 'violence' we might say — and pretend that enforcement and violation are the central issues, we will — regardless of our intentions — render the rule of law meaningless, for it is the function of the law, not violence, that defines enforcement as such and excludes from consideration arguments that the offender is a victim of the law.

Coercion seems primary when 'government' and 'society' are represented as in opposition to the individual and hence violation of the law as an aspect of 'freedom'. In theory, the rise of democratic States has supposedly disposed of such problems, but events of the last two or three decades suggest they are now more deeply felt than ever. This can hardly be the result of any actual increase in the power and arbitrariness of democratic governments. Analyses of the relations between individual members of society and social organization suggest that no matter how much 'bigger' government has grown, it has much less control than formerly. Laws regulating government have grown at least as fast as laws regulating the citizen. Although the actual relations between the State and its citizens do not explain the new attitude to government and laws, yet more and more people are thinking of the government as 'them' and hence the law as the 'will of the stronger' and consequently as essentially coercive. How can one explain the development of such an attitude to law and government in a democratic State? Is there perhaps a normative system as strong as — if not stronger than — the democratic system, which implies that the laws of a democratic State cannot conflict with self-interest?

Most defences of democracy tend to see the main threats to the system in terms of the Marxian historical determinism, forgetting that *any* deterministic school of thought is in fundamental conflict with the individualism and freedom on which democracy is premised. If human behaviour is determined, any attempt to regulate it must by nature be coercive and those affected must see it as a violation of the 'self'.[11] The point at issue is that the rule of law will not work if it is presented as primarily an act of coercion. Even if prudential arguments can be raised for obeying it, prudential reasons can be offered for disregarding it and there is no prudential — or any other system of normative reasoning — for mediating between the two. The conflict between the self and the rule of law becomes absolute.

If, as seems likely, deterministic interpretations of human behaviour have profoundly affected popular attitudes to the law, the effects are not the result of any direct teaching of such a doctrine. Though a large number of psychologists and psychiatrists do advise the 'release' of aggression, few if any directly set their patients against society: the opposition of the individual and society is a premise rather than an aim. Most, indeed, see their task as the 'adjustment' of the individual to the rules of his society (a rather hopeless task in view of the premise!). There can be little doubt, however, that in popular thinking the premise has now become at least as important as the premises of democracy.

More direct damage is being done to the rule of law by the determinist attack on the concept of 'justice'. Since the rule of law is based on the concept of free choice and responsibility, the doctrine that human behaviour is determined by one's biological inheritance and early environmental influences on the 'self'

[11] In one of history's more curious ironies, the society which most firmly rejected Marx gave its whole-hearted support to Freud, who explained human behaviour in terms of biological drives in conflict with social controls over them. The reason is not far to seek. Freud's system is certainly a thorough-going individualistic one and its talk of the dangers of inhibition and repression is of the kind that would appeal to an individualistic society. What was not recognized is that its 'individualism' is really egoism and that the 'self' is always in opposition to society; the stability of the system is represented as requiring the expression or release of hostility. Indeed, it has been pointed out that one can always detect those who have undergone 'therapy' by their rudeness and hostility. Only a small percentage of Americans have actually undergone therapy, but the fundamental opposition of self and society is now an article of faith in the USA, even among the adherents of psychological systems in opposition to Freud.

and not by anything that deserves the name of rational or prudential choice, the penalties for wrong-doing are by the nature of the assumption 'unjust'; that is, determinism converts the concept of 'punishment' into that of 'violence sanctioned by the State'[12] — an idea which played a prominent part in the debates on the abolition of capital punishment. The judicial system cannot of course accept such a view, but since the latter is now presented as 'scientific fact' (which it is not) rather than a consequence of determinism, the requirement that the rule of law be just has led to accommodations in the applications of sentencing which effectively destroy the rule of law. As a formal procedure, arraignment, trial and sentencing are much the same as they were at the beginning of the century, except that 'reports of the prison psychiatrist or social worker' now play a major part in some courts. The real change lies in the fact that this formal procedure, which used to reflect the presence in society of the rule of law, is now merely ritualistic. Sentences as laid down by the court are rarely carried out: they are rendered meaningless by the concepts of parole and remission, as most judges and criminals know.

[12] How does determinism convert punishment into the concept of violence? Punishment — as distinct from 'retaliation' or 'revenge' — rests on the assumption that penalties for wrong-doing can affect behaviour: knowledge of the fact that certain behaviour is subject to punishment can instruct one about the society's attitude to certain acts and can result in the inhibition of impulses to engage in such acts by shifting the sum of advantages and disadvantages. Some determinists deny the validity of this assumption: for them 'character' (the tendency to act in certain ways) is set by biology and early experience and this cannot be altered by rational calculation of advantages and disadvantages. For them, man is not in any meaningful sense 'rational' and hence 'punishment', because it presupposes rationality — and thus is not applied to infants, idiots or madmen — is not really rational. But if you remove the rational element — the intention of punishment — it is not possible to distinguish between fining a thief and robbing a bank, or hanging a man and murdering him. Following this line of thought, all partake of the same nature — violence — and it is the task of the reformer to correct behaviour not only of the thief but of the judge who sentences him.

Other determinists accept the body of evidence in support of the view that punishment can indeed influence behaviour; but being determinists, they do not see any element of 'free-will' in the matter. All behaviour is 'conditioned' for them, and if the social rules embodied in the law are not effectively a part of a child's conditioning, the sanctions of the law could be effective only if they could be applied immediately and certainly after every violation. But this is impossible in a democratic state, which to the bewilderment of this school of thought, seems more interested in ensuring that *only* the guilty will be punished, rather than that *all* the guilty will be. Such a concept of 'justice' is contrary to their concept of 'punishment', which they see as the essence of law. But what then is 'punishment' when detached from 'justice'? What can it be except coercion — 'violence sanctioned by the State for the purposes of the State'?

Still, the determinist school, through its behaviourist-instrumentalist branch, has had an even more important influence on the rule of law by directing attention from the judicial system to conditions in society. According to this school of thought, the courts are not only unjust but ineffective. If there is to be a 'rule of law' — and the determinists are quite ready to accept this — what we need is to manipulate the individual and his environment in such a way that no one will be able to choose any other course of action than obeying the law. People following this line of thought are largely responsible for the enormous sums spent on public housing, justified on the grounds that slum areas have a higher crime rate than middle-class neighbourhoods. (It is ironic that these efforts have now given us a new social statistic: public housing projects have a higher crime rate than slums!) The determinists have also developed in the name of the rule of law various techniques of behavioural modification; and because some of their techniques can be shown to work more effectively than 'punishment', they have diverted a good deal of attention and funds away from the traditional system of justice. With all this, they have not solved the problem of the rising crime rate. Why is that so, even though in specific cases the behaviourist school employs more effective methods of altering behaviour?

The answer is that the 'rule of law' is not merely a system of penalties for misbehaviour. It is a system of justice, not coercion, resting on the assumption of rational choice, and it is undermined in everyone's eyes if it is represented as a technique of control by the State over its own members. The demonstration by instrumentalists and behaviourists that the State can manipulate its members does not inspire confidence but rebellion.

Instrumentalist Revolution

Knowledge gained by science has enabled us to solve so many problems that it is not surprising that a society which is markedly relativistic and values 'efficiency', would promote science's findings (the 'facts') as an actual standard of value. Hence the current vogue of instrumentalism. In recent years perhaps the most prominent exponent of instrumentalist ideas has been B. F. Skinner. His advocacy of the type of society described in

Walden Two (1948) and the method of achieving it by behavioural psychology is in effect a proposal for a systematic revolution (without violence). To the political theorist, the existence of such proposals, the wide interest aroused by them, and the attempt to implement them raise some important issues. One of these is the problem of understanding the norms of democracy and their implications for one's personal life.

Both Orwell in *1984* and Huxley in *Brave New World* make a point that repeatedly has to be made in anti-intellectual, anti-rationalist societies: the road to hell is paved with good intentions. To the end of his life, Orwell remained a convinced socialist — an advocate of non-violent revolution — but he saw quite clearly that the attempt to impose such principles requires a non-egalitarian power structure which necessarily becomes more and more tyrannical as it is given more and more power to introduce the 'good life' of egalitarianism. The thesis is evidently not based on Acton's view that power corrupts or any supposition of an innate hunger for power which overrides all ethical principles, but on the commonsense observation that those who believe they are acting in the interest of others — men of goodwill — will value the means to attain their goal. The means in question is power, including the power to stifle or dismiss objections, which — by definition — are false or misguided. There is nothing intricate about such a line of thought. Orwell thought the point could be made simply by picturing a society which had already gone through the process.

Judging from the reception of his book, he was successful at the time, but since then something seems to have happened to our capacity to read and analyse the normative implications of behavioural engineering. People have become more naîve, more anti-intellectual, anti-analytic and anti-rational. Here is the response of Kathleen Kinkade, who helped induce several other well-intentioned, intelligent individuals to set up a community on the principles of Skinner's Walden Two[13] (and thus to use the method of trial and error when the means already exist to avoid this very predicament — the means provided by political and social theory): 'We have never been hindered by the usual conception of behavioural engineering as the manipulation of

---

[13]Skinner himself seems to have read both *Brave New World* and *1984* without discovering any 'message'.

people's desires and preferences by a group of scientists in white coats.... We have read *Brave New World* and *1984* and were not impressed. The writing is great, the logic downright silly. If there were to be manipulators, we were it. But we would also be the manipulated.... The logic of egalitarianism is inescapable on the point.'[14]

Kinkade, like Skinner, himself, seems to have missed the point made in the two books: even if you begin with egalitarianism, the power to manipulate the behaviour of others will produce a class system of manipulators and manipulated; 'equality' will be redefined in terms of this situation: 'Some are more equal than others'. What Kinkade seems to have done is to see that *1984* and *Brave New World* were class societies, reason that Walden Two was not a class society and conclude that no problem existed.

Now the interesting point is that the man who supplied the financing for the Walden experiment — and was, even in Kinkade's estimation, the ablest member of the founding group — found himself forced to leave precisely because Kinkade and two other board members insisted on making decisions and enforcing them on the other members without explaining or even analysing the basis of their actions, so that no true democratic election or control of the board was possible. Far from seeing the justice of the accusations, Kinkade argues that in her opinion the protests were founded upon the psychological shortcomings of the critic and his lack of commitment to 'equality'.

How is this typical 1984 'double-think' possible? The answer probably lies in the very attitude to rationality implicit in both books. Both Orwell and Huxley obviously responded to Pavlov's conditioned response experiments, Watson's behaviourism (Skinner's predecessor in the field) and Freud's deterministic, anti-rationalist model of the mind. All these men acted on the assumption that 'free-will' and 'reason' are illusory: 'reason' is always necessarily 'rationalization'. Neither Huxley nor Orwell accepted the full implications of such views, although their preference for the fictional presentation of ideas shows that they felt 'emotion' was most important in the acceptance of ideas. Both, however, retained the traditional European respect for the mind, as is shown by the direction their satires take.

[14]Kathleen Kinkade, *A Walden Two Experiment* (New York, 1973), p. 148.

In the USA, however, 'reason' has never been an important norm. The only indigenous 'philosophy' that has developed — pragmatism — is not recognized as genuine philosophy even by Americans: it is not sufficiently systematic or tightly enough reasoned.[15] Yet, within such a climate of opinion, reason will still have a place, provided it is limited to the analysis of something other than human behaviour: Americans have been pre-eminent in the physical sciences. But if the assumption is made that human behaviour is basically irrational, it follows that thinking about the rational consequences of types of behaviour — expressed by norms — is a waste of time. The point is 'commitment' to certain types of behaviour — for example equality — and so long as one can honestly say one 'believes' or 'is committed to' such a norm, nothing else matters. In Kinkade's eyes, Orwell's analysis of the consequences of trying to induce absolute equality will indeed be 'silly'. It will, in fact, prove to her that Orwell was not really 'committed'. If pressed, she would doubtless come up with a 'psychological' explanation of why Orwell expressed his particular views, for to her mind it would be impossible for him to have genuine reasons. This, in a nutshell, is the problem faced by political theorists in North America: most people are convinced that speculative theorizing is a waste of time and a mere reflection of personal prejudices — a commitment to certain norms which is either too strong or not strong enough.

---

[15] America, too is the place where Freudian determinism reigns supreme as 'science' instead of being recognized for what it is — a medico-mystical faith which has a lower cure rate than that practised by shamans and African witch doctors.

V
The Insufficiency Of Apologetics

Defenders of democracy characteristically appeal to the norms of democracy, to 'equality', 'individualism', 'freedom', 'majority rule' and 'natural rights', so that they cannot convince anyone who is not already committed, or answer those critics — appalled by the inefficiency and relativism of present-day democracies — who have come to feel that this form of government is only one more regrettable episode in man's unfortunate history. Yet democracy, both as an ideology and a social and political structure, has wrought changes in man's outlook and in society that even the uncommitted and the skeptic must see as worthwhile contributions, even though it has also brought changes that are of doubtful advantage.

One of the most notable of the positive contributions is that democracy has established the electoral system, which (with one exception) is the best method known to man, or conceivable, of ensuring an orderly succession of governments.[1]

The only real alternative to an electoral system has been hereditary rule, which might have continued indefinitely, despite its manifest disadvantages, if the logic of democracy had not established an alternative method of transferring power which eliminated the shortcomings. The latter include the ever-present possibility that the ruler will be born mentally incompetent, become insane or grow senile, and that having power by virtue of birth, may not fulfil his responsibilities. As history shows, the latter is not nearly so common as the 'power corrupts' school pretends, for the responsibility of office tends to become ingrained. Nevertheless, if society, or that part of it which

---

[1] There have been other systems, such as the casting of lots and the laying on of hands, but they have rested on the primitive belief in 'fate' and 'mana' peculiar to very primitive communities.

influences the ruler, is hedonistically oriented, he is much more likely to become corrupt than to be a source of reform. The hereditary method of transferring power can ensure order, but it has never been able to ensure competence.

The democratic electoral system has solved the problem of achieving an orderly succession of governments while at the same time, it is claimed, ensuring that the government is not merely competent according to its own lights, as is the case when authority is usurped or imposed. This has been a major contribution, but it is very easy to misunderstand its nature. We must remember that though historically the electoral system spread throughout Europe along with democracy, it is not peculiar to democracy. The critic of the democratic system will have no difficulty is postulating an electoral system that is superior, no matter what norms are used, provided one of them is not equality as a supposed fact.

Electoral Systems and H.B. Mayo's Justification of Democracy

In his 'justification' of democracy, H.B. Mayo seems to identify the advantages gained by an electoral system with the particular kind of electoral system peculiar to democracy. He lists 'the orderly succession of rulers' as his third value (the other two being 'peaceful adjustment' and 'peaceful change'), arguing that 'the methods of self- appointment, of hereditary succession, of co-option by an élite, and of the *coup d'état* are not contemporaneously plausible in their philosophic justifications, apart altogether from the practical difficulties inherent in them, to which abundant historical experience testifies.'[2]

This blending of ways of attaining power — self-appointment and the *coup d'état* — with methods of ensuring continuity of government, is certainly not the best way of making clear what the democratic contribution has been. The *coup d'état* and self-appointment can hardly be called systems of government, for they fail to ensure an orderly succession of rulers, which is surely the first requirement of any system that is to be called a system of government.

[2]H.B. Mayo, *An Introduction to Democratic Theory* (New York, 1960), p. 222.

H.B. Mayo's Justification of Democracy 119

Mayo has mentioned only two such systems: hereditary succession and co-option by an élite. In respect of the first, it is possible that the 'practical difficulties' to which he refers are the points made above and perhaps the fact that such an apparently simple rule as hereditary succession is not sufficient in itself. The rule of primogeniture (rarely ultimogeniture) coupled with an intricate kinship system, for instance, must be incorporated so as to ensure an orderly transference of power should the ruler have more than one, or no, children.

Mayo's second alternative to the democratic electoral system, 'co-option by an élite', obscures the nature of the democratic contribution to government. The assertion that the democratic electoral system is the only one that is 'contemporaneously plausible' is misleading, if not untrue. Given that the people should govern, or at least control the government, and that direct democracy is not possible in a modern State, a system in which there are elections at fairly regular intervals and where the candidate who receives the most votes gains office, does seem logical at first sight. But is is precisely the notions of majority rule and government by the people that are being questioned today. Discussions of government and democracy are likely to become muddled if we assume that the orderly succession of rulers achieved by an election system implies that only the particular kind of elective system now operating in liberal democracies can be 'contemporaneously plausible'. It is not 'plausible' at all philosophically, unless one is an egalitarian and a relativist. Indeed, it is so difficult to defend the majority system under the so-called universal franchise, that one of the commonest methods of defending current practice is to argue that the system precludes genuine majority rule and government by the people.

Mayo's identification of the advantages of an elective system with those of the democratic one seems, however, to be quite deliberate. His reference to 'co-option' (by an élite) shows that he is quite aware of other possibilities. Because he does not develop his view or define the élite', it is difficult to understand precisely what he means, though there can be little doubt that he at least partly believes it is not possible in a democracy to restrict the franchise further or to restrict those eligible for office. Such restrictions could be said to convert the democratic electoral system into that 'co-option by an élite' which Mayo dismisses as philosophically unacceptable. Since these two restrictions have repeatedly been put forward as solutions to the problems — both practical and theoretical — facing democracies, the matter cannot be brushed aside.

Obviously, at some point a restriction on the franchise and on those eligible for office will keep an electoral system from being democratic: we cannot call the Holy Roman Emperors democratic rulers simply on the ground that the office was elective. But at what point does the change occur? Is it a purely arbitrary one on a continuum, or is it decided by normative considerations associated with the norms that decide whether the government will be hereditary, appointive or elective?

C.B. Macpherson in *The Real World of Democracy* seems at first to support a view based on the logic of the egalitarian norm. He sees 'democracy' as a late addition to the liberal state, his ground being that the franchise was restricted until late in the nineteenth century. Since women did not have the franchise until the twentieth century, it is possible that if he were completely frank, he would admit that Canada, Britain and the USA did not achieve democracy until after the USSR had conferred its blessings upon the world. The exact nature of his position is not clear, for he seems willing to call a State democratic if eligibility for office is open. In discussing the 'underdeveloped variant' of 'non-liberal democracy' he does not mention the franchise, which in the earlier part of his discussion was the determining factor in converting the 'liberal' state into a 'liberal-democratic' one. Perhaps he is simply assuming that the reader will understand him to imply that there must also be enfranchisement of all adults. In any case, the point raised is interesting. In the first place, is it possible to call a State democratic if one of the elements in the electoral system, the franchise or eligibility for office, is restricted? Secondly, (the question originally posed), what is the degree of restriction which deprives the system of the right to be called democratic? If we cannot answer these questions, we must call any system 'democratic' (except the hereditary one) which provides an orderly transfer of power.

Mayo in his defence of democracy, and Macpherson in his classification of dissimilar political orders as democracies, imply that restrictions on the franchise or on eligibility for office can exist without invalidating a society's claim to be democratic. Elsewhere, however, Mayo specifically denies that either the franchise or eligibility for office can be restricted in a democracy. When defending it against the charge that its basis is incompetent, he simply forgets that his rebuttal of this charge must be consonant with the rest of his analysis.

Electoral System as a Norm

Taking as his true position his assertion that 'democratic theory [starts] with a method of choosing and controlling decision-makers',[3] let us see what Mayo has to say about restrictions on the franchise and eligibility for office. By defining democracy in terms of the electoral system, by making the latter the fundamental norm, as it were, Mayo raises serious theoretic difficulties, for the electoral system is not by its nature democratic, as we have observed before. Apart from institutions in very primitive communities and a few relics of the monarchic system in others, the electoral system is now the general method of maintaining an orderly succession of governments, but it can hardly be said — without ignoring clear differences — that democracy is the usual form of government today. If we are to begin an analysis of democracy in terms of the method of attaining a government rather than in terms of the norms that prescribe the method, we must see restrictions or the lack of them as the true index of whether the system is democratic or not. We must then take Mayo to mean that democratic theory starts with an electoral system which in theory has a universal adult franchise and unrestricted eligibility for office.

Mayo offers six arguments for an unrestricted adult franchise, but we will disregard those that he himself finds dubious.

The first argument in which Mayo finds any merit is that of justice: since a government imposes duties, the individual should have the right to decide the duties. Mayo sees the argument as having considerable force and objects only that there are practices inconsistent with it. He misses the main objections entirely. If duties imply rights, they do so only under special conditions and special assumptions. If the duties are imposed

---

[3]*Ibid.*, p. 110.

by the government for the government's benefit, it could be argued — though it certainly need not be — that some 'rights' for the citizen ought to ensue. On the assumption of a marketplace morality of fair trade, he should get something back of equal value. Needless to say, such a position assumes that government and society are separate interest groups. But the duties a democratic government imposes are supposed to be in the interest of society, so that the concept of reciprocation lying behind the duty-right argument is of course invalidated. Mayo seems to have confused an argument for right derived from duty with the case for its converse: duty derived from right. The argument that rights entail duties simply recognizes that the concept of rights necessarily implies some kind of contract. The concept of duty, on the other hand, most certainly does not. What possible right can I demand, and from whom, if I fulfil what I regard as a moral duty?

A second objection to the justice argument is that even if we suppose that duties entail rights, one of the rights need not be that of deciding who shall specify the duties. Indeed, to regard government in this way would make the imposition of unwanted duties almost impossible, even if they were to the advantage of those required to perform them. If Mayo can see difficulties in arguing from choice — which he does in relation to one of the arguments — he certainly ought to be able to see difficulties in arguing from duty, for the practical effect of the two is the same. Far from being 'an argument of considerable force', the argument from justice is one of the weakest.

Another argument for universal adult suffrage which Mayo sees as having merit is that of self-protection: 'Any section of society is likely to have its opinions and interests overlooked and perhaps trampled upon unless it has the vote to ensure its share of the control of government and hence of policy.'[4] Mayo rightly sees the argument as likely to lead toward functional representation, but raises no other objection. However, the assumption underlying the argument is rather dubious and certainly antisocial: man is said to be so narrowly selfish and self-seeking by nature that any decision ostensibly made on behalf of another will really be made for the benefit of the decision-maker unless

[4]*Ibid.*, p. 118.

he is in some way under the control of those affected, whose own selfishness and self-interest will ensure that they are neither neglected nor oppressed. This Hobbesian view of man, of course, has always constituted one of the primary objections to the concept of sovereignty among those who have not troubled to follow Hobbes's logic. Historically, it has accounted for the complex system of checks and balances operating in some democratic systems.

Unfortunately, it is not possible to reject out of hand the view of man's nature on which such controls are based. We have to admit that enough men have behaved as if they were Darwinian animals in a jungle society that we must think twice about taking any bars off the cages we have made for them. However, if man were as completely individualistic and selfish as the view implies, it is difficult to see how society and government ever came into being or how they managed to operate before the imposition of democratic controls. We can agree that some men have acted as if sympathy, friendship, love, cooperation and principle were for them restrictions on their 'natural' impulses, but it is less likely that their behaviour is 'natural' than that it has in some way been imparted to them through education. Indeed, I suspect that one of the best ways to promote their thoroughly anti-social attitude is to defend social institutions on the supposition that men's attitude is the natural one: acceptance of the institution entails acceptance of the attitude. By arguing that the franchise permits self-defence for those capable of forming power blocs, you are ensuring that those not capable of doing so will be disregarded, perhaps even oppressed. In short, to base the argument for universal adult franchise on self-protection is really to argue indirectly in favour of the 'might is right' school of justice.

The arguments Mayo accepts are not convincing. Like all examples of apologetics, they take the wrong direction: the problem is not to prove that current practice is justifiable. What should be obvious is that practices do not need to be justified unless they come under attack and when they do the justification must meet the objections, must show they they are unfounded or, if they are sound, that the practices objected to are an integral part of the system and that their removal would involve the rejection of an entire system which can be successfully defended on other grounds. Mayo has not done this. The objection to universal adult suffrage is that the general public are incompetent. It does not solve the problem to argue that they do not in fact govern, as Mayo does elsewhere. His argument for this view is based upon an analysis of the electoral system that in effect demonstrates an absence of the 'free choice' which he puts forward as a defence of the system. Whether the reference is to government by the people, public control of the government or simply public influence on the government, the charge of incompetence stands. A man who cannot drive has even less excuse to fiddle with the controls while someone else is driving than he has to set off on a jaunt by himself. If we admit the charge of incompetence, we cannot approve of control or influence unless it can be shown that they are so important or beneficial from other standpoints that the question of competence is overridden. Mayo has not done this either, or even attempted to. He summarizes his opinion with the assertion, 'I am inclined to think that today the universal adult suffrage is merely an inseparable part of the wider argument for democracy',[5] but he offers no explanation for his inclination. In view of the very serious objections to universal adult suffrage and the convincing argument that can be made for an electoral system in which the franchise is not universal, we must ask ourselves whether the democratic political and social order is indeed inextricably bound up with universal adult franchise.

There is one argument for the universal franchise which Mayo does not raise — the egalitarian one. On the assumption that men are by nature equal, the universal adult franchise follows logically. Indeed, it is then one of the very conditions necessary to attain the ideal of equality. However, Mayo wisely avoids the argument, probably because it is no longer possible to believe in the possibility of factual equality. But if we abandon the argument that has broadened the franchise, can we now reverse direction and begin to limit it? Can we, for instance, shift from eligibility at the chronological age of eighteen to eligibility at the mental age of eighteen? Would this entail a shift in the public's feeling that a democratic government is 'our' government to the belief that the government is 'their' (the egg-heads') govern-

[5]*Ibid.*, p. 120.

ment and thus destroy the sense of democracy as well as change its definition? Could the present policy of making voting as convenient as possible be reversed so that it would become highly inconvenient except for those with a high level of intelligence and knowledge? Could votes be weighted in favour of the latter?

Mayo objects to restrictions, 'fitness tests of any kind', on the ground that such tests imply four propositions: '(a) Some political decisions are wiser than others. (b) Some people know which decisions are wiser. (c) These people can be found by fitness tests of some kind. (d) All adults can be persuaded to accept the first three propositions, and hence to accept the legitimacy of restricted voting.' Mayo maintains that the propositions 'mistake the purpose of elections, which is not and should not be to decide the many complex issues, but to give everyone an equal vote in choosing decision-makers.'[6] As I have argued before, however, it is not necessary to assume that the public — rather than the government — makes decisions in order to raise the question of competence. If it can be shown that voters in any way influence the government, fitness tests become necessary. Mayo patently begs the question when he asserts that the purpose of elections is to give an equal vote to everyone and that once this is granted, fitness tests become irrelevant. It is not possible to answer an objection to equality of voting by merely asserting that everyone must have an equal vote. Such an electoral system is not necessary to ensure an orderly succession of governments, nor does it appear necessary to democratic theory now that 'equality' can no longer be regarded as a fact.

Mayo evidently feels a little uneasy about his argument, for he next attempts to answer the four propositions. He argues first that though we can accept the proposition that some decisions are wiser, it is not possible to know beforehand whose decisions will prove to be wiser. This, of course, is tantamount to saying that there are no discernible patterns of intelligence, knowledge or principle: the common man is as likely to seek medical advice from an idiot child as from a doctor. He remains completely unaware of the probable quality of the advice until it is given, whereupon his eyes are mysteriously opened, only to close again

[6]*Ibid.*, p. 110.

before he can ask the next question. I can only say that when a defence of democratic practice falls to this level, we are no longer dealing with a genuine attempt to appraise it. Mayo's effort here is low-level apologetics.

His objection to 'proposition (d)' is not so readily answered, since he says only that it is 'absurd' to believe that the public can be persuaded to accept restricted voting. But how can he be so sure? If there are cogent reasons for his belief, why does he not advance them?

Theory as a Justification of Practice

There can be no doubt that universal adult suffrage has become strongly associated with democracy. It is clear from Mayo's statements that for him and, likely enough, the great mass of the public, or particular electoral system *is* democracy. This conversion of particular practices into principles of the system is, of course, a well-known phenomenon: going to church comes to be the essence of piety. It is one of the basic reasons why analyses of social institutions have shifted from pure theory to pragmatic studies of actual practices. When practices in effect become the theory, there may not seem to be much point in analysing the abstract requirements of the normative order. Yet there is a point beyond which practice and justification cannot diverge further. The great 'reform' movements in Church and State have unquestionably been attempts to bring theory and practice closer together and it is theory which has been the initiating factor. We may also suspect, though the evidence is less clear, that when a practice loses all possible justification, when it becomes a mere custom that is at odds with common sense, it withers. Is this the present state of the universal adult franchise? Many no doubt accept it because they see it as the essence of democracy itself. These are the pharisees of democracy who are completely indifferent to the traditional norms, quite baffled by talk of freedom of speech and so forth. Others may still believe firmly in the universal adult franchise because they retain a belief in literal equality, which is still a necessary belief among fundamentalist sects. Still others may do so because they confuse the franchise with the electoral system itself and hence suppose that the alternative is an hereditary system or a tyranny. Again, many others undoubtedly support the franchise because men like Mayo seek to justify it by perpetuating the myth that self-interest necessitates self-protective devices. Nonetheless, the system of universal adult suffrage has no clear and sound justification today. The possibility of a return to a restricted franchise will depend, of course, on the future of the egalitarian norm and the particular construction placed upon it. It was egalitarianism that required the universal franchise; its current interpretations do not.

It is not likely that change in the franchise will soon be made. Changes in eligibility for office, however, are a rather different case. It might be felt that they should be treated in the same way as the franchise, since they are part of the same electoral system. After all, what is the point of universal franchise if the choices are limited? As Mayo says, 'Choice at the polls further depends upon whether there is a meaningful choice or live option among candidates, and this is turn depends on whether candidates are free to offer themselves for election.'[7] This seems sound enough until we recall that Mayo did not defend the franchise on the grounds of freedom of choice. His argument comes down to the simple assertion that one man-one vote is democratic practice. As such, of course, it need have no meaningful function whatsoever. Those inclined to the pragmatic interpretation are usually reduced to such illogicalities. However, since a franchise is part of an electoral system and this is one of the two possible ways of obtaining an orderly succession of rulers, voting *must* be meaningful. If it is not, the system is dangerously unstable, for the method of finding successors to rulers becomes irregular, part of some other system; if the latter is not an electoral or hereditary one, it will introduce its own instability. This a major weakness of the communistic systems. Despite the façade of an electoral process, they lack a clear-cut method of supplying an orderly succession of rulers. In the Western democracies, the party system — which Mayo sees as a valuable means of reducing objections to the democratic franchise — introduces an inconsistency into the electoral system that makes for some disorder. Though the parties are ostensibly miniature democratic systems — systems of co-option — it is in practice quite

[7] *Ibid.*, pp. 138-9.

difficult to get rid of ageing and incompetent party leaders or to acquire new ones without creating rather serious divisions in the party. Until the features that experience has shown to be necessary to the electoral system as a whole are introduced — the secret ballot and regular elections, for instance — the system will tend to be unstable. The need for these features has nothing whatever to do with making the elections 'democratic'. It is absurd to use such a term with reference to what is certainly election by an élite, and which can therefore only be called co-option by an élite. The need arises from the nature of an electoral system, which cannot logically allow potential leaders to influence the chances of their own selection. Such pressure introduces the element of force and hence the instability that stems from the unpredictable nature of force.

But although it is true that voting must be meaningful if the system is to be stable and that it is consequently not possible to solve the problems of democracy by making the franchise a mere form while making the source of government succession quite different, it is not true that restrictions on eligibility for office are impossible.

So long as government was not felt to require any specialized skill or training because of its very limited functions, limitations on those eligible for office were not defensible. They appeared to be, and were, simply methods of defending privilege. If all men were really equal, all men could hold office. But the increasing complexity of government and the widely recognized need for the equality of democracy to be regarded as other than a statement about human nature have since made it possible for access to government office to be restricted without a sense of departure from democratic norms. The restrictions are at present informal: the need for a considerable degree of wealth, or a position that will enlist it; an occupation such as the law which permits absence for the purpose of politicking; and a few others. It is quite possible that some formal restrictions could be imposed: a minimum standard of intelligence and education, perhaps even a test of psychological stability. The increasing demand that an authority in the organizational sense (viz. holding a leading position in the political hierarchy) also be an authority in the sense of having expert knowledge may well promote changes of this kind. As a result, those problems in a democracy which arise from its traditional open office system could be resolved without any sense of a failure to meet normative requirements: the logic of egalitarianism would simply be cancelled by the logic of government.

It must be remembered, however, that such restrictions will not solve the major problems of democracy, which can hardly be traced to lack of competence in the leaders. There is no particular reason to suppose that an aristocratic revolution tomorrow would have any marked effect on the makeup of Parliament. A few football players and ageing entrepreneurs might be thrown out, but on the whole those at present in politics are probably the persons who are most interested in government. One of the main problems of democracy lies in the influence of the general public on policy. This difficulty can be resolved only by restricting the franchise, but since it cannot be restricted so far as to make it meaningless, the problem for the future will be that of deciding the extent of restriction. This will be determined by the norms associated with democracy. It was, after all, egalitarianism that brought universal adult suffrage. What will happen as a result of the changes in interpretation is a matter for speculation.

We have seen that the electoral system spread across the world by democracy has solved the practical problems inherent in other systems of government but that the electoral system itself has defects that need to be removed if democracy is to remain viable.

Democratic Apologetics and the Democratic Ideology

'That the people determine', announces David Spitz in his appraisal of the works of Walter Lippmann and Ralph A. Cram, 'through the free expression of competing ideas the broad patterns of policy and the composition of central personnel is undeniably the very heart of the democratic principle. But that "the people" are, as Cram contends, "average men", is a proposition subject to serious disputation.' Spitz then argues that 'there is nowhere a man or a group of men to whom we can point and unqualifiedly say: There is average man'[8] and ends with a pretty picture of mechanics and shopkeepers, lawyers and

[8]David Spitz, *Patterns of Anti-Democratic Thought* (Revised Edition) (New York, 1965), p. 144.

scholars debating together, as dreamers and utopians once hoped they would, in democracies yet to come: 'From public discussions in lecture halls and private conversations across the dinner table, from incidental talk in the barber shop and passing comment in the streetcar, from the multitudinous organs of propaganda...men derive new and sometimes challenging ideas.'[9] The startling part of this vision, however, is that it is described as a reality and is put forward as an answer to Lippmann.

How did a political scientist familiar with the facts of political behaviour manage to reach a conclusion opposed to the facts of democratic life and how can he suppose that he is defending 'democracy'? What kind of democracy is he defending?

Spitz begins by professing to find the concept of 'average man' a dubious one. Most of us would say that if you can talk about 'the majority of men', you can certainly talk about 'the average man'. (This is true, if the majority are identical — or closely similar — as regards those attributes which are relevant to the subject under discussion.) The latter refers to members of the majority regarded as individuals, and the attributes of 'the average man' are determined by whatever classifying system has been used to define 'majority'. Spitz pretends he is puzzled: 'Is he [the average man] alike or uniform in all things to all men?' Lippmann or Cram, the men Spitz professes to be opposing, would be embarrassed by such a question, but not because they could not answer it. There is worse to come, of course. Having established for himself that 'Democracy knows no average man',[10] he proceeds to argue that there is also no such thing as 'rationality' or 'competence', on the grounds that they are always manifested in particular instances, and that 'values are related to social organization' and consequently 'it follows that group opinion...is the result of prolonged discussion.'[11]

One cannot help feeling that democracy would be better off without such 'defences'. The mischief in Spitz's argument does not lie in its particular fallacies, but in its general tenor: the type of 'democracy' he is defending is not the same as the system of democracy operating in the USA. His democracy tolerates

[9]*Ibid*, p. 148.
[10]*Ibid.*, p. 146.
[11]*Ibid.*, p. 147.

Apologetics and the Democratic Ideology 131

anything done in the name of authority, provided that authority is 'democratic' in his sense. It is a relativistic system incapable of anything remotely resembling the 'public philosophy' conceived (later) by Lippmann.

Spitz sees Lippmann as a man who argued that 'the public governs but is incapable of governing'[12] and he has no difficulty in establishing that such a criticism is irrelevant. For him, democracy is 'in essence, control by all men of political power exercised by a few.'[13] Lippmann, it seems to me, would not reject this interpretation, although he would probably substitute 'ideally' for 'in essence', and he would argue that it is precisely this concept of 'democracy' which he is criticizing, not the unrealistic notion of 'majority rule'. Whether one speaks of 'rule', 'control' or (as many critics do today) 'influence', the charge that the average man is 'incompetent' is a valid objection. No word juggling can change the fact that most people lack the interest, norms and degree of rationality needed to control or influence a government for their good as private citizens or for that of the society as a whole. The point is not that some people have more knowledge, higher intelligence or stricter ethics than others, but that most people do not have enough of these qualities to function in the way required by the concept of 'majority rule'.

When Lippmann questions the 'competence' of the average man he is not arguing that we should abandon democracy, but that we should reappraise those defences of democracy which take no account of what freedom, equality and other norms mean. To him, norms are not expressions of private interest and group relations — as they seem to be for Spitz — but the distinguishing characteristic of the political order called democracy. To him, society's norms are necessarily public, not private. Spitz is more of a relativist and consequently cannot use norms to define democracy. His idea of democracy is some kind of haphazardly-determined mean on a scale of government ranging from absolutism to anarchy.

The objection of men of Lippmann's persuasion to those who argue for the 'competence' of the average man is that they are trying to make the electoral system perform a function for which it was not designed. By insisting on the centrality of the electoral

[12]*Ibid.*, p. 138.
[13]*Ibid.*, p. 143.

system to the democratic conception of government and by directing reforms of the electoral system in such a way as to make it more meaningful as an expression of public opinion, they are trying to make the electoral system a source of norms. But this cannot be so, for as a source of norms — as a 'control of' or 'influence on' policy — the electoral system satisfies neither the relativist nor the normativist.

In as much as relativists are convinced that the good is what the individual believes it to be, they can hardly accept a system which encourages the attitude but removes one of the benefits. If one votes as one pleases, chance determines whether one gets what is desired, for if you grant 'the people' the power of influencing the government, you deprive the individual of the right to influence his fellow-citizens. As an attempt to impose one's own desires and interests on others, such influence becomes illegitimate. Under such a conception, *all* techniques of influencing one's fellow-citizens, including the use of 'reason', are illegitimate, for here 'the good' has been defined in terms of private will. But in a democracy it is the 'public will' rather than the individual will which is supposed to influence the government. Instead of arguing for democracy in terms of the norms of 'liberty' and 'individualism', the relativist is compelled to replace them with the norm 'majority rule' or 'respect for the electoral system' or 'the law'. Given that norm, the gap can be bridged, but only at the expense of his initial relativist assumptions. Now 'the good' is likely to be the Constitution to which the individual must submit his will. The relativist has argued himself into a quasi-'absolutist' position (based on a single absolute).

It is the arbitrariness of this absolute that normativists like Lippmann object to. Elections were not designed to serve as a source of society's norms. Originally, they had to work within a framework of norms, not create them. Arguments that members of the voting public are as individuals 'competent' to create normative systems for a society are spurious. Under the conception of democracy suggested by their proponents, it is the electoral system which becomes the normative source and — whether the individual is competent at inventing normative systems or not — it is manifestly impossible for a normative system to create normative systems. Voting is a process within a normative system, not a system-making scheme in its own right.

Beyond Justification: Thorson's Challenge to Epistemological Assumptions

In his *Biopolitics*[14](1970), Thorson makes the contribution of substituting an 'evolutionary-developmental' for a 'universal generalization' paradigm and challenging the epistemological basis of democratic theory. He stands by the conclusions of an earlier book, *The Logic of Democracy*[15] (1962) — as I think he should — but he does so by professedly deriving 'experiential rules' from both the practice of science in our society and those of democracy and then generalizing from the rules and reapplying them to science and democracy as rules of procedure.[16] The questions which arise are: in what way are the rules 'experiential' and how do they establish their 'authenticity'? (Thorson prefers this term to 'validity' or 'authority'.)

Nothing Thorson says enables us to arrive at rules which can be learnt and taught in the way approved by our society. It was once possible for Thorson's critics to object to the argument in his earlier book on the ground 'that the recognition of human fallibility...is in fact nothing more than a covert place of metaphysical deduction and thus falls prey to the arguments against deduction.'[17] However, it is no longer possible to do this, since 'the logic of recommendation' on which the argument is based is no longer regarded by him as 'a static set of rules for "truth getting" like deduction or induction, but the time-oriented, experience-oriented logic of life.' 'The fact is,' says Thorson, 'that scientific method and democratic method are justified as a matter of life and not a truth.'[18] Such a defence permits no argument. Knowledge and art become one and, seemingly, we must now respond to a political theory much as we respond to a poem — we either feel its 'truth' or we do not. If we accept

---

[14]Thomas Landon Thorson, *Biopolitics* (New York, 1970).

[15]In which, as Thorson says, 'The core of the argument was based on the logical parallel between the *justification* of scientific method and the *justification* of democratic method.' *Ibid.*, p. 201.

[16]See *ibid.*, the diagrams on pp. 204-06.

[17]*Ibid.*, p. 203.

[18]*Ibid.*, pp. 203-04.

Thorson's view, we have no means of transcending the level of individual experience.

The problem of political theory is that of relating the truth and knowledge of individual experience to that approved by society. Thorson recognizes this when he says that 'the mode and content of communication is at the centre of culture and therefore of any account of cultural change.'[19] But the direction which he subsequently follows seems to be essentially 'non-political': his concern is with epistemology.

Any society is confronted with a set of beliefs and values that arise as a result of individual experience, in addition to another set — not necessarily related to individual experience — defining society *qua* society. If we do not have a technique for mediating conflicts between the two sets, a technique which is related to the 'authority', 'logic', or 'authenticity', we must impose some other kind of authority in order to make the social system viable. In other words, if a society does not have a generally acceptable way of arriving at 'truth', the political system must extend its jurisdiction over the minds. Under such conditions, 'education' becomes a technique of imposing beliefs and values on the greatest possible number of people; certain ideas are excluded by censorship; and the law serves to enforce politically acceptable opinions. As in Plato's Republic — one thinks of the importance of Forms and education — political theory then finds it necessary to incorporate a 'truth' into its system.

Hitherto political theory has had little or no concern with epistemology. It has been taken for granted that its epistemological basis is generally acceptable. Now Thorson believes that we cannot make this assumption any longer: the idea that a political system can be based on 'reason' or 'science' alone no longer carries conviction. This also means that the problem engendered by relativism is not limited to norms but embraces beliefs in general.[20]

---

[19] *Ibid.*, p. 140.

[20] One could note here that the difference between Thorson and David Easton is not a difference in 'paradigms' but in the attitude to paradigms. Where Easton believes that his model permits us to organize our knowledge of political systems in a pattern that is 'like' the system itself and as a result gain new insights into its working, Thorson denies that such knowledge is possible. According to him, political systems are a part of culture and must derive their 'authenticity' from the culture as a whole, not merely from the

Thorson's Challenge

Thorson's approach to political theory poses the following difficulty. Irrespective of whether we have an assured method of arriving at norms and knowledge, if we want to talk about existing political orders rather than what 'should be', we have to recognize that these orders are faced with relativism as a practical problem. To be a working system, a political order must take into account the fact of relativism. Apart from the coercive method under which the State is the supreme arbiter of norms and beliefs, one of the possible ways of arriving at norms is for the State to acknowledge for the time being differences in beliefs and values. Under this system, we do not have to hold the same values but we do need to suppose that it is not enough to put forward the proposition that our 'conscience' or 'reason' tells us what is true or good. We have to assume a general belief in 'epistemological possibilities' — that our system of knowledge will one day produce a 'truth' and a 'natural law' that everyone will accept.[21]

Thorson's shift from the 'universal generalization' paradigm to an 'evolutionary-developmental' speculation entails not only a change in the attitude to 'truth' or 'knowledge' but also in the technique of communication. Because Thorson denies the validity of traditional logical schemes one cannot infer from his writings that if the conclusions he reaches appear false, the particular directions of thought which led him there can be dismissed. In consequence, scattered throughout his book are some exceptionally interesting ideas, undeveloped from the point of

---

minute relation between the categories of biological and political systems. When Thorson raises logical objections to Easton's 'system', he is not claiming that we have in logic an assured method of arriving at 'truth'; he is pointing out to Easton an aspect of our culture that Easton has neglected.

[21] We do not pretend that this day has already arrived. The democratic State does not even insist on its fundamental norms. For instance, an individual is perfectly free to question the nature of equality and the value of majority rule. He is free to do this not because it is his privilege as a member of a minority in a State made stable by the rule of the majority. Rather, he is free to question the norms because there is a general agreement about the *methods* he uses. He can be countered without being suppressed or coerced, even though he may advocate violence, because the real basis of appeal is to 'reason' and not to the norm of 'violence'. Whether we actually order our norms and beliefs rationally is a moot point; what matters is that as individuals we attempt to propagate them by what passes for rational argument. We have no choice in the matter. Non-rational techniques — like propaganda — are known, but are not open to the private citizen; and they are, of course, under grave suspicion.

view of the traditional 'universal generalization' scheme and also unrelated to one another.

The problem implied by Thorson's 'evolutionary-developmental' scheme is primarily that of communication: although we have a large number of different techniques of communication — printing, music, poetry, gesture — what we define as 'knowledge' has so far been communicated by one particular method, the logical analytical generalization scheme (questioned by Thorson). The reason is that this method alone enables us to agree on what has been communicated. It is quite possible that the poet, the mystic or Thorson himself, for that matter, is capable of arriving at a 'greater' truth than the philosopher. Such truth, however, requires a special technique of communication which has not yet been agreed upon. Until such a special technique has been found, we have to discuss the scheme itself not as false but as unintelligible.

One particular issue introduced by Thorson requires special attention because it raises the problem of scientism and the marked current tendency to explain human behaviour in terms of man's biological inheritance. As Thorson observes: 'the evolutionary-developmental paradigm calls direct and crucial attention to the question of the relationship between biological evolution and social-cultural evolution, whereas this is not a question at all for structural-functional analysis or systems theory.'[22] How does it do so? Thorson draws on Teilhard de Chardin's argument and confronts us with the alternative of the special creation of man and the supposition that 'human consciousness and all that is connected with it [was] somehow implicit in the historical development of the universe from the beginning.' He opts for the view that we are 'obliged to look actively for the connection between man's biological development and his intellectual and cultural development.'[23] He does not believe that human evolution stopped when *homo sapiens* developed: 'the evidence is substantial that in the human passageway nature found a new method of information transfer, namely, that product of human learning and teaching that we call culture. And through this system of information-transfer evolution has continued.'[24]

[22] *Ibid.*, p. 101.
[23] *Ibid.*, p. 100.
[24] *Ibid.*, pp. 110-11.

For Thorson 'the mode and content of communication is at the centre of culture.'[25] Indeed, cultural evolution is by him equated to ('at the core of') information transmission.[26] He makes much of the distinction between 'print' and 'oral' cultures and argues, for instance, that an oral culture is family-oriented in morality and hence its behaviour — compared with a print culture such as our own — is corrupt: nepotism is rampant in most 'developing' countries.

There is no point in making an issue of such a loose association of ideas. It is not a vital issue in *Biopolitics*. But it is important to understand why such an astute thinker as its author should suppose it valuable enough to set down, yet not support it with logical analysis. To him, the manipulation of words is what traditional science and philosophy are about[27] and they have misled us. Like McLuhan, he wants to enlarge our concepts of communication and with the enlargement, change our thought processes. Logical analyses of what one perceives would be a retreat to the past.

Thorson seems to forget that if the function — even in part — of political science is to describe things as they are, we must attend to the words and thoughts of our present culture. He himself has not evolved a new language nor has our culture done so. The fact that our words and logic have no necessary relation to the nature of the universe is irrelevant to the social scientist, no matter how disturbing this may be to the physical scientist. Traditional language and logic have an essential relation to human culture. Indeed, language has been called 'pure culture'. It embodies almost everything in our culture precisely because it is the basic means of transmitting it.

---

[25]*Ibid.*, p. 140.
[26]See *ibid.*, p. 148.
[27]See *ibid.*, p. 165.

VI
The Insufficiency Of Empirical Theory

Partial Theories

Empirical theories which are not applicable to all societies or to all political behaviour are termed 'partial'. Unlike classical, 'overarching' theories, they approach political phenomena as the physical sciences do — as something that can be divided into areas of research, within which models can be constructed and tested against the facts. Implicit in this view is the belief that just as it is possible to enrich our understanding of, say, electromagnetic phenomena by applying models derived from the study of visible light, so one should be able to bring to the study of political behaviour established models drawn from other areas of investigation. The fact that they do not explain everything is irrelevant.

Theories are 'partial' because they do not give a full account of such activities as the attaining of power and the making of political decisions: activities that fit the proposed models are 'explained'; those that do not must await the construction of another model. At first sight, this seems reasonable, but as soon as we ask just what it is that needs explaining, the inadequacies of partial theories become apparent.

Advocates of games theory can make an apparently convincing case for its analysis of international relations and it is also of some use in the study of party politics and labour-management relations. Although it has otherwise no clear bearing on the problem of domestic policy, it might perhaps be said that here at least is a way of understanding part of the decision-making process and that subsequently other models could be introduced to supplement it. However, the reason why this piecemeal approach to political behaviour is unsatisfactory may be seen by analysing the role played by games theory in decision-making. The problem we face is that of making decisions within a system set up to make decisions: any workable theory of political behaviour will be put into practice by those whose behaviour it professes to describe. The difficulty with evolving this kind of political theory is that it can never be entirely true as a description, unless men are consciously aware of it as a working model. (Otherwise, one is forced to assume that men are not capable of choice and, like atoms, are forced to carry out predetermined actions.)

Before the application of games theory to political behaviour, a rough approximation to it was certainly being used in international relations. It was never, however, a conscious policy for reasons born of long experience. It presupposes an attitude of perpetual rivalry in foreign affairs, although attitudes such as cooperation and indifference are equally possible and indeed can be found to have existed in the history of international relations over long periods. The impact of the games theory has been remarkable. Its very usefulness in giving government an indication of what policy to pursue in situations of rivalry and conflict has enabled governments to pursue the policies of 'cold-war' and 'brinkmanship'. Games theory supplied the principles which converted one of several possible attitudes into a policy and, by offering a 'reward' to the successful contestant, it has helped to preserve international tensions.

Some students of political science consider games theory to be incompatible with the direction of our civilization. It has the serious weakness of being limited to situations of rivalry or potential conflict. It has the odd characteristic of avoiding conflict while commonly using the threat of it as a weapon. There is now a realization that games theory supplies a basis for policy only where conditions of rivalry or conflict exist. The theory has the deficiency of requiring opposition between elements where no such opposition is sought or desired. Over-stressing the 'opposition' aspect, it distorts the image of democracy and raises some serious questions about the nature of democracy. On the whole, it remains valid only insofar as the theories of power politics apply and when all motivation except strict self-interest is excluded from consideration. It presupposes that some particular situation prevails without taking into account the norms prevailing in society — a fundamental requirement of any theory of foreign policy-making.

The defect of all 'partial' theories is that they seek to give an orderly description of a situation which does not exist as an orderly phenomenon. Furthermore, policy-making is not just the application of some more or less orderly normative scheme, such as an ideology. Thus, the policy of a democratic government cannot be a mere implementation of democratic ideology. Foreign policy-making requires recognition that the norms of democracy are not the only norms and that the State is not an isolated entity. A sovereign power is confronted, for instance, with the need to pursue a policy which will maintain a viable economy, preserve its independence among sovereign powers of different ideological persuasions, and also act in accordance with the ideology and legal system on which its own legitimacy is based. When shaping its foreign policy, a government has to integrate some widely differing normative requirements.

Partial theories are not just partial explanations; they are inadequate templates for action. Partial theories, dealing with specific areas of policy-making rather than policy in general, compound the problem of policy-making by fragmenting it. The problem for government is to arrive at an *integrated* system of policy-making — an unattainable goal for the adherents of partial theories. The latter reinforces the tendency of government members to think of their role in the same way as a bureaucrat or a technocrat thinks of his — as the carrying out of a limited task which is inevitably compatible with the other parts of a wider system. Partial theories do not even touch on the crucial aspect of decision-making — that of the sovereign power.

Traditionally, the policy-making norms of the sovereign power have been called 'justice' and philosophers trying to give an explanation have resorted to 'overarching' or 'grand' theories. Such theories linking a number of 'supreme' norms were expected to provide the needed normative system. Our failure to arrive at a plausible outline of such a system can be attributed to the fact that we have focused our attention primarily on analyses and defences of sub-sets — ideologies, economic values, legal codes, etc. This trend is largely due to self-interest. Those who advance the ideals of democracy or the requirements of the market place as supreme norms have sought to influence government decisions in favour of their beliefs. Although they may be sincere in this respect, they fail to see that none of these sets of norms can become the chief consideration in government decisions.

The reasons for the current trend are also professional and methodological. The direction of modern political science is towards understanding the particular influences that shaped particular policy decisions — an approach which presupposes that no general principles exist. (This is so even though the defence of particular studies is often that a sufficient body of them will enable us to grasp general principles.) It seems that particularistic studies can only tend towards the conclusion that no supreme norms — or methods of decision-making — exist; that principles are illusions. It also appears that despite the professed need for an 'overarching' theory, the most commonly employed methodology of the social sciences prevents us from getting one.

Systems Theories

Until recently, the use of general systems theories as a tool of analysis was limited. (The reasons why their use as a tool of analysis was minor and why they have not become popular will be given later.) Unlike social and political theories, they are often put into practice before being fully formulated. Quite frequently, 'systemic' models of society — or of parts of society — are employed as vehicles of social criticism. This is important to all those who use systems theories for analysis. Various Utopian designs found in literature can serve satiric purposes and expose the shortcomings of the norms and institutions of actual societies by making clear the fallacy in all presuppositions about systems — the notion that an institutionalized expression of a norm embodies that norm and that therefore no further attention need be paid to society's goals and ideals.

In Part IV of *Gulliver's Travels* Swift presented the Utopian society of the Houyhnhnms — an institutionalized form of the ideals of reason, moderation and humanitarianism, a society superior in these matters to any actual society. Swift's main point is not that this imaginary system is superior but rather that a system designed to express certain 'primary' norms cannot be actually guided by them. The system becomes a thing in itself, static with regard to those 'primary' norms and working according to some different set of norms. By being institutionalized in Swift's satire, the reason, moderation and humanitarianism of the Houyhnhnms are made ritualistic. When confronted by a situation demanding to apply their principles, they are unable to do so. The stability of the system is more important to them than the norms on which it is supposed to rest. This very notion requires them to reject — despite the principles of reason, moderation and humanitarianism — anything that does not fit the system. As their 'reason' has no category into which Gulliver can fit, he is sent off to what they imagine to be his death, despite all his appeals to their ideals.

Interestingly enough, Gulliver himself is unable to see the shortcomings of the system (and, by implication, of the systems approach). Of all the societies he visits, he is converted only to the Houyhnhnms. Though rejected, he wants to be a Houyhnhnm, convinced by the orderliness of the system which is the epitome of reason and humanitarianism. He scorns the reason and sympathy of members of his society and cultivates the companionship of horses, making himself ridiculous by acting like a horse. This conversion of Gulliver to what might be called the systems point of view makes him the target of satire. It is clear from the bitter mood of the book that Swift interpreted such conversions as abortive attempts to attain the 'good society' or understand its nature.

Swift is not alone in this respect. In similar fashion, Aldous Huxley used the institutionalization of an ideal — the concept of 'happiness' in this case — to show that any system which attempts to reach the ideal by setting up a system meant to embody this ideal, becomes a horror even to those who believe in the ideal. Huxley knew quite well that he could expect most of his readers to agree that it would be good if everyone were happy. He could then proceed to show that a systematic attempt to attain the goal makes it impossible to agree that 'happiness' and 'pleasure' are the goals to be sought by the social system. They are destroyed as meaningful norms.

This fact about systems — or, more accurately, this widely held belief of sensitive and discerning critics of society — is unknown to all those today who are convinced that the way to attain an ideal (or a set of ideals) is to attempt to give it institutional expression — to make society itself the ideal. How else — despite its lack of logic — can we interpret the demands for government by the people? Advocates of primitive democracy wish to convert democratic societies into democratic systems in which all institutions and personal relationships accord with the democratic ideals of equality and individualism. It cannot be done, of course, but the people concerned can make themselves very unhappy in trying; they can also cause serious disruptions and changes of no benefit to anyone and which must ultimately necessitate a reversion to the original condition. One thinks, for instance of schools being run on democratic principles of equality and individualism — a system which must please those who like 'participatory' democracy but not those who are concerned with education: one system excludes the other.

It is rather odd that the concept of systems should be revived as a tool of social analysis despite the evidence provided by our experience with systems in the fields of literary analysis and actual historical experiments. One suspects that what lies behind the revival is modern scientism — the desire to unify science by applying models derived from the physical sciences, the area which constitutes the core of scientific knowledge. Whether this is so or not, one thing is obvious; the result is never more than a static description of a particular society at a particular moment. Systems theory has no room for change.

Change is excluded from systems theory for one of two reasons. When the system applied derives from the attempt to institutionalize an ideal — as in most literary satires — it is the institution that resists change. It is required to do so as the supposed embodiment of the norm or norms, even when those demanding change appeal to norms. Whether or not stability was originally an ideal, it becomes one, in fact it becomes even more of an 'ideal' than the ideal supposedly embodied in the system. Such a system 'changes' only in the sense that it acts to resist change. The 'model' then becomes useless as a device for describing the operation of the system: we get a static model in which all change comes from outside. To understand any change which occurs, we must look to something unknown and (by definition) alien to the system: in other words, in this case models do not 'work'.

When the system derives from a model taken from the physical sciences, change is excluded because the transference from the physical to the social sphere leaves behind the part that permits the original system to 'work' in the sense of responding to changes in its environment. A biological, chemical, or mechanical model can describe the changes taking place in real organisms and machines because implicitly or explicitly they incorporate in the system the concept of cause and effect. Gear X moves in a certain way because of gear U; response R is made because of stimulus S. But when we talk of a society as an organism or machine we cannot use the cause and effect assumption to explain its operation. It does not seem true that man's behaviour in isolation or in a group is 'caused' in the sense that changes are 'caused' in the physical world. Such models give us useful ways of classifying our knowledge and of bringing some sort of order to the data obtained from an empirical investigation. We can talk about the nerves of government and the machine of the market economy. But the difficulty with this method of organizing information is that one has to assume that the machine is not working or that the organism is 'dead'. In theory, we could bring 'life' to the system by an infinite number of static descriptions which, when juxtaposed, would allow us to see the model changing just as still photographs of a doll in different positions can make it appear to move if they are run rapidly through a movie projector. Yet, even if it were possible to analyse and categorize changes in a society rapidly enough to achieve such a result, we would know that it was all an illusion. The actual working of the model would remain unknown. The prime defect of systems is that by nature they are not working models and, since all the 'systems' we are interested in investigating are 'working' models whose process of 'working' we are trying to explore, we have to conclude that analysed models do not fit our requirements, no matter how neat they are.

Structural Functionalism and Input-Output Analysis

Among the most frequently used systems approaches in politics are structural functionalism and input-output analysis. Certain inherent limitations of the former prevent it from providing a 'basic framework for analysis', although this fact does not make 'functionally-oriented' political scientists reluctant to dismiss the more serious theoretical objections. Such is the case of Oran R. Young who lumps these objections[1] together as weaknesses of the practitioners rather than inherent weaknesses of the system. He feels that such objections are precluded by the modifications introduced into the original system: rejection of the 'postulate of the functional unity of society'; of the 'postulate of universal functionalism'; and of the 'postulate of indispensability'.[2] But the question arises: can the system allow such limitations and still continue as a system of analysis? Are the 'modifications' merely an acknowledgement of difficulties made by the practitioners of functionalism themselves, so that they can carry on as if the difficulties did not exist?

As Young says, 'The conceptual framework of the structural-functional approach centres around the question, What structures fulfill what basic functions and under what conditions in any given system?'[3] Such an approach implied that observable structures have functions. Although it is a plausible proposition, it is unfortunately an all-or-nothing postulate. It is not possible to analyse function if the proposition is 'Some structures have a function'.

So long as one talks about 'all structures', it is possible to make shrewd guesses about 'function' that will contain a grain of truth. Behind a proposition about 'all structures' are other propositions which seem to have empirical support. When making it, we say in effect that man is capable of making choices in a meaningful sense; that his choices are purposeful; and that when the structures evolve to serve these purposes and are not adapted to serve any other, they cease to exist. In other words, choice and change — two necessary elements in any discussion of human behaviour — are fundamental to the proposition about 'all structures'. (It is likely then that one man's guess about the 'function' of a structure may well reflect other men's purpose and if we make the further assumption that the guess about

---

[1] Under such headings as the 'fallacy of functional teleology', the 'fallacy of deductive functionalism' and the 'justification of the status quo'. Oran R. Young, *Systems of Political Science* (Englewood Cliffs, N.J., 1968), pp. 35-6.
[2] *Ibid.*, pp. 32-3.
[3] *Ibid.*, p. 28.

function reflects the purposes of those having some power to change or use structures, we are well on the way to making useful comments on society.)

The approach is more suited to the analysis of primitive, highly stable societies where the number of purposes is limited. It is less useful for the analysis of modern democracy in which the system of power distribution is so complex that speculation about function always involves two guesses combined in one: a guess as to whose purpose is being served and another about its nature. Such analysis is very difficult, but in conjunction with studies of power distribution it could still be useful.

Matters are changed, however, when the proposition is about 'some structures'. Behind the proposition are quite untenable propositions about human behaviour: some behaviour is chosen and some arises from factors unknown. If this is so, we can no longer talk of purpose, and 'functions' becomes an exceedingly obscure term. Young, aware of this, tries to define function as 'the objective consequence(s) of a pattern of action for the system' which 'may be perceived as objectives, processes, or results from various points of view and for various purposes.'[4] It seems hardly necessary to point out that 'consequences' are not observable. If they were, structural-functionalists would be able to make an irrefutable case based on empirical evidence — there is the structure and there is the consequence!

What the structural-functionalists overlook is that if you cannot be a strict empiricist — which they are not, since 'function' is not observable — then you must be a strict logician. The non-empirical basis of your system must accord with the principles of logic. It is not aesthetic consideration, 'theoretical neatness' that, to use Young's words, leads some structural-functionalists to 'an unwarranted twisting and distorting of empirical realities'.[5] It is inherent in the system. Those who do the twisting can at least lay claim to a consistent application of what is, after all, a methodology. If logical application results in recognizable distortions of empirical reality, it is the fault of functionalism, not the fault of the investigators. It is not possible to use structural-functionalism modified by empirical realities

[4] *Ibid.*, p. 29.
[5] *Ibid.*, p. 36.

as a logical starting point.

The general objection to systems is that they are essentially static. Young sees this as a 'relevant limitation' rather than 'a critical inadequacy of the approach', though he oddly admits that the corollary — that 'the structural-functional approach tends to lead to the rationalization and/or justification of the status quo' — is 'the most damning of the criticisms'.[6] What is striking about this view is that the normative objection is considered of more moment than the logical objection (which ought to form the basis of any logical normative objection). 'A justification of the status quo' can be said to be normatively 'wrong' only if the system is 'wrong' and cannot become 'right'. Why should justification of the status quo be in itself a 'damning criticism' when an analysis of things as they are is not? The political theorist finds the absence of a mechanism for change damning and avoids normative judgements about it.

Young's view plainly represents the peculiar consequence of the democratic version of relativism: in a democracy we have in principle the kind of society we want, but it is not what we want because we keep changing our mind. This normlessness — fuzzy as it is — allows one to feel that the lack of a force for change is of no consequence, whereas a defence of immutability is damning: people are obviously not satisfied — consequently, a system that implies satisfaction is unacceptable.

To the political theorist, the defect of functionalism is that it is static in a world of change. It talks of 'function' in a way that implies interacting forces which do not really interact and may not even exist.

Like all system models, David Easton's input-output system immediately raises doubts among theorists because the operating principle is cause-effect: the 'system' is the mechanism which makes the principle plausible in its application to human behaviour. We see the cause-effect basis most clearly in the diagram: A Simplified Model of a Political System[7] in which the 'political system' represents the mysterious black box which converts stimuli into response. The complications introduced into

[6]*Ibid.*
[7]David Easton, *A Systems Analysis of Political Life* (New York, 1965), p. 32.

the simplified scheme — the 'gate-keeping', 'channel capacity', 'cleavage', 'feedback', etc. — serve to explain why a steady input of 'demands' and 'support' does not produce a steady output directly and obviously related to input. As Easton says, 'it is most difficult to extricate any single demand and watch its progress through a telephone network....Nevertheless, it is quite feasible to abstract, from the multiplicity of reality, a typical pattern for demand networks in all political systems, from the moment demands are given birth in the form of an ambiguous, restless want, felt need, hope or desire, to the time they ultimately find their way to points of political decision and implementation.'[8]

What a normative theorist finds objectionable in this statement is that while it leaves room for the normative considerations — which to him are crucial for the understanding of human behaviour — it converts them into some kind of 'causative' phenomena — one group among many — and thus destroys what he considers their most significant feature.

To the theorist norms represent goals sought and hence explain the choices made in particular circumstances. The key issue in understanding human behaviour is the apparent fact of choice. So far as he can see, nothing in human behaviour need happen as it does. The theorist is not a determinist who supposes that full knowledge of a situation would make accurate prediction possible. Yet he believes prediction to be feasible — and theorizing worthwhile — because the norms are goals which will be attained if and when circumstances permit. The norms have a kind of permanence that cirumstances do not have. Hence any attempt to give permanence to circumstances, by erecting a system embodying certain supposed permanencies of circumstances, is at best a secondary enterprise. To be valid, it must relate directly to the known permanencies of norms, as in the case of political structures relatable to ideologies. When the system is not so related — but instead seeks to make the structure describing the circumstances permanent and to make the norms and ideology a part of this structure — the theorist must see the enterprise as more of an attempt to fit behaviour into the cause-effect pattern of physical science than as one grounded on

[8]*Ibid.*, p. 71.

empirical observation or an attempt to provide an adequate set of categories for ordering empirical observations.

In Easton's input-output system, concepts such as norm, value, ideology, authority, legitimacy — all concepts of traditional political analysis — have a place. He does not explicitly dismiss as irrelevant the entire body of political theory which preceded him. Yet, when we consider the function of norms and values in his system, it becomes clear that he might just as well have dismissed them. Consider, for instance, the following statement:

> Values serve as broad limits with regard to what can be taken for granted in the guidance of day-to-day policy without violating deep feelings of important segments of the community. The norms specify the kinds of procedures that are expected and acceptable in the processing and implementation of demands. The structures of authority designate the formal and informal patterns in which power is distributed and organized with regard to the authoritative making and implementing of decisions — the roles and their relationships through which authority is distributed and exercised. The goals, norms, and structure of authority both limit and validate political actions and in this way provide what tends to become a context for *political interactions*.[9]

It is clear that in Easton's system concepts that were once primary are now secondary: 'political interaction' has some other operating force than goals, norms and authority. What force can this be? What makes the system an operating one? Like all system analysts, Easton does not say. Although, unlike other systems, his system implies change — it is intended to move — the change is illusory. A political system is represented as a method man has devised for introducing cause and effect into human behaviour: an input of demands 'causes' an output, a part of which becomes part of the input again and thus the machine is made to run on, presumably forever.

Easton's system resembles a perpetual motion machine but it has no real place for any kind of continuous change. In the real world, the principle of cause and effect allows for continuous

---

[9]*Ibid.*, p. 193. Emphasis added.

change because in any particular set of phenomena we choose to abstract we recognize that the set is not self-contained, that it is subject to 'causes' that are 'effects' in some other contiguous system. We cannot, however, adopt this attitude towards a political system and pretend that we are giving a realistic and intelligible account of the changes that continually occur. In most systems there is no place whatsoever for change because the cause-effect principle on which they are based describes only such change as has occurred. They are static by nature. Easton's theory, by leaving the input — except for 'feedback' — outside of the system of cause and effect, allows for a moving, but not really the changing system, required by empirical observation.

A system in which 'input' accords with what we know of the role of wants in human behaviour and 'output' accords with the principle of cause and effect modified by conjectures about the complications of a political system may at first sight appear attractive. If we stop to ask ourselves why, we begin to realize that the system may fit our conception of what a government 'should' be — responsive to the demands made upon it as a government, while not functioning merely as a 'servant' of the people. That is how many people would like to think of government but can such a system describe adequately any political order? We can agree with Easton's assumptions that all governments are in part responsive to demands from the governed and we can believe that particular differences in expectations and wants, of input and differences in structure can lead to differences in responsiveness. Easton's system, however, does not seem to give the sovereign power any real initiative unless we identify it with the principal source of input — the community. It is the community's wants and expectations which supply the motivating force of a system that is otherwise a cause-effect, static one. It would follow that the closer a political order approximates the traditional concept of democracy, the more initiative it will have. But this does not accord with known facts. It is at odds with the concept of sovereignty which would have to be refuted before Easton's system could be seriously considered.

Behaviouralist Images of Democracy

The behaviouralists attempt to develop theories of democracy based on observable facts, rather than on the investigator's preconception of what he or others feel it should be. Although their attempts to see things as they are may appear admirable, it is clear from the rising tide of objections that this approach is failing to fulfil its purpose. The democracy so revealed does not resemble the structure in which adherents of democracy believe.

Unfortunately for the behaviouralists, it is not possible for them to say: 'Well, now your eyes have been opened, you will have to alter your beliefs.' When we talk of 'belief in' democracy (or anything else) we are not talking about preconceptions about an empirically observable situation. (An exception is those who define democracy in terms of the practices of their State. A behaviouralist study showing, say, that the public has little knowledge of political issues — although 'primitive' democratic theory requires them to have a substantial knowledge — may well change their 'belief in' democracy to accommodate this.) Most people who talk of a 'belief in' democracy do not mean acceptance of things as they are in a society which calls itself democratic. A discrepancy between the ideal and actuality for them does not call for a change in the ideal but in the actuality or, at most, a change in the theory designed to actualize the ideal. By failing to understand the distinction between 'belief in' and 'belief about' the behaviouralists cannot escape representing 'democracy' as if it had the characteristics which the most naïve citizens 'believe in' (= accept).

This tendency within empirical studies of normative behaviour to define the norms by the behaviour rather than classify the behaviour in terms of the norms is reinforced by the fact that according to the editors of a relatively recent collection of readings, *Empirical Democratic Theory* (1969), 'the choice of research strategies represents the taste of the researchers'.[10] This is another way of saying that the 'significance' of the studies must in fact depend on something else: a researcher's 'taste' has no room in science or behavioural research.[11]

[10]Charles F. Cnudde and Deane E. Neubauer (eds.), *Empirical Democratic Theory* (Chicago, 1969), p. 9.

[11]The 'significance' of an empirical study selected by such a criterion will ultimately depend upon the use to which it is put, presumably by those — like the 'power élite' — who are in a position to apply it. It may not be a coincidence that behaviouralism is considered to be essentially conservative. Behavioural studies often reinforce an image of democracy which is autocratic and stratified.

Nelson Polsby has shown[12] that the concept of stratified power typical of a great deal of literature cannot be substantiated by strict empirical studies or theoretical analysis. (An opportunity is thereby provided for establishing links between assumptions about power and the researcher's 'taste'.) But Polsby's alternative — pluralism — while in a sense more acceptable to many normative theorists, is not likely to escape the problem that behaviouralists (empiricists) pose for themselves.

In traditional theory, the concept of power ultimately rests on normative assumptions; thus the whole theory of sovereignty rests on premises about what man wants most (which in turn rests on the empirical observation that we all do in fact live in society under a government and hence can be said to desire this state of affairs). Now if we try to get rid of the normative assumptions and focus on the 'facts' alone, we do not end with a strict empirical statement about 'power' but an unintelligible concept. Where the theory of power under sovereignty makes sense because it seeks to answer the question 'How can anyone prevail?', a concept of power which seeks to answer 'Who prevails?', while at the same time assuming that nobody need prevail,[13] makes 'power' a description of personal relations only — someone or some group induces another to do something. How so primitive a concept of social relations can be related to government is not explained. Presumably, the relation between friend and friend, parent and child, court and criminal, president and public are all somehow assumed to be the same. Empirical observation, of course, does not allow us to lump together such diverse relations; and — no matter what behaviouralists maintain — such a concept of power is not usable in political analysis. Theoretical considerations do not allow us to ignore the element of 'consent' almost always present in manifestations of power.

The real difficulty with any empirical approach to social concepts is that they focus on only part of the situation and pretend it is the whole. An empirical concept of power sees only that someone has prevailed and ignores the fact that this is so because someone else has in some way 'consented'. 'Power', on

---

[12]See Nelson W. Polsby, *Community Power and Political Theory* (New Haven, 1963).
[13]This is Polsby's 'presupposition' in presenting his 'Pluralist Alternative'. See *ibid.*, p. 113.

the other hand, makes sense in the theory of sovereignty because it takes into account both coercive and consenting aspects of social relations and does not weight the evidence in favour of certain norms, as is the case with empirical approaches.

Despite Cnudde's and Neubauer's belief that 'empirical theories are descriptive and explanatory',[14] it is well-known that empiricism can supply only descriptions. Explanations are excluded by the nature of empiricism unless 'description' and 'explanation' are somehow identified. (This becomes possible when the situation chosen for empirical investigation has been conjectured to have a specified nature, as when it is argued that 'the success of democratic political organizations is dependent upon such diverse factors as the absence of extreme conflict, a relative equality of social and economic condition, the predominant distribution throughout the population of so-called "democratic personalities"...'[15] and so forth.)

What are the major tasks of empirical theories of democracy? Cnudde and Neubauer give an answer: 'Empirical democratic theory attempts to (a) determine the empirical veracity of...causal assertions in their simple form, and (b) specify those factors which appear to be causally pre-eminent in the determination of democratic government.'[16] Although aware of the difficulties and complications involved in accomplishing these tasks, empiricists in general are not aware of the following major objection: the propositions they set out to test are seldom part of the body of political theory proper. Furthermore, selecting these propositions for empirical testing distorts them out of all recognition. The nature of the 'theory' tested and the peculiar image of democracy that arises from it can be seen in Almond and Verba's study *The Civic Culture: Political Attitudes and Democracy in Five Nations*.

Curiously, Almond and Verba do not disclose their definition of democracy until their work is quite advanced. In their definition they rely heavily on Robert Dahl: 'The common thread running through the many definitions of democracy is that a democracy is a society in which "...ordinary citizens exert a

---

[14]Cnudde and Neubauer (eds.), *op. cit.*, p. 1.
[15]*Ibid.*, p. 3.
[16]*Ibid.*, p. 4.

relatively high degree of control over leaders." [17] It is this definition that accounts for their preoccupation with citizens' active part in government affairs, 'participation', as well as questionnaires designed to establish facts about participation in several democracies. It is the image of democracy they thus create which is faulty.

Dahl's concept of 'relative popular control' as the 'minimal' definition of democracy, represented as its essence, is not so much a reflection of a theory as an accommodation to theory and fact of what was essentially a political slogan: government of the people, by the people. It has never been a theory because it is self-contradictory. It has always, however, had a strong appeal to members of a democratic society who want a simple way of looking at their society and a simple goal. The slogan can be adjusted to accord with logical requirements of 'government' and observable similarities and differences between governments, by speaking of 'control' rather than government, and 'relative control' rather than simple control. The result represents democracy as a point on a continuum called 'government', at one end of which is non-government or 'anarchy' (the mythical government of and by the people) and the other end an absolute or total control of the people. Under this conception, democracy is represented as a form of government on a scale that is not recognizable as 'government', because the latter cannot be thought of as simply the giving of orders which are automatically obeyed — the push-button theory of the social machine.

What Almond and Verba are concerned with in their fact-gathering capacity is not so much Dahl's view of 'democracy' as a normative conclusion that can be drawn from it. Thus if it is true that 'democracy' requires 'relative control', this control will be of a 'good' kind (rational) if the people were informed about and interested in the activities of their government. It becomes possible to test the quality of a democracy by gathering information about attitudes towards the government and society and classifying the information under the heading 'participation' (which under the 'theory' being tested has now become a central

---

[17]Gabriel A. Almond and Sidney Verba, *The Civic Culture* (Boston, 1965), pp. 118-19. The quotation within the definition is from Robert A. Dahl, *A Preface to Democratic Theory* (1956).

concept). Devising questions, the behaviouralist makes conjectures about possible attitudes and Almond and Verba duly provide a classification with this in mind.[18]

Whether the attitudes singled out cover all the possibilities and whether the questions asked best reveal them is beside the point. What is important is that writings of this kind reinforce a common but naïve view of democratic political behaviour and political phenomena. The common man in the USA would have no difficulty in relating the tables provided in *The Civic Culture* — and showing expectations and attitudes in different countries — to his own conviction that the USA is a democratic country with a high degree of popular 'participation' in government and respect for it. He has come to believe that that is what 'democracy' means and, being under no compulsion to fit such a view into a theory of government, he can be satisfied with it. Indeed, most of the propositions tested in behavioural analyses are not *political theories* but the naïve conjectures of members of democratic societies. The reason lies in the nature of political theory which is based on 'ought' and not on 'is' propositions. The former make complex patterns that cannot be understood as if they were statements of fact taking the form $X = Y$. The latter propositions can be investigated by the empiricist and, if they are held by some members of a democratic society, he can even convince himself that he is studying 'democratic theory'.[19]

The Camera Artists

If one were to give an account of Gulliver's journey to Behaviora,

---

[18] See Almond and Verba's types of political culture: 'parochial', 'subject' and 'participant'. *Op. cit.*, p. 16.

[19] What he is really studying is democratic opinion. Consider, for instance Table IX. 2 (in Almond and Verba, *ibid.*, p. 213) which seeks to estimate social trust and distrust. We are given two statements that are supposed to have equal weight in estimating distrust, but in the USA only 38 per cent agreed with the first statement whereas 68 per cent concurred with the second. Of the three statements (again presumably of equal value) expressing trust in the USA, the percentages of agreement were 55, 31 and 80. Altogether, there were five different answers whereas, if the questionnaire had expressed what was presumably intended, only two would have been possible. Furthermore, these two would have to bear a clear mathematical relation to one another! Such results are possible when one is testing opinion, but if that opinion is supposed to have a bearing on some theoretical consideration, we must conclude that something has gone wrong. But what has gone wrong? The behaviouralist has no way of knowing. He can see from the results that he cannot have tested what he wanted to test. Nonetheless, he must be satisfied with the results: sense must somehow be extracted from them.

a modern land in which the Behavioural School reigns supreme, the result might be as follows:

...The people of Behaviora seem both vainer and more humble than those anywhere else in the Universe. They express the utmost humility, deprecating strongly the behaviour of their ancestors, who, it would seem, were so vain that they imagined human motives and principles to be the force behind the Universe. In the past, they conjectured a sort of gaseous version of themself which ordered and operated the Universe in accordance with their own principles. Since then, they say, they have acquired humility, though their fondness for being photographed seems to imply that they are as vain as ever.

They frequently explained to me, however, that their predilection for being photographed is not a manifestation of vanity but of science. They wanted only — they said — to discover the principles behind their behaviour, to see how they fitted into the Universe now that their humility would not allow them to conceive of the Universe as fitting into them. Their professions of humility would have carried more weight with me if they had gone on to explain why, in giving up their belief that the Universe acted in accordance with their principles, they should also give up the belief that they themselves acted in accordance with them, and therefore must record their own behaviour with the same minute attention to detail that they expended on the analysis of the physical world. I could not escape the feeling that they wanted an excuse to be noticed, questioned and photographed.

The reader may note that they have a class of professional photographers who devote themselves exclusively to taking pictures of the citizens of the country at work and at play. They say this is not mere vanity but a scientific enterprise of great moment. When enough photographs have been taken it will be possible to discover patterns of behaviour that will reveal how very humble they really are — how much the creatures of unknown forces. Until that moment arrives, they realize that the employment of photographers must make them seem as vain as they were when they thought that their own motives actuated the Universe.

I candidly confess to be somewhat doubtful about their explanation of what seems mere vanity, the more so as the school for photographers, called the Behaviouralist School, trains its members solely in camera work. It has no department for teaching the interpretation of pictures, though it is only the possibility of interpretation that can keep the camera work from being mere vanity. The absence of an interpretive department became more puzzling when I discovered that the camera artists trained by the School were not in the least hesitant to make conjectures about what they recorded and that many of the photographic studies they made were selected because the artists thought they might prove interesting or useful. Indeed, completely candid, unposed photographs seemed very rare, though I admit it is sometimes hard to decide just what the artist's intentions were when he pointed the camera and operated the shutter. I thought that the School must surely offer some guidance in selecting a subject for study, but it appears true that the individual artist alone decides what the choice is to be and is under no necessity to explain his choice to either his subjects or his School. So long as he can prove that he has recorded his subjects' behaviour as accurately as the camera permits, he is entitled to be regarded as a genuine camera artist.

Limitations of Empirical Democratic Theory

Empiricism has always been a method of testing theory rather than evolving it. Those who have attempted to make it a self-sufficient theory of knowledge have not been able to supply an adequate defence. Some of the special difficulties facing 'empirical democratic theory' have been set forth by Cnudde and Neubauer, who seem to believe that they are not insurmountable.

In the first place, they argue, 'prior to any empirical examination of...phenomena [encompassed by the concept 'democratic'] it is necessary to impose closure upon that segment of behaviour to be investigated.'[20] They compare the process of delineation to 'the ubiquitous "definitional problem" wherein a

[20]Cnudde and Neubauer (eds.), *op. cit.*, p. 9.

given author provides a definition for a concept which in fact delimits by attribution the range of phenomena in which he is interested.'[21] The theorist who limits the concept of democracy devotes a part of his analysis to the reasons for setting the limitations. His study will be rejected as worthless if he assumes he can limit the definition of democracy as he pleases in order to study it as he pleases. What matters are the limitations distinguishing democracy from other forms of government and the defence he offers. The behaviouralist, on the other, does not begin with a field of interest — a vague idea called democracy which he proposes to make less vague — but a methodology which provides no similar way of limiting the phenomena to be studied. As a rule he begins with some system called democratic and then proceeds to exclude most of the system from examination. The factor which keeps most behaviouralist studies even within the range of phenomena the theorist calls 'democratic' is that one of the countries best able to support extensive research happens to be democratic and economic factors also limit many behaviouralist studies to what happens there. So far, 'theories' of democracy deriving from behaviouralism relate mostly to the USA.

How relevant can a study be that excludes the greater part of the system it assumes to be democratic? Behaviouralist methodology provides no way of criticizing the limitations the researcher imposed in order to conduct his research. Another behaviouralist can as a rule only criticize the research method, not the limitation, unless he wishes to abandon behaviouralism and become a theoretician.

According to the above-mentioned authors, another problem in developing empirical democratic theory is that of 'operationalizing very abstract concepts'. As they put it: 'Many of the concepts utilized in democratic theory are...normative or maximizational concepts....Thus, the concept "political equality", while basic to almost any discussion of democracy, has no literal empirical referent.' Yet, despite this objection, the authors believe that 'the concept does...provide a basis for constructing a measurement, the degree to which actual, existing democratic political organizations approximate the condition of political equality. Thus, one can cite elections as

---

[21]*Ibid.*, p. 10.

Limitations of Empirical Democratic Theory

instances in which individual citizens are permitted to express their preferences on certain issues. Since elections differ considerably with respect to who is allowed to vote, how equally the votes are treated, and the like, the examination of various features of elections provides one with an empirical indicator of the degree to which political equality is realized in democratic politics.'[22]

Theorists, of course, do not think that matters are so simple. A theorist cannot assume that equality means having a vote and offer no justification for this simplification. Behaviouralists, instead of defending what seems naïveté, offer surveys and statistics based on simplistic assumptions. Somehow the rigour of their methodology is supposed to compensate for their simplicity. The 'theory' we obtain from their research is no more significant than the opinion we would get from any untrained, unreflecting member of our society.[23]

---

[22]*Ibid.*, pp. 11-12.

[23]The trouble is that the costly procedures required for testing 'theories' makes the more naïve views the most acceptable, because they are cheaper to test. Cnudde and Neubauer call this economic factor and absurd method of choice 'data constraint'. Consequently, a huge number of research projects is based on electoral data. This leads to the view that 'democracy' and 'equality' consist in an electoral system. There seem to be too few non-behaviouralists to point out that this view is simplistic.

VII
'Participation' in Democratic Theory

A curious aspect of 'participation' is that some of its advocates do not represent it as a new insight into the nature of democracy but rather as a revival, a return to the true path after an 'undemocratic' interlude which was introduced by Schumpeter's calm acceptance of the facts of limited public participation in democratic government. The assumption of the advocates of participation is that 'classical theory' was a theory of participation. Even Carole Pateman — to whom 'the notion of a classical theory of democracy is a myth'[1] — argues that analysis of some typical theorists — Rousseau, J.S. Mill and G.D.H. Cole — shows them to be proponents of participation.

Although Pateman does not need to twist meanings or distort evidence in order to show that Rousseau and Mill could both be said to be supporters of 'participation', the concept nonetheless can be described as a normative novelty which can lead to a serious misunderstanding of classical theories as well as of the nature of our political order.

That participation is a norm paralleling other norms such as equality and freedom does not seem to be denied by any of its proponents. Instead, the question has been whether it is a part of the 'classical' normative system of democracy or a recent development. The proponents of participation, conscious of its normativeness, recognize that it can be defended only as a part of the definition of an existing system. It is clearly not enough to introduce it as something that will make the system 'better'. It must have been there from the beginning — inherent in the actual working system of democracy. Hence efforts such as Pateman's to show that the concept is part of 'classical theories'.

[1] Carole Pateman, *Participation and Democratic Theory*, p. 17.

160

The logical consequence of this position is that those who oppose it must be represented as having derived their own notions of 'democracy' from non-classical sources (in practice — from empirical studies of what democracy 'is' at present).

Opponents of 'participation' as a democratic norm do not deny that a great deal of support for a concept of participation can be found in the writings of most democratic theorists. It should be clear that equality — an acknowledged norm of classical democracy — includes a good deal of the type of behaviour required for 'participation'. If all men are equal, it follows that no man is better qualified than another to direct human affairs, so that if government is felt to be necessary, it must be representative, the result of a universal franchise and open office. Each man has the right to vote and if the system is to be called a democracy, that right must be respected.

In order to arrive at precisely the same institutional system, it is not necessary to begin with 'equality': one can begin with 'participation'. The two concepts appear interchangeable. There is, however, an important difference. Whereas the type of behaviour deriving from 'equality' leads to statements about 'rights', that deriving from 'participation' leads to statement about 'duty'. Thus egalitarian democracy gives the individual a right that the State must recognize if it is to be a democracy. Participation, however, gives the State a right that the citizen must recognize. This difference has far-reaching consequences. Although in one respect the hand of the State is strengthened by the concept of participation, on the whole one strikes at the very foundations of the State by holding it up as the ideal: maximum participation becomes the sovereignty of the people, a concept that was excluded from 'classical' democratic theory by the logical requirements of sovereignty. Indeed, 'participation' would never have developed as a norm if the logical requirements of sovereignty had been more widely accepted.

Participation and Democratization

Proponents of participation demand what opponents of it cannot concede — 'democratization' of the social structure. Thus Pateman maintains that 'the argument that...the participatory process...requires...that the [non-governmental authority] structures should be democratized, looks...plausible',[2] whereas to anyone familiar with the logic of sovereignty such an argument is false. What in classical theory is excluded by the nature of political organization is that 'democracy' can somehow be extended to social structures. A purely 'democratic', participatory type of decision-making is feasible only when the question is one of greater or lesser desirability: 'Which is preferable: X, Y, or Z?' No structure of authority is then necessary. Thus a family can democratically plan how to use its leisure time. But as regards keeping the family's house clean, the 'democratic' decision-making process has to be foregone. The reason is that when the activity is not intrinsically desirable, possibly no one will do it unless there is someone who can ensure that all necessary steps are taken and that someone does. One suspects that the more 'democratic' the group (in the sense of having goals acceptable to all), the more elaborate must be the structure of authority to ensure that all required action is taken and that the burden is equitably distributed throughout the group.

Given 'democratic' ends, decisions cannot be left to individuals or to their collective expression, majority rule. The reason is that in respect to ends, the isolated individual and the member of a group are in a different position. To an isolated individual, his ends are scarcely distinguishable from his means: he takes the means into account when deciding upon his ends. In a group, means and ends are dissociated for the individual: a decision about ends does not automatically require a decision about means. The fact is that under majority rule no question about means need enter in so far as each member of the group is concerned. However, for the group as a whole, the relation between means and ends remains what it was for the individual: they must be taken into account. If the group is to achieve its ends, majority rule is not enough. What is necessary is a structure of authority to make decisions which include concepts of means; a method of distributing tasks, ensuring that they are done and modifying goals in terms of available resources.

Now, however, democratic societies are being told that for the good of their members the structure which incorporates the principle of authority should be abandoned. Everyone, to the

[2]*Ibid.*, p. 45.

best of his ability, should participate in decision-making. This, of course, is another way of saying that he should not permit others to tell him what to do or to make decisions on his behalf. 'Participation' is designed by and for those who do not want to believe in a structure of authority; it is also a method of doing away with the latter. In our argument against 'participation' we should go one step beyond Hobbes, while holding to his basic line of thought. Whereas Hobbes argued for a structure to society on the ground that there is a structure to man's wants, we must go further and argue that there is a structure to society because norms held by a group acutely raise the problem of means and ends. Agreement about ends requires the apportionment of means and this requires an authoritative social structure, not participatory egalitarianism. Participation requires us to accept a particular hypothesis of relativism — that all man's behaviour expresses immediate want-satisfaction and that there is no distinction between means and ends.

The Illusion of Participation

Jacques Ellul's argument that participation is a political illusion[3] — that it does not exist by reason of man's nature and the nature of organized activity — is important and relevant. It does indeed matter to the case made by the participationists whether the rank and file members of a group, by engaging in any of the activities generally called participation, actually make or influence the policy of the group. If in fact they do not, the advocates of participation must go far beyond their present position: if Ellul is correct, then in order to advocate participation they must develop a new technique of social organization which allows 'participation' to be more than a mere ritual.

Ellul helps make clear the following important point:[4] the advocates of participation are not arguing for more of what we already have (as, for instance, an extension of the political and social activity of leaders to members), but for a totally different

[3] See Jacques Ellul, *The Political Illusion* (New York, 1967), pp. 188ff.

[4] The point is obscured, however, because Ellul is talking about 'is' and participationists are talking about 'ought', so that the relation between the two arguments is not really apparent.

kind of society and social organization. Although the latter is unspecified, it will (they say) be true democracy. The argument for participation is thus an argument for a change in our social and political order.

The basic objection to the participationists' view is that society is much too important to be meddled with for the sake of 'educational' goals — the assumption behind the latter being that 'participation' develops political competence: one learns 'on the job', as it were. Society is much too complex and fragile a body to permit a trial and error approach to change. Participationists wish to manipulate social organization rather than ideas with a recklessness that arouses suspicion. To answer them it is necessary to show not that men lack competence — advocates of participation recognize this — but that an attempt to give competence through permitting or encouraging participation is irresponsible. Traditional democratic theory has always been open to the view that men can be — should be, even — better than they are, but it has also assumed that such improvements as are possible must not threaten the very structure of society. A theory which views the political and social order as a place for experimentation may properly be looked on in the same light as an ideology which insists the system must be suspended. Hence, both the advocates of 'participation' and the communists ask for a kind of change which goes beyond the capacity of the system to undergo changes and still retain its identity. Each group must know this: they are both talking about 'true' democracy. What the advocates of participation must supply is a logical analysis of the probable consequences of their views and not arguments based simply on what 'ought' to be.

Participation and Radicalization

Advocates of 'participation' are not likely to be pleased by the suggestion that what they seek is not markedly different from the radical views of the author of *The New Democratic Theory*.[5] They could argue that the opposite is true — that the very concept of participation implies acceptance of the present structure and norms of democratic society and that the changes they

---

[5]Kenneth A. Megill, *The New Democratic Theory* (New York, 1970).

advocate relate to human behaviour, not to political systems. In view of the fact that their principal argument is that 'participation' has an educative function, it seems that they find the 'goods' of democratic society in the establishment and seek to extend those goods by encouraging others to become members of the establishment themselves, in fact and spirit, by acting as the existing members do. The ideal is to make universal the behaviour of those now in power.

To a radical such as Megill, this view would be an outrage. Those in power are in his eyes responsible for the ills of those not in power and hence are scarcely to be imitated. The system which allows this corruption at the top is at fault and needs to be replaced; society needs to be restructured. In short, it may be argued that because the advocates of participation see the ruling élite as worthy of imitation, they accept the system as a whole and seek to improve it only by extending its benefits, whereas the radical, seeing those at the top as exploiters, sees the system as faulty and seeks to replace it with a new system whose nature is not yet clear. That is why Megill speaks of 'experiments in a new form of living'.[6] On the face of things, then, we could describe the participationists as 'conservatives' and their opponents as radicals.

But this distinction is not an analytical one. It has no solid theoretical base. In making it, we have pretended that there is a meaningful difference between those who wish to extend the good and those who wish to limit the evil. Logically there might be, but not until we have more information about the ends and means in each case.

About the ends of the radicals one really knows nothing. They tell us about the evils of society and argue that some good will come if the present system is replaced with a new one whose only known feature is a lack of resemblance to what we have now. Belief in anything so vague requires such a great amount of faith that it can hardly be treated as a rational objective. It seems a purely emotional reaction: the reflection of an unhappy mental state. The position, on the other hand, of the advocates of participation is not much clearer. Focusing on the goods rather than the evils of our society, they want greater participation in

[6]*Ibid.*, p. 138.

the 'good'. But how their kind of goods are to receive wider distribution is dismissed as a mere theoretical objection. As with the radicals, the emphasis is on action alone. Each is impatient with theory and analysis because each is quite certain of his single objective. One says: 'I know the good — extend it.' The other says: 'I know the evil — eliminate it.'

It is quite irrational to talk of evil without talking about good, of ends without means and means without ends, as the radicals and participationists do. It looks as if in talking about the good and evil in the system, both are talking about exactly the same thing from different points of view and that the ostensible difference in their ends — extend the system *versus* eliminate it — results from their failure to analyse the consequences of their position. Those who desire more 'participation' refuse to recognize that the 'ideal' of participation is necessarily the structureless society of anarchism, which is no society at all. The radical, on the other hand, does not strive for anything specific, but reacts against society and hopes that some unknown good will come out of the anarchism he advocates as a method. For the participationist, 'anarchism' is the ideal of full participation, arrived at as a result of appreciating what our society offers to only a few; beyond that ideal he does not attempt to see. For the radical, anarchism is a way-station on the road to the unknown, arrived at as a result of detesting what our society offers to only a few.

Participatory Democracy and Citizenship

What is missing from the discussion of participation is that while the demand for participation was at its height, political participation in the democratic process did not become greater even though this was possible under existing arrangements. What is a possible explanation? One can argue that the 'greater' possible or available participation was somehow seen not as a real involvement in decision-making — and would therefore not improve the democratic process. If, on the one hand, the demand for participation implied criticism of the democratic system, this (sense of distance from the democratic process) is indeed a plausible conjecture; but if so, the demand for participatory democracy would be a disguised demand for revolution.

If, on the other hand, one rejects the view that most advocates of 'participation' were simply victims of some large-scale manipulation, it is difficult to see how any rational person could hope to gain adherents for a policy whose methods and aims were concealed from those he sought to influence. It would seem probable that the demand for participation usually implied acceptance of the democratic process. If so, then the lack of new participation at the time of a demand for it would seem to be the result of an 'apolitical' trend as well as ignorance of the fact that the present system already provides satisfying opportunities for greater participation.

The movement towards greater participation is linked with the concept of 'citizenship'. According to George Kateb's summary of the 'new idealism': 'the aim is to rehabilitate the idea of citizenship and to extend the practice of citizenship into as many areas of life as possible.'[7] In other words, the issue is really the sense of being part of a community. The evidence, moreover, suggests that unfamiliarity with present opportunities plays more of a part in the making of the demand than does some recognized shortcoming in the system itself. People feel left out because they do not know how to join in. If that is the situation, no organizational change could possibly alter it. What needs to be changed is the awareness of how to join in and act. This awareness is concealed from most by the concepts and methods we use to instruct people in the meaning of citizenship. They already feel that citizenship ought to entail some sense of being part of a community — 'part of a social formation', to use van Gunsteren's words.[8] But what they are in fact taught about citizenship and democracy is concepts of rights and legal processes. In consequence, although one feels oneself to be a member of a democratic State — subject to its laws — one does not feel that one is a member of a democratic community. The concepts of State and community have become separated.

In his outline if the theory of citizenship, van Gunsteren

[7] George Kateb, 'Comments on David Braybrooke's "The Meaning of Participation and of Demands for It" ' in J. Roland Pennock and John W. Chapman (eds.), NOMOS XVI: *Participation in Politics* (New York, 1975), p. 91.

[8] Herman van Gunsteren, 'Notes on a Theory of Citizenship' in Pierre Birnbaum, Jack Lively and Geraint Parry (eds.), *Democracy, Consensus and Social Contract* (London and Beverly Hills, 1978), p. 11.

expresses the view that not all acts of the individual's will, even though performed within an institutional framework that defines them as acts of a citizen, are in reality acts of citizenship. Only acts related to some notion of the common good can be so considered. In making his judgement we must look to how the 'will' was formed and what the outcome will be. He maintains that 'In order to qualify as actions of citizens, actions should at least either tend to improve...existing possibilities of citizen action, or help to develop new ones, or tend to make full citizenship available to more members of the polity.'[9]

What evidently troubles van Gunsteren is that demands for greater 'participation' could be demands for willful expression of 'citizen will' in democratic procedures, but — as was suggested earlier — such demands appear to be expressions of a sense of isolation, of not being involved in the political order, rather than demands for greater control. However, the normative issue van Gunsteren raises is certainly relevant. We might consider, for instance, the issue of 'pluralism', of demanding representation on the grounds that as a member of a special class (group) one has special interests that the present system does not take into account.

To those who view norms as expressions of individual or class interest, such a demand cannot be dismissed. The problem for a democratic society is that of adjusting the special interests so that a balance is struck and the 'common good' or 'justice' is achieved. While not denying that interest groups can indeed make a legitimate claim, the normativist tends to be suspicious of the basis of such claims to be 'represented' or to 'participate' in the decision-making process as classes. If the claim rests on the view that norms are by nature expressions of individual or class interest, it has to be dismissed as a form of determinism incompatible with political — or ethical — theory. (It is not possible to be both a political theorist and a determinist. If what happens in history is determined by pre-existing conditions and not by man's conceptions and goals, there is no point in analysing the process; it lies outside our control. Hence knowledge of what is happening will not affect the ultimate outcome.) The view favouring special interests is not acceptable to van Gunsteren,

---

[9] *Ibid.*, p. 27.

who thinks of the common good (and general will) essentially in Rousseau's terms: the will of all, of special interests — whether cooperating or conflicting — will not achieve it. Some other normative term is necessary.

C.B. Macpherson appears to have been influenced by both Marx and Rousseau while not recognizing that their views are largely incompatible. Marx's historical determinism can achieve the common good only when the special interests arising from class disappear, as the classes that give rise to them disappear as the result of historical processes. For Rousseau it can conceptually exist and be sought entirely apart from the condition in which man finds himself, so that it is by no means dependent on the existence or non-existence of class.

Macpherson, like H.J. Laski before him, is not enough of a determinist to suppose that the processes of history have already decided for us what will happen; for both of them 'will', 'choice', 'reason' and 'norms' are still meaningful terms. But whereas Laski can conceive of democracy in terms of a pluralism which balances special interests in order to achieve the common good, Macpherson's 'class interests' are politically relevant and therefore eradicable. His 'common good', moreover, depends on the eventual elimination of these interests by removing the inequalities of private property. Class interests are for Macpherson what they are for Marx — economic interests. Far from seeing pluralism as a solution to the question of participatory democracy, he sees attempts at pluralism as hindering participatory democracy. 'Such division', he says, 'requires that the political system, in order to hold the society together, be able to perform the function of continual compromise between class interests, and that function makes it impossible to have clear and strong lines of responsibility from the upper elected levels downwards.'[10] To Macpherson, 'some significant amount of direct democracy is required for anything that can be called participatory democracy.'[11] However, he can also conceive of a party system as 'positively desirable', once its present function of 'blurring of class opposition' vanishes as classes vanish, so that

[10] C.B. Macpherson, *The Life and Times of Liberal Democracy* (Oxford, 1977), p. 110.
[11] *Ibid.*, p. 112.

political parties become truly representative. In short, for Macpherson participatory democracy could be based on party representation provided the society were classless. Such a view of 'participatory' democracy does not seem remotely to resemble what was recently being demanded. Obscure as the nature of the demands has been, the concept of 'fraternity' rather than 'equality' would seem to cover it better. Indeed, if one sometimes wonders what happened to the concept of citizenship, one might well also wonder what happened to the third member of the revolutionary slogan *Liberté, égalité, fraternité*.

Participation and Human Nature

Whatever construction one places upon demands for 'participation' or however one interprets the factors 'causing' the demand, one thing is clear. As mentioned earlier, a demand for participation in any type of organization usually implies some kind of acceptance[12] of that organization as an effective social force capable of advancing the interests of the individual. It is not in opposition to the 'self' unless the self is in some way left out. Such a view of political and social organization does not entail the view that the given organization is necessary to social order — the demand for 'participation' can be subversive if the organization one demands to participate in is seen as merely a social power structure that can be dispensed with when 'natural' relations are restored. Or, if one assumes that human beings are 'naturally' social animals who recognize their equality and interdependence, and who see the 'self' as an illusion similar to the illusion of 'will', one will certainly be ready to use particular social organizations having power to bring about the 'natural' situation that particular historical circumstances have corrupted.

Thus Marcuse works on the premise of a corrupt social order which permits a demand for the tolerance of intolerance and participation by those who refuse participation to others. For him, there is no normative problem: those making the demand ask only that the inequalities created by society be adjusted in favour of 'natural' equality. The ensuing state of affairs will

---

[12] The 'acceptance' may be only 'up to a point' — as in the case of the radical elements which dissent from present arrangements, yet clamour for 'participation'.

allow the natural interdependance of man to express itself in what in fact would be a denial of the biological egoism taught by the Freudian school.

Freudian determinism has neither attempted to find nor produced a satisfactory explanation of the State. It begins with the biological organism as a set of drives which must be satisfied if the organism is to survive and reproduce itself. As such, the organism is necessarily 'selfish' and aggressive; it *must* assert itself to survive. It is opposed by other biological organisms with like requirements which have evolved prudential arrangements that must be enforced upon the new-born biological egoist. How this happened is not explained under Freudianism. Opposition between individual and society is simply assumed.

But the opposition between the biological entity and the State — which Freud assumed as a fact — had already been analysed by Hobbes, who formulated the concept of a social contract. Hobbes has been criticized on the grounds that he ignored the social elements in human psychology and demanded that the prudential and rational aspects be overemphasized if the 'contract' were to work. Both objections — if one begins with biological egoism — are quite unsound: there are no 'altruistic' elements until society is created by the compact; the 'prudential' element is merely an expression of the supreme importance of the self. The consequence of the Hobbesian analysis is that the State and society are by no means as opposed to the individual as they appear to be in Freudian analysis. Transplanted to Hobbes's theory, the superego of Freud is not the guilt-making source of mental problems but an integral part of the self in time.

Marx — a determinist of different persuasion — ignores the individual and focuses on the fact of society. To him, it does not matter where the individual or entity or organism came from: the fact is that what we call individuals are a part of a sequence of cause and effect. Consequently, if we are to look at individuals we must first look at that which allows them to exist — the State or society — and ultimately at their capacity to exploit the environment or exist as a class. As individuals they cannot exist. Therefore, anything that distinguishes them as individuals (e.g. property) is an aberration that militates against their existence.

Neither Freud nor Marx attempted to mediate between the

concept of the biological egoist and the fact of society and the State. But the contractualists did so. They argued that this is the essential problem, no matter how we think of human nature and the State. If we talk about 'participation', that — in effect — is what we are talking about. The truth is that if we speak of law and order, human rights, democracy, totalitarianism or (focusing on the individual) of mental aberration and crime, we are always talking about the relationship between the individual and the State — and hence always of the contract.

Social Contract and Participation

In Kenneth Minogue's view 'the currency of social contract theories is a litmus paper indicating the fear of a social breakdown.'[13] Much of the same could of course be said of almost any theory or proposition about man and the State; therefore, what seems to provide a more interesting link between historical conditions and political theory is the observation he rather casually introduces and leaves undeveloped: 'Wherever individualist assumptions about life are current, it [the contractarian question about the nature of obligation] is never far from the surface of thought.'[14]

Now, if this is true historically, it goes far to explain why contract theory has been revived: current psychological theory is utterly individualistic. Man is seen as either a biological egoist or a culturally-patterned egoist (such as a member of one race or culture required to make some kind of political accommodation to the presence of a different race or culture, as in Africa, where demands for application of the majority rule principle in a democracy produce social conflict rather than settle it). Contractualist theory would expect this, for the operation of democratic principles can be considered legitimate only if there is a prior sense of contract — or the prior fact of one in the form of a constitution — establishing the relations between the individual and the State. Without this, the demand to participate in accordance with democratic principles could produce

---

[13]Kenneth R. Minogue, 'Social Contract and Social Breakdown' in Pierre Birnbaum, Jack Lively and Geraint Parry (eds.), *Democracy, Consensus and Social Contract*, p. 143.
[14]*Ibid.*, p. 134.

social policy which — although in the immediate interest of the majority — would in the long run destroy the State.

Democratic principles work only because there is an overriding constitution — a contract, in effect, written or unwritten — that prevents their being the only principles. Obviously, the concepts of government and state must take precedence over views about who shall have power and how it is to be distributed. Yet we lose sight of this elementary fact until demands for 'participation' by groups dissenting from present arrangements force us to reconsider just what the relation between the individual and the State necessarily is. In this sense Minogue is correct: the fear of social breakdown does induce us to revive social contract theory. But if we rest content with this linking of psychology and social conditions, we have abandoned political theory for behaviouralist determinism and eschewed the very question that modern psychology poses and political theory has to answer: how can the biological egoist possibly have come to accept the society's (and State's) interference with his egoism?

Darwinian theory — as it has been interpreted — represents man as being as egoistical as he was in Hobbes's view, quite unlike the social animal he was felt to be in eighteenth and early nineteenth-century conceptions. The consequence was fully realized by the early psychologists: if man is a biological egoist then either he is by nature in opposition to his society or he has — in addition to his biological drives — a set of social instincts which enables him to live together in reasonable harmony with his fellow men. Thus an instinct of 'gregariousness' was postulated to account for the fact that we prefer to live in a society rather than in the solitude that would be our principal protection against our fellow egoists. An instinct of philoprogenitiveness accounted for the raising of children despite their egoistic interference with the egoistic interests of their parents. An instinct of mother love accounted for the necessary nurturing and protection of the infant and so on. The 'instinct school', however, never discovered a satisfactory instinct to explain the acceptance of authority; it seemed satisfied that once a society was made possible through the instinct of gregariousness, no further problem existed.

For good reasons the instinct school has now been rejected by reputable social scientists, but its disappearance has left a gap between the individual and his urges and the State and its demands. Not only is there no explanation of how State and society came into existence, but the ills of the individual are seen as the product of a conflict between the drives of the individual and the controls exercised by State and society. Yet the latter are regarded as essential not only to the survival of the individual but to his own identity. (Thus not only is one unable to survive as black or white without one's society, but one cannot think of oneself as having separate interests without the society's process of socialization.)

Long before the discrediting of the instinct school — that solved only some of the problems — social contract theory offered the only satisfactory alternative to the notion of instinct. Though it is true that both Locke's and Rousseau's versions of the contract postulate social instincts in man, their views — like Hobbes's — rest primarily on a characteristic of man that can be considered an alternative to instinct as a method of adaptation: reason. Where instinct seems the only possible explanation of the behaviour of social insects such as bees and ants, reason seems the main explanation of the social behaviour of man. We need only suppose that human beings — instead of being sets of biological drives — have in fact become conscious of a 'self' which possesses and has some measure of control over those drives and will exercise such control because of the consciousness of the self as having an extension in time. This may be an illusion — determinists think it is — but empirical evidence supports it; it can hardly be dismissed as invalid except by doctrinaire behaviouralists. The contractual argument, then, begins with the concept of 'self' rather than the biological egoism propagated by the social sciences. It argues that the very sense of self as the supremely important fact of consciousness requires us to take into account the existence of other selves capable of cooperating with or acting against us and that it is obviously to our advantage to cooperate. But as in Hobbes's analysis of the state of nature or in the modern Prisoner's Dilemma, we cannot trust each other and must therefore devise a strategy which will enable us to pursue our own interests.

The point that needs to be made about contract theory is that, no matter which version appears the most plausible, it is the only theory that enables us to reconcile the fact of individualism with the fact that we are clearly social beings; even more important, the theory makes it clear that the State and society are not in opposition to the individual self.

The modern contractualist theorist advances what might be called 'contractual psychology' — in opposition to the biological egoism of current psychology. Is this intrusion into the territory of another discipline legitimate? The political theorist must reply that it is absolutely necessary. Social organization cannot just be assumed to exist, as psychologists assume: conclusions about the relations between individual and State cannot be legitimately derived solely from assumptions about the biological nature of individuals. One must first explain what these relations are — and not assume they are in every case hostile. Indeed, the political theorist has good reason to believe that many of the social disorders that occur are attributable to psychological and sociological theories being represented as a sound basis for political action when in fact they are misrepresentations of the true situation. It is more correct to say that behavioural psychologists illegitimately intrude into the political arena than to assert that political theorists have no justification for discussing the nature of man and society. As an example, let us consider the demands for 'participation'.

Many of those who favour greater participation clearly assume that the government is against their interests as members of interest groups inasmuch as its policies do not reflect those interests and that these interests must therefore be proportionately represented in a democracy. But contractual theory denies that government is an agglomeration of separate interest groups: there is only one interest group — society as a whole; it is the interest of society as a whole — the common good — that determines (in theory) the government's policy. Once particular interest groups begin to determine policy, the contract breaks down and conflict between the individual and the State develops — the government is seen as a coercive institution serving special interests rather than as an institution serving the long-term interests of the 'self' in relation to the other 'selfs' in the society. We move back towards biological egoism (regarded by contract theory as psychologically unsound and theoretically absurd) as the basis of social organization. Now contract theory does not 'work' if it is considered to be a desription of some supposed historical event. Rather it purports to describe the attitude a normal 'self' adopts when considering its relationship to other selfs and the State. The relationship is not hostile and is coercive only insofar as I am coerced by my own reason when I control a momentary impulse for the sake of my long-term interests. Consequently, contract theory requires us to see a process of change in that fundamental conception of the State and society as the result of other normative considerations. What must come first is the recognition of the theory of sovereignty. This is the pattern into which everything else must fit, if we are not to destroy ourselves. The demands for participation do not fully recognize this; yet, if they are to be acted on at all, they must be examined very carefully in the light of contract theory. It is absurd to consider them only in terms of basic democratic principles, as if these could exist apart from the State and somehow be more important.

Participation and Relativism

In John Ladd's view 'Participation...cannot be understood apart from various conceptions of moral responsibility.'[15] The political theorist would of course expect that each analysis of the meaning of participation and the objections to and statements in support of particular aspects of proposals — such as those discussed in the NOMOS XVI symposium — rests on certain normative assumptions. His premise is that man's concepts about himself and society — of which norms are a particular variety — represent the only possible explanation of complex human behaviour. We act in accordance with our beliefs, which are not necessarily the same as the 'facts'; hence it is misleading to attempt — as behaviouralists do — to discover the objective facts of a situation and offer them as an explanation. It is also sheer folly to pretend — as behaviouralists do — that norms and beliefs are not 'facts' or that they are in some way derived from facts and hence best ignored.

To the theorist, Ladd's statement is virtually a truism with regard to its introduction of an ethical concept — yet is poten-

---

[15]John Ladd, 'The Ethics of Participation' in J. Roland Pennock and John W. Chapman (eds.), *Participation in Politics*, p. 103.

tially misleading because it focuses on the single notion of 'responsibility'. It seems improbable from the psychological viewpoint that the demand for participation can be linked predominantly to the concept of moral responsibility. Often the reverse is true. There can be little doubt that many people refrain from expressing their true normative position precisely because such an expression implies moral responsibility.

The fact that a great many of the people who demand participation have indeed made an ethical commitment suggests we are looking at some very strong ethical objection to decision-making in our society that can hardly be explained in terms of the relativist concept of 'interest groups'. 'Participation' appears to be not so much a demand that a particular interest group be recognized (or that more interest groups be recognized) as a protest that somehow the decision-making process takes place without considering the fact of citizenship. In modern democracy, decision-making seems to be a purely relativist process that tries to balance off conflicting interests, whereas in all of us — even members of interest groups — there remains an inner conviction that such relativism is contrary to both our own best interests and the common good (even though we may not be able to define the latter precisely).

Most people probably believe that the norms embodied in the criminal code and the structure of our political and social order are absolute, and tend to act accordingly. Consequently, when government policy is clearly determined by the interest groups involved — whereas ethical considerations seem to require a different type of decision, as in the case of the slaughter of seals for fur — the general public is made aware that the decision-making process has gone astray. Not everyone will join Greenpeace demonstrations — moral responsibility, as was said earlier, does play a part in political activism — but even the most law-abiding will not approve of a government policy which condones seal-killing, though there is no doubt that in terms of 'interest groups' the latter may be 'correct' and 'just'. It simply happens to be morally unacceptable to a great many people; as such it arouses a strong sense that the government is not 'of the people' but a separate establishment influenced by the same motives that govern psychopaths.

Other examples can be given where the issues clearly do not

involve a clash of 'interest groups' in any meaningful sense and yet arouse more public interest than any others, as in the case of capital punishment, abortion, and the use of marijuana. It is significant that when such ethical issues were openly debated and members of parliament were free to act in accordance with their consciences — as in regard to the abolition of capital punishment — the results have since been accepted in several countries as evidence of the working out of the democratic process despite the realization that the legislation runs counter to the wishes of the majority: most people now want the legislation changed. Yet legislation abolishing capital punishment is not used as an example of some weakness in democracy but rather as a mistaken judgement that can be corrected. So long as a decision can be seen to be based on the type of considerations one uses oneself — or thinks one uses — in arriving at decisions, one does not object to decisions made by 'representatives'. They are indeed acting as representatives when they use the methods we ideally use — the rational weighing of normative issues. But when the decision-making appears to leave out ethical considerations entirely, we ourselves feel left out of the process and demand 'participation'. It is our norms that define us as individuals. Hence arguments for greater representation of interest groups overlook the basic issue, which is that, as a citizen who believes in reason and norms, I am not represented when decisions are made as if the only objective were the balancing-off of interest groups. At least some demands for participation would appear to be a protest against pure relativism in democratic decision-making rather than an objection to present democratic processes and institutions.

VIII
Whither Democratic Theory?

The Insufficiency of 'Realism'

What has been done to assess the sufficiency or insufficiency of 'realism' in democratic theory? To those who have not made 'efforts to restate democratic political theory in terms which would be more satisfactory to the needs of the present day'[1] Lane Davis's criticism of political realism is likely to make a strong appeal. But will the 'realists' find his appeals to classical norms of democracy 'unrealistic'?

In answer to the charge that classical democratic theory 'fails as a descriptive and explanatory tool', Davis enters a plea of *nolo contendere*: the classical theory was not created to describe but to prescribe. Realists are almost certain to say, 'But the facts are...,' to which Davis has no answer, for he has made no attempt to relate his prescriptive democracy to the realist's conception of democracy. In order to make an effective case against 'realism' one has to demonstrate that what the political realists are overlooking is a part of the political reality of democracy — 'the distinctive moral function of democratic politics and government'. Davis has not discussed the essential issue of just how realistic political realism is.

Assuming that there is a prescriptive element in classical democratic theory, the issue for theory is not whether we should uphold the prescriptions or abandon them, but rather what the relation is between the 'reality' found by political realists and the prescriptions that are supposed to have established the reality. Did the prescriptions cease to operate once a democratic govern-

---

[1] Lane Davis, 'The Cost of Realism: Contemporary Restatements of Democracy,' in Charles A. McCoy and John Playford (eds.), *Apolitical Politics: A Critique of Behaviouralism* (New York, 1967), p. 185.

ment was set up? Are they still present but of subordinate influence? Have new ones, as Davis implies, taken their place? If one fails to ask these questions one weakens one's defence of classical theory, for the issue then becomes one between (on the one hand) realism in the sense of objective empirical investigation of what actually exists and is known of democracy and (on the other hand) theory in the sense of an emotional attachment to traditional hopes and beliefs about man. But the basic issue is how realistic political realism is.

The problem confounding the 'realist' is not that his account of democracy differs from the classical theorist's — he may well argue that the difference is a problem for the theorist only — but that in his approach there is no place at all for norms. They are not, apparently, manifest in the institutions and practices of democracies in a way that behaviouralism can detect. Political theory does not require a direct and unequivocal relation between norm and practice. A political theorist, for instance, would not be troubled by the thought that a random set of trials studied empirically might suggest the institutions of feudalism rather than democracy. The 'realist', however, either has to suppose that there is a direct relation — for example, that courtroom trials in a democracy are unmistakably 'democratic' — or that norms are irrelevant.

It is the latter position that the 'realist' usually adopts. In order to maintain that his account is both complete and accurate, he must argue that the 'norms' of democracy *are* the institutions and practices he perceives. Here one's objection is not to a different conception of democracy but to the fact that the 'realist' view compels us to believe that democratic norms once operated — as in setting up democratic practices — and then stopped, or that they never operated at all and that democratic societies are the result of forces which were present within societies long before anyone ever heard the word democracy.

The notion of norms serving to set up democratic institutions and then ceasing to function is not tenable. It provides no explanation of how norms could operate so as to have effects and then be supplanted by the effects, and it inevitably raises questions as to where the norms came from and why the new norms have not produced new effects. It is a bad blend of Hegel and Marx which, although it has not been expressed as a viable theory, must have been assumed by those behaviouralists whose studies were conducted as if it were true. The alternative view — a form of historical determinism — has more plausibility, and is probably the basis of most current 'realism'. But it does have the awkward consequence of implying that mankind cannot have aspirations or make prescriptions that can be followed.

We cannot solve the problem of accounting for norms by pretending that they are illusory — a mere reflection of institutions, habits and attitudes which already exist. The absence of norms from behaviouralist studies is not evidence of 'realism' but a serious deficiency.[2] The question is not whether we should believe certain things or follow certain goals, but of the function assigned to norms. They must be given some function because they are part of the present empirical democratic situation; if they are not to be given the importance assigned to them by classical theory, a theory of norms explaining the change is necessary. Simple relativism will not suffice.

To pursue their studies, 'realists' need a theory which requires that norms represent non-realizable hopes or, if these hopes are realizable, requires that the institutions and practices be directly related in form and content to the norms. Since the latter is another way of saying that all desires must be specific, it can be dismissed as false and we are left with the requirement for non-realizable hopes. But I do not believe that 'realists' can prove that this represents the true nature of norms.

The Insufficiency of the 'Pure Politics' Approach to Democratic Theory

All exact sciences shade into one another. Thus pure chemistry can hardly be distinguished from pure physics and the distinction between the two is largely a matter of administrative convenience within academic and research organizations. Matters are not quite the same in the social sciences, largely

[2] If democratic prescriptions have affected democratic institutions — and there is convincing evidence for this, for instance in the USA and France, where revolutions produced sudden changes which cannot be explained solely in terms of antecedent institutions and practices — the political 'realist' who professes to give a complete description and explanation without reference to the original prescriptions must provide a satisfactory reason for the omission if he wishes to be considered a true realist.

because no decision has yet been reached as to what constitutes the fundamental phenomenon(a). The social sciences have no equivalent of the atomic theory which makes physics and chemistry branches of a single science. Instead, there is a strong tendency for particular branches of the social sciences to replace one another *as if* they were fundamentally different disciplines. Political science has at times been approached as if it were a branch of sociology, biology, or psychology; and, of course, sociology and psychology have at times been considered to be no more than an aspect of something else.

Under such circumstances, the concept of 'pure politics' can be a useful device for political scientists to disassociate their investigations from outside influences. If we consider, for instance, behaviouralist studies of political phenomena — there is little, if anything, in behaviouralist methodology or assumptions to distinguish them from social psychology. But there is a way in which political science as conducted by behaviouralists can be differentiated from social psychology. Although the social psychologists venture freely into areas which may be considered the province of political science, the reverse is not true. The range of behaviouralist studies is depressingly narrow.

The behaviouralists achieve this by limiting the definition of political phenomena much more than has traditionally been the case; they also avoid speculation and the intrusion of normative influence into their studies. To them, the notion 'pure politics' becomes a convenient label that can be attached to the restricted area of political activities seen as 'researchable propositions'.

Behaviouralists are singularly unfit to pronounce on democratic theory. That the study of democratic theory cannot be limited to the study of purely political processes — voting, gaining power and keeping it — becomes apparent when one realizes that in the modern State democratic norms have become the all-permeating norms of its society. Thus *all* social organizations in a democracy — from labour unions to amateur theatre groups — are expected to imitate the kind of social organization that comes from accepting the principle of democracy along with its organizational norms: the principles of open office, universal franchise (within the membership), majority rule, fixed terms of office, and so on. Few people question the

Group Theory and Neo-Pluralism

general application of democratic organization, no matter how inappropriate it may seem in some instances, as in the family or the school system. The reason why anything so bizarre as a 'democratic' family making democratic decisions is conceivable is that the norms behind it are assumed to be not purely political. 'Democracy' cannot be limited to a number of political processes. Its norms are about man and his relation to society, and they make the notion of 'pure politics' unintelligible.

Group Theory and Neo-Pluralism

Group Theory and Human Rights

Political theory has always been concerned with supplying an explanation of two tendencies in human behaviour: the egoistic pursuit of self-interest and the acceptance of governmental authority that restricts the citizen's freedom to seek the former. No study of human behaviour made without reference to an explanatory framework, such as contract theory, or an analysis that denies the truth of one (or both) of the two tendencies, can be a satisfactory political theory. Thus the theory of the 'sick society'[3] which derived from psychotherapy is not a true political theory — even though the resultant attitude to the State with which it deals lay behind a good deal of directionless violence of the Sixties. This is because the particular discipline involved does not include a theory of the State (except as it constitutes a force in conflict with the individual). What, then, can be said of group theory?

As G. David Garson observes, 'But where group theory excelled in describing the new realities of private power, it contained no real theory of government.'[4] Why should a description of power politics without a theory of government be any more relevant to political science than psychiatry's equally accurate descriptions of internal conflicts which are supposed to be brought about by society? Group theory begins with the same pursuit of private interest that psychiatric theory postulates.

---

[3] According to this theory, the mentally ill are victims of conflicts induced by a society which — if 'healthy' — ought to be so constituted that such conflicts between biological organisms and social norms are not induced.

[4] G. David Garson, *Group Theories of Politics* (Beverly Hills and London, 1978), p. 166.

What is necessary, however — and missing — is an explanation of our acceptance of the framework in which the pursuit takes place — the framework of the State that makes organization into an interest group both possible and effective in attaining its ends.

Group theorists were able to show that interest groups play a major role in policy-making, but once the policy is instituted, they are unable to explain why the policy should be accepted by anyone other than the interest group itself: the concept of power was well described, but the concept of authority was ignored.

In an empiricist (and relativist)-oriented climate of opinion, it was felt that this deficiency might be remedied by further empirical studies. Yet group theory was undermining itself. The very effort to show that 'power' was widely distributed made it difficult to understand why the same was true of conflict. Against whom was the latter directed? If the conflict was between interest groups having power, then the fact of distributed power reflected the need for a sovereign power. If, on the one hand, it was directed against the 'government' or sovereign power, then group theory was clearly supplying a misleading description about the facts of power. What was the 'government' that seemed to be recognized as the only effective power — the one worth pressing one's demands on? As Garson puts it, 'The group approach...was undermined by numerous studies empirically refuting various group-theory hypotheses.'[5] Since the principal claim made by the theory was that it reflected the actual facts about the distribution of power, the studies Garson mentions were telling blows; an 'empirically-based' theory that can be shown to be in fact non-empirical has nothing left to recommend it.

While organization into a group is an effective way for individuals to obtain certain ends — e.g., full civil rights for a minority group — it is not the fact of their being an organized group that ultimately decides whether the demands will be met. It is inconceivable, for instance, that in the Western democracies even the best organized and most militant group of drug-

---

[5] *Ibid.*, pp. 175-6. Among the authors of the relevant studies published in the Sixties mentioned by Garson are McCloskey, Luttbeg and Zeigler, Milbrath, Olson, Pye and Verba, Walker.

users could obtain the repeal of discriminatory laws against their habit or that the rights of minorities could be abrogated by well-organized bigots, irrespective of whether these rights are set out explicitly in a constitution. Such rights exist so long as the minority is recognized as having citizenship — and citizenship is recognized as inalienable. Group theory, which interprets social relations in terms of power or the enforcement of one's 'rights' (=interests) upon others, cannot explain the facts of citizenship. One of these is that minorities which are not organized and hence — in terms of group theory — do not have power, nonetheless quite clearly have enforceable rights. Yet being a minority is not enough to give one any kind of rights, if only because of the great number of potential minorities (increased by permutations of their norms and interests). What matters is whether the supposed rights fit a normative pattern that defines them as 'just' — which implies 'deserving recognition'. If they do not — as with the use of drugs — they cannot be enforced without destroying the fabric of the State: through a successful revolution. If they do, the rights of the minority will be enforced even by those who are not themselves members of the group (as when slavery was abolished). Here group theory offers no explanation: one feels that even the best attested empirical descriptions of the effectiveness of organized groups on policy-making are misleading accounts of what has in reality taken place.

The essential problem with group theories is that their views of human 'rights' are Thrasymachian and thus lack a concept of 'legitimacy'; without the latter their very 'power' evaporates. The 'power' that an organized interest group has in our society is obviously not the same as that of an armed band. A group has power only inasmuch as its 'interest' is recognized as legitimate. Hence group theory does not so much offer an explanation of politics as it poses a problem for the theory of sovereignty. If the 'interest' of interest groups is already defined as 'legitimate', why should it matter whether it receives expression through an organized group or not? (This question has not been adequately dealt with either by group theory — put forward as a rival to the theory of sovereignty — or by the theory of sovereignty itself.) In sum, what group theory lacks is an adequate theory of the State, legitimacy and human rights.

Neo-pluralism as a Theory of Power: the Dilemma of Actual and Potential Power

To use David Ricci's words, 'interrelated presumptions about the nature of power'[6] underlie the pluralist theory (a version of the group theory), notably that of its chief exponent Robert Dahl. Ricci — a contemporary student of the neo-pluralist scene — is highly critical of Dahl's decision-oriented methodology. Dahl emphasizes the distinction between actual and potential power: the actual power a man wields has no obvious relation to the potential power he enjoys. Ricci points out, however, that 'Potential power is a factor in political decisions because of what political scientists call "the rule of anticipated reactions". The rule states that politicians anticipate the needs and responses of other men and act so as to fulfill those needs'.[7] In other words, potential power is actual power. Indeed, Dahl himself seems to treat it as such in his concept of 'slack' power. The theoretical problem here is that the two parties to the dispute both make a distinction between actual and potential power and yet at some point each treats it as if it were not valid. (We must ask whether political theory can make a distinction about power analogous to that needed in physics in regard to potential and kinetic energy.)

Although the neo-pluralists emphasize the distinction between two kinds in order to justify their methodology, they do not analyse the theoretical implications of their position. The first question they need to ask is: What effect (if any) does potential power have on actual decision-making or 'active' power? If the answer is 'none', what is the justification for calling it 'potential'? If it does have an influence, why call it 'potential' rather than influential power? The neo-pluralist intention appears to have been to question the theory of sovereignty; the failure to relate the distinction to the latter makes the concept of potential power either illusory or simply another way of referring to influential power. Neo-pluralists like Dahl either violate their own 'cardinal negative rule of pluralist theory' (as formulated by Nelson W. Polsby: 'Nothing categorical can be

---

[6] David Ricci, *Community Power and Democratic Theory: The Logic of Political Analysis* (New York, 1971), p. 126.
[7] *Ibid.*, p. 170.

assumed about power in any community') or stress distinctions merely to justify a methodology, which — being capable of analysing only one aspect of power — is insufficient even within the confines of their own theory. In effect, they proceed as if 'potential' or influential power exists as a valid concept only if manifested in decisions that are actually implemented.

Even if we ignore all questions about the relation between decisions made within a community and those made under the State's sovereignty, there is a serious methodological problem. The neo-pluralist argument is that the only power open to empirical observations is the kind manifest in working to achieve a goal requiring at least the acquiescence of others and actually achieving that goal. But in order to argue that such behaviour represents power, we have to assume that it represents the result of will or decision-making power — and this we most certainly cannot do. Dahl would surely recognize the absurdity of saying that because office workers make decisions without the observable intervention of a superior will, the result of their efforts can be called their 'power'; it would be even more absurd to assert that this kind of 'power' is the only kind that exists — that the nature of a bureaucratic structure embodies a rule that those who implement decisions must have originated them because they implement them. Yet this type of reasoning is necessary if we adopt the view that the study of outcomes determines who prevails, and that those who *do* are those who have 'power'.

The weakness of the neo-pluralist view is that pluralists have no all-encompassing theory of the community or State into which they can fit the decision-making they observe; there seems no way of constructing one by studying isolated instances where decisions are made and carried into effect. A single instance of an implemented decision that does not originate with the group studied but governs the latter raises the question whether the 'power' perceived has any relevance at all to the concept of power as applied in the theory of sovereignty. The theory seeks to explain not the fact that 'power' exists — in the sense that the 'will' of others is obeyed — but that the process has an observable structure and orderliness that cannot be explained by particular instances. It is this orderliness and structure that neo-pluralists leave unexplained — yet it is clear that without some concept of structure their methodology collapses. How can we apply their findings about particular instances of power in particular communities to others, unless we assume a structural connection? How can neo-pluralists establish that the instances of power they observe are not instances of delegated authority paralleling that of the office workers just mentioned, unless they advance a theory that observable power structures are in some way illusory? Yet, if they do that, what can 'power' mean? Does it not become a synonym for success in 'goal-achievement' — when the real issue for political science is not such a psychological concept, but a different kind of 'power' observable in the structured relations between members of a State?

Neo-pluralism and Relativism

In what sense are relativistic norms relative? The extreme 'relativistic' view that the contradictory of any norm has as valid a claim as the norm itself is patently false so long as we keep in mind the standard (or point of reference) being applied. How can we escape relativism? We cannot escape the fact that norms are *relative* to a central point of reference. What can this point be? It must obviously be fixed or 'absolute' — as absolute as, for instance, the assumption that our sensory receptors are giving us an accurate record of something other than the working of the observer's mind. There is only one thing that fulfills this condition: the standard of 'good' is the same as that of 'truth' — namely the 'self'.

If this seems a lame conclusion which invites pure relativism — the good is what I think it is — the fault lies as much with the inadequacies of empiricism as with normative analysis. As C. E. M. Joad among others has observed, empiricism — as usually put forward — cannot escape the problems of solipsism. If 'truth' were really based on a self-objective reality distinction alone, the truths of science would have to be regarded as being as subjective as norms. In fact, however, we demand that all statements about truth be verifiable: they must always yield the same observations under the same conditions. Thus science avoids solipsism because it rests on two fundamental propositions: the *self-it* distinction and the *self-other*, and the latter is vital to its defence of objective truth.

The self-other proposition necessary to empirical truths

assumes that the self not only makes a distinction between self and not-self but also between self and 'things-not-the-self-but-like-the-self', and that it uses this distinction in its verifications. The self gives the observations of the other about the 'it' of objective reality a weight equal to its own (even though the other is but an aspect of objective reality insofar as the self is concerned). If we did not do this, we would be solipsists.

Science, then, escapes solipsism through a self-other dichotomy. If it has validity in converting relative truths to absolutes, there is no reason not to use the same principle to convert relative goods to absolutes, as in fact mankind appears to have been doing throughout history.[8]

The 'self' accepts as a standard of good its own welfare, just as it accepts as a standard of 'truth' its own perceptions and converts these from relative standards to absolutes by means of substantiations or verifications; the latter are made possible by the self-other identification. If we deny the validity of this technique our science becomes solipsistic and our ethics relativistic. If we accept it, then both 'truth' and the 'good' are verifiable.

How does the above view apply to neo-pluralism? Neo-

[8]It is evidently not prudential reasoning, for instance, which makes murder universally wrong — a sort of 'If I kill him, then others may feel free to kill me, so I will contract with others not to murder in order to guarantee my safety'. There are far too many objections to such prudential considerations for the latter to serve as an adequate explanation of the known facts about norms. Our security would be too dependent on the policing powers of the State; on our confidence that State power would be used purely for our protection and not exploitation; and on the quite unreasonable view that everyone would act in terms of their own long-range security rather than the immediate situation. Above all, we would find war or organized violence utterly inexplicable: if prudence were the normative basis of our objections to killing, we would certainly expect war to have been suppressed long before murder. Nor could prudential considerations explain the fact that murder produces a deep sense of shock (which the murderer himself often feels), whereas killing in war or capital punishment give normally many people what can only be called moral satisfaction.

The *self-other* identification has no difficulty in explaining such facts. In war the enemy has usually been excluded from the concept of 'other'. In fact, not until the rise of the major religions and their doctrine of the brotherhood of man was it even conceivable for those outside the community to be regarded as members of the same species. They could be hunted and even eaten like any other animal. Similarly, capital punishment for murder has been regarded favourably precisely because murder is so fundamental a violation of the self-other concept that the murderer clearly shows himself to be outside the category of 'other' and poses a serious threat to the community because he is otherwise indistinguishable.

pluralism is the quintessence of relativism. It assumes that normative standards must be relativistic and that the 'real' or 'scientific' issue is not *what* standards are applied — they will vary over time and from place to place — but *who* applies them. The concepts applied in analysis are 'will' and 'power'; and like many concepts, these seemingly simple terms are treacherous. Neo-pluralists have rightly recognized the problem inherent in the concept of 'power' by drawing an analogy between potential and kinetic energy: power that is not used may be present in the same way as the conditions for an avalanche threatening a community; but if we are examining what is actually happening, we must ignore the potential until it is actualized. This is good behaviouralism: it is what is — not what might theoretically be — that matters.

There is also a problem with 'will', which is as necessary as 'power' to the neo-pluralist position. It also allows a distinction similar to that made by the neo-pluralists with regard to 'power'. There is 'will' in the sense of 'acting according to one's drives and interest' — paralleling actual 'power'; and 'will' in the sense of 'having the drive and interest but not in fact acting', which is given a separate term 'apathy', though that term seems to mean something like 'potential will'. (It clearly does not mean 'having no interest in and hence no will' with regard to a situation, but rather 'not acting in one's interest though the potential is there'.)[9]

But if we start making the distinction between actual and potential will, as the neo-pluralists do with the actual-potential power dichotomy, we make a theoretic distinction whose sole justification is that it enables us to undertake a (behavioural) study of one of the terms and dismiss objections on the grounds that the other term is not open to investigation. This is what the neo-pluralists have done with power: they make a theoretical distinction between two kinds of power, argue that only the one that manifests itself in decision-making is open to investigation

[9]In his *Community Power and Democratic Theory* David Ricci points out — unfortunately without drawing a parallel to the neo-pluralist distinction between actual and potential power — that neo-pluralists are forced to assume that the lack of public outcry over atomic stockpiles reveals 'apathy' in the sense of no self-interest, whereas there can be no doubt that no one in his senses can be or is complacent about the situation. Obviously, if we are going to make a distinction between actual and potential power we should make a distinction between actual and potential will and not call 'potential will' by so misleading a term as 'apathy'.

and then proceed as if it were the only kind of power (except when they need the unanalysable aspect to answer theoretical objections to their methodology). With regard to 'will', which also allows an 'actual-potential' dichotomy, the neo-pluralists use a substitute of 'potential' will (in the form of 'apathy') for purposes of theory, while in fact identifying 'will', 'power' and 'decision-making'. The result is an unsatisfactory hodge-podge of behaviouralist and non-behavioural analysis.

How do we get out of such a morass? We got into it by assuming that in examining decision-making we cannot focus on the 'norms' because they are relativistic — a matter of 'will' — and since this is not analysable, we must focus on power or capacity to exercise the will, and since *this* in turn is not observable except when exercised, we must look at decision-making and wherever we find it assume that we have discovered the one observable set of facts that will enable us to retrace our steps to the theoretical distinctions with which we began. The pitfalls and shortcomings of following so tenuous a clue to truth are so obvious that no one would be likely to put it forward if the assumption were not relativistic, or if he were not convinced that to begin at the beginning (by analysing the normative basis of decision-making and power) was impossible. But we have reason to believe that norms are relative only if truth is relative; that the important issue confronting us is not that of 'will' and 'power' detached from norms — in that case they do not even make sense — but the issue of *self-other* and the limitations we set on this concept.[10]

Kelso's Three Types of Pluralism

On the face of it, Kelso's distinction between laissez-faire

---

[10] Political science has long been the Cinderella of ethics and of the latter's ugly stepdaughter, relativism. Historically it has never accepted the ethical view of philosophy or the major religions that there is a universal standard for mankind. The norms of political science have usually stopped at the borders of the State. The norms or laws of the State have repeatedly been presented as overriding those of its individuals and communities: State sovereignty does not strictly speaking allow for 'pluralism' in any meaningful sense. The ensuing conflict between the will of the individual and the will of the State was instrumental in raising the issue of 'relativism' in a most acute form. Now if we follow the lead of scientific methodology and argue that people do not in fact make the two-fold distinction between *self* and *it* but rather a three-fold distinction between self-other-it, the problem of the relationship between self and State acquires a new aspect which has yet to be explored.

pluralism, corporate pluralism and public pluralism[11] seems promising; but if one hopes to resolve the objections to pluralism, one must be fully aware of the various underlying assumptions that make pluralism an issue. In Kelso's book, however, the assumption underlying pluralism is tossed off in a subordinate clause as it it were a self-evident truth: 'Even though democracy has always been defined in terms of popular participation in government policy making...'[12]

If this were true, we could understand why in the recent century participatory democracy and pluralism (a theoretical way of increasing participation) have been prominent and why the theory of sovereignty has been under such vigorous attack; but we certainly could not understand the lack of emphasis on participation in the history of democratic theory. Historical evidence shows that it is not true that 'democracy has always been defined in terms of popular participation'. In fact, it does not seem to have occurred to anyone that such a definition could be meaningful until relativism claimed that the normative definition of democracy was meaningless.

Under the normative conception of democracy, the theorist considers legislation, institutions and practices — present or ideal — in terms of their compatibility with normative requirements, but is not committed to anything except the compatibility. Under relativism, a normative position *is* a commitment; if this raises normative problems of the compatibility of the particular commitment with other normative positions, the problems have to be concealed. This is why a great deal of what passes for political theory today is of doubtful value. Much of it is intellectually dishonest because the norms assailed by relativist proponents are not concepts for them but attitudes towards practices or institutions to which they are committed. Thus, as Kelso realizes, pluralism raises serious difficulties about the problems of decision-making. Consequently, he defines laissez-faire pluralism as one which is dominated by the very problem of decision-making; corporate pluralism, as a device for solving the problems by 'capturing government authority', so that it ceases to be a representative interest group; and public pluralism, as

---

[11] William Alton Kelso, *American Democratic Theory: Pluralism and Its Critics* (Westport, Conn., 1978), Ch. 2.

[12] *Ibid.*, p. 37.

a means of solving the problem by 'central direction'. But although Kelso presents a clear discussion of pluralism in terms of an equitable distribution of power and suggests how this can be achieved, he does not give an equally adequate account of the 'central direction' which purportedly distinguishes public from laissez-faire pluralism. Indeed, the concept of 'central direction' appears to be a mere technical device to dispose of a known objection to pluralism. Thus the conceptual difficulty with regard to the distribution of power has been converted into a normative difficulty — a commitment to something else. Kelso says that it is a commitment to 'efficiency' and rightly disposes of the latter as an objection. But the problem posed by pluralism is that raised by the concept of sovereignty when power is distributed; it is therefore wrong to pretend that the conceptual problem is the normative issue of 'efficiency' versus democratic pluralism.

Pluralism has a number of advantages. Instead of defining democracy in terms of set institutional forms, the institutions are considered as flexible as the legislation, so long as analysis shows that they effectively fulfill desired requirements. Though pluralist theory is based on competition and uses economic theory for support (if not as a model), it recognizes that cooperation is possible (which is particularly apparent in Kelso's 'corporate pluralism') when particular interests coincide and are in competition with alternative interests. Because of the focus on individual interests, the class conflict of Marxism is dismissed as an illusion: individual identity is never submerged in the group, for the interest group is understood to represent only small aspects of the member's total personality and to tend to dissolve when goals are achieved. Clearly, as a description of political behaviour, pluralism is markedly superior to theories of class behaviour based on the criterion of property ownership; this is because, despite use of the market model, the actual interests represented in pluralist theory are not only economic but cover a wider range of human values. Pluralist theory will probably continue to attract attention as it fits observable facts and is not in conflict with relativism.

Kelso's classification of various types of pluralism frankly recognizes the market-place model employed by pluralist theory and the refinements made on the original model by modern economic theory. Outmoded as pure laissez-faire economic theory is, Kelso rightly objects to criticisms of laissez-faire political theory as criticisms of pluralism. The market-place model of pluralism does not commit it to either laissez-faire theory or corporate theory. Indeed, there is no reason why the relationship between interests groups in general and government should not be like that between economic interest groups and government (the basis of the 'public pluralism' advocated by Kelso).

On the other hand, the theory underlying pluralism is still the eighteenth-century view that the 'common good' results from free competition between private interests. This view has been made obsolete by the modern belief that some government regulation is indispensable. Kelso's own position concerning the concept of 'common good' is necessarily subject to limitations. He rejects the original economic laissez-faire theory or its political parallels, but he cannot use the economist's technique of waiting for the political theorist to supply one (he is himself such a theorist). Nor can he assume that the concept is the result of competition between private interests without abandoning the very distinction between laissez-faire pluralism and the public pluralism that he himself advocates.

The problem can be reduced to the fact — not recognized by the pluralists — that insistence on private interest or egoism as a fundamental principle of human relations makes social relations meaningless. Given the absolute dependence of men from birth to death on the fact of society, strict 'egoism' becomes a problem to be questioned. What makes us think that we are in competition with one another when the plain fact is that we often cannot be so?

Private interest or egoist assumptions are the basis of both Hobbesian and Freudian theories, though their respective conclusions differ. Hobbes's theory suggests that the social contract changes man's relationships and ultimately his 'nature': trust and cooperation become possible once the conditions which prevent them are removed. In Freud's theory there is an enduring conflict between biological egoism and the restraints imposed on individuals by society. Which view does pluralism accept? How can it be related to Hobbes and Freud? Its emphasis on interest groups and power relations accords quite well with egoist assumptions — hence its primary appeal — but it is not a complete political theory. To be one — which is more than a convenient way of describing certain political phenomena — it must incorporate itself into the theory of State and sovereignty. By itself it is as inadequate as Freudian theory. We have to know the nature of the State within which pluralist relationships are taking place. This is where pluralism is most deficient.

As Kelso himself admits, the studies on which pluralism is based are for the most part studies of municipal politics. As was said earlier, pluralists do not offer us a theory of the State, even though their assumptions about egoism make such a theory essential to their analysis. In conclusion, one could venture a statement that pluralism looks more like a modernized version of Hobbes's 'state of nature' than a fully-fledged political theory. This in itself does not discredit pluralist theory. But some of its arguments may prove to be much more valuable if they can be integrated into a modernized, neo-classical version of the theory of sovereignty.

Democracy as a Formal Machinery of Rights, Obligations and Procedures

Although in his Preface to *Democracy and Illusion* Plamenatz professes to be neutral,[13] such a stance is hardly possible. The direction of his arguments shows that the norms of democracy and their implications are not so important to him as the institutions and processes. He reduces democracy to the formal machinery for free elections and competition between rival political parties.[14] The view that permeates his analysis is expressed as follows: 'Democracy is a matter of rights and obligations and of procedures that secure rights and ensure that obligations are, or can be, fulfilled. Whoever seeks to explain it, no matter how much his purpose is merely to explain and not

[13]John Plamenatz, *Democracy and Illusion* (London, 1973), p. X.
[14]Democracy then becomes a system 'where rulers are politically responsible to their subjects'. 'Responsibility' is guaranteed if two conditions are met: (1) that there is freedom to criticize rulers, to come together to make demands on them and to win support for competing policies and beliefs (2) that supreme policy- and law-makers are elected to office at free, periodic elections. *Ibid.*, pp. 184-5.

also to justify, cannot avoid a kind of exercise which is more properly called philosophy than science; especially if the natural sciences are taken to be models of what science should be.'[15] Each of these two ideas deserves analysis.

It is an article of belief among many contemporary social scientists that for children norms are internalized commands deriving from their parents. To be sure, this is not an entirely adequate explanation: most children readily recognize the difference between an arbitrary household rule and a norm of the society. Even children raised by criminal or indifferent parents know and usually observe the norms. Norms are argued about whereas rules are simply obeyed or disobeyed, depending on whether one thinks one can get away with it.

Social scientists, however, have adopted the above explanation of norms and this for at least two reasons. Firstly, it enables them to hold to their fundamental position that human beings are motivated only by biological drives: norms are internalized as a result of the child's fear that the principal source of the satisfaction of bodily needs — the love and approval of his parents — will be withheld if he disobeys. The second reason — the one which immediately concerns us — is that norms are much more binding than laws because they become as much a part of us as our fundamental drives — that is, a normal person does not need a policeman or a criminal law to keep him from murdering someone.

Now a legalistic interpretation of democracy is prone to deny the above-mentioned views of social scientists and go against such evidence as we have of the nature of norms. In effect, the legalist attempts to *externalize* norms rather than *internalize* them and this has profound effects on society.

In countries like the UK or Canada — which lack a written constitution defining democracy — the norms are internalized: they exist within the individual as part of the mental framework defining him and his society. Now let us assume that we adopt Plamenatz's view that 'democracy is a matter of rights, obligations and procedures'. Does anything change?

With respect to 'rights' one might be tempted to say 'no'. The man who believes in the two fundamental democratic norms of

[15]*Ibid.*, p. 181.

egalitarianism and individualism is likely to define the meaning of democracy in terms of rights. He would be prone to say either that it does not matter whether they are given legal expression in some 'Bill of Rights' or that such legislation is a good thing. Indeed, taken by itself, it is hard to think of it as bad or mistaken.

Matters, of course, are quite different when it comes to duties: prescribed duty breaks the natural connection between rights and duties and makes it an act of oppression even if it is well meant.[16] Plamenatz's third element — procedures that secure rights and ensure that obligations are, or can be, fulfilled — cannot be easily related to anything that a member of a parliamentary system would normally think of as essentially democratic. It is pure legalism.

It is perhaps understandable that societies which have strong relativistic tendencies — as is the case with modern democratic societies — and yet which recognize that the norms defining them must be left out of the relativistic system, will be attracted towards the legalistic solution. It is difficult to account for the Canadian Bill of Rights legislation on any other grounds. Nonetheless, I believe that such 'solutions' represent a fundamental misunderstanding both of democracy and the relativism that appears to threaten it. 'Majority rule' deriving from egalitarianism is unquestionably relativistic in tendency. So is individualism, with its emphasis on the rights of private conscience. Since egalitarianism and individualism are the two basic norms of Western democracies, we might expect an irreconcilable conflict both within individual members and within the society itself. But this is not what happens at all. So long as the norms remain norms and are not externalized into specific rights, duties and procedures, the two norms in conflict give rise to a third norm — toleration — which enables us both to accept legislation based on majority rule and to oppose it if that happens to accord with our conscience. Not only is toleration in this sense not relativistic, but it is opposed to the tendency towards relativism created by the two norms.

[16]Consider the history of compulsory voting, which converts a right into a duty. Where it does not exist, any proposal to introduce it is resisted as oppressive; where it does, it is regarded as proof of some serious fault in the system — as proof that there is no real belief in democratic processes.

What would happen if we decided that the norms of democracy held by its members are not an adequate foundation for a State? In the first place we would inevitably have to give up toleration as a norm, for it is by no means implicit in procedures, rights and duties; furthermore, there is no legal way of prescribing such an attitude. Indeed, one of the reasons, perhaps even the principal one, why the USA has throughout its history been considerably less tolerant of out-groups and more conformist in attitude than other Western democracies, despite its lack of a clear tradition of 'right' behaviour, is that Americans tend to look at democracy in the way Plamenatz does. Democracy for them is less a matter of norms than of legally prescribed rights, duties and procedures. It is the Constitution which supposedly determines what is right and wrong.

Americans must, of course, admit that it is not the American Constitution that made the USA a democracy but the normative attitude that lay behind and guided the drawing up of the Constitution and made it acceptable to the citizens. The fact is that no legal statement could set forth all possible interactions between norms and particular social conditions. When the Supreme Court attempts to justify or disallow legislation in terms of the Constitution, it is trying to rationalize behaviour prescribed by the norms of democracy, not by the Constitution. Perhaps the last outstanding case in which the Constitution did indeed motivate the decision was the Dred Scott case (1857), in which the Court with perfect propriety insisted that a man could not be deprived of his property, which in this case turned out to be a human being, an escaped slave. That decision, however, violated the norms of democracy and one of the consequences was a civil war that might well have been avoided if concepts of right and wrong had been based on internalized norms of democracy rather than constitutional legalism. Indeed, the exacerbation of conflict seems an inevitable result of attempts to externalize norms. So long as they exist within us, as a part of our very being, we are open to reason, doubt, and choice. Narrow them down to sets of prohibitions and restrictions and you set man against man and against the society which is restricting him.

We have so far been talking as if Plamenatz were hostile to norms and hence, at least in part to political theory. In fact, he asserts what few will admit today: 'The modern State is to a

Democracy as a Formal Machinery 199

considerable extent a product of political theory.'[17] But, he says, in the minds of its critics, such theory 'had been superseded by a type of theory superior to it' and he draws an analogy between this change and the replacement of Ptolemaic theory by Copernican.[18] Now this is rather odd. Copernican theory replaced Ptolemaic theory precisely because the latter was *not* the foundation of the solar system. In what way can modern political theory be superior to 'old-fashioned theory' (Plamenatz's term) if the latter is the foundation of the modern democratic State? Has any fundamental change taken place in the State? Not necessarily, but a fundamental change has taken place in the theorist's attitude to his tools of analysis — norms — and this is implicit in the second sentence of the quotation from Plamenatz with which we began: 'Whoever seeks to explain it...cannot avoid a kind of exercise which is more properly called philosophy than science, especially if the natural sciences are taken to be models.'

That is the crux of the problem. Plamenatz wants to talk about 'rights and obligations and procedures' precisely because the normative element which makes them significant can then be ignored:[19] they can be treated as facts about the State and be analysed without reference to the norms. Such an approach can make political theory superficially resemble the physical sciences or rather what physical scientists pretend to be doing — namely dealing with the facts. But as Bronowski — among many others — has pointed out in relation to the physical sciences: 'A scientific theory cannot be constructed from the facts by any procedure which can be laid down in advance.'[20] In effect, Bronowski argues that every science has norms which form the basis of its explanations and that without explanation we do not have anything that can be called a science. If pursued further, Plamenatz's half-formulated

---
[17] Plamenatz, *op. cit.*, p. 30.
[18] *Ibid.*
[19] Plamenatz's 'realism' leaves out virtually all substantive and normative debates of contemporary democratic theorists: there is, for instance, no discussion of the critiques of 'democratic elitism' (by Bachrach, Baratz, Bay, Connolly and others), while the arguments of Michels, Mosca, Pareto and Schumpeter are assumed to be true once Plamenatz has made his own rather minor revisions.
[20] J. Bronowski, 'The Creative Process', *Scientific American*, Vol. 199, No. 3 (September 1958), p. 62.

preference for scientism would have led him into the cul-de-sac of being unscientific. At least his argument can serve as a warning that a false conception of the physical sciences can produce a misleading conception of political theory.

Property, Equality and Freedom

The conviction that the 'wrongness' of liberal democracy derives not from its principles but from the incorporation of a concept of property which is at odds with those principles — and, further, that the 'wrong' element can be eliminated without seriously disrupting the liberal democratic system — is one of the beliefs widely accepted by the critics of democracy. If we are to understand C.B. Macpherson's position in this respect and expose any fallacies in it, before tackling his models of democracy, we must first look at what can be called his thesis.

The 'thesis' is contained in the opening paragraph of *The Life and Times of Liberal Democracy* (1977): 'The subject's life is over...if liberal democracy is taken to mean...the democracy of a capitalist market society' but 'not necessarily if liberal democracy is taken to mean...a society striving to ensure that all its members are equally free to realize their capabilities.'[21]

Macpherson, like many who substantially accept the Marxist analysis of property, says that if one limits one's case for security of property to security for the fruits of one's labour, 'he [Bentham, whom Macpherson is specifically discussing] would have...a fairly effective case. But...he went on to a very different proposition: that security of any existing kind of established property, including that which could not possibly be the fruits of one's labour, must be guaranteed.'[22] Macpherson sees this as reflecting a lack of historical sense.

Macpherson's Protective Model of Democracy

In Macpherson's view, the democratic franchise provisions were 'put into the model' of 'protective' democracy belatedly, perhaps because of 'the sheer logic of their own case for reform, resting as it did on the assumption of conflicting self-interested

---

[21] C.B. Macpherson, *The Life and Times of Liberal Democracy* (Oxford, 1977), p. 1.
[22] *Ibid.*, p. 31.

maximizing individuals.' In other words, [the founders] 'allowed themselves a democratic conclusion only because they had convinced themselves that a vast majority of the working class would be sure to follow the advice and example...of the middle class.... The founding model of liberal democracy took man as he was, man as he had been shaped by market society, and assumed that he was unalterable.'[23]

The portrait of market-place man drawn by Macpherson is by no means attractive. That it can hardly reflect man's 'nature' is clear from the fact it is descriptive only of a particular class at a particular period in history. So far, Macpherson is certainly correct. But what he is looking for is the elevation of a concept — property — to the status of a norm: one of the most important, if not the most important, of the norms held by man and society. That in fact it has been so — and still is — for a great many can be shown by pointing out that classical economics has been able to develop working 'laws' of behaviour based on the premise of the 'norm's' importance. Conversely, the fact that the 'laws' do not work with respect to many primitive societies and do not give us a clear understanding of human behaviour before the Industrial Revolution shows that there is some substance in Macpherson's views.

The difficulty, however, is that Macpherson's account of the influence of 'bourgeois' norms requires us to presuppose the dominant power of the bourgeois class itself, whereas what we really have to explain is just how such supposedly class-based norms could attain such influence in the face of the two entrenched classes — ecclesiastical and aristocratic. It would thus appear that we must examine the 'norm' of property rather than its source in a particular influential class if we are seeking an explanation of the influence of class. Yet if we look to the property 'norm' as an explanation we adopt an essentially Marxian view of history, a view that is so unpalatable to Marxists themselves that, like Macpherson, they predict a time when the norm will cease to function so that the norm they want to believe in — equality — will have the field to itself. The only way to do this is to insist that the norm is a class norm and will vanish with the class, but — as pointed out before — that requires at the outset the unhistorical influential power of the bourgeoisie,

[23]*Ibid.*, pp. 42-3.

whereas the attainment of power would seem possible only if 'property' constituted something more than a class norm. Thus it would seem that the bourgeoisie attained power because it acquired property and that a change in its status would be possible only if property were associated with power — apart from what society said about the nature of social organization.

Yet even if there was no apparent change in the consequences of being propertied, there was an unmistakable increase in the number of property owners from the Renaissance onwards. To attribute this to economic factors — increased opportunities in trade and manufacturing — is to adopt the unrealistic view that property accumulates under certain conditions whether you want it or not. Obviously, one must first desire property before employing the means — trade and manufacturing — that will attain it. When we see normative shifts we must look for the norms to explain them.

What occurred in the seventeenth century was a normative change — the emergence of such normative concepts as equality and individualism which preceded the development of a capitalist economy. Is there anything in either of these concepts which could possibly affect attitudes to property? Can we reverse Macpherson's analysis and argue that democratic norms had developed first and that this led to a shift in the importance of property?

Now the concept of equality does not merely change one's attitude to those in power. It changes one's concept of the self in relation to others. Once the concept of equality is accepted, both those given by society a high status and those given a low one are in effect required to redefine their position. The most obvious way, which is open to everyone, is through the pursuit of property; for by its very nature property enhances the self. A naïve way of looking at equality is that under egalitarianism each man would simply accept the other as of equal worth. Such an interpretation, however, is equivalent to redefining 'equality' as *aquality*, a denial of the significance of qualitative differences, or a denial of the concept of the 'good'. It has certainly never meant that to anyone. The strictest egalitarian is capable of admiring — and desiring — such qualities as strength and intelligence, and is bound to look with suspicion at anyone who argues that property — a 'good' attainable by one's own efforts — should be so distributed that it will cease to be desirable as a goal to be attained. There is something wrong with the reasoning of an egalitarian who supposes that human beings not only could modify their desire for property in this way, but as egalitarians 'naturally' would so, if their attitude to property had not been influenced by society's conditioning. But the evidence of history and the psychological desirability of property seen in its relation to the self falsify Macpherson's predictions about the future of liberal democracy.

What Macpherson is really arguing is that there is a normative conflict between the concepts of property and equality and that consequently 'property' will have to be modified. Such reasoning parallels attempts to solve the problem of euthanasia by pretending that one can ignore either the requirements of the death taboo or those of mercy. Norms cannot be treated in this high-handed fashion, for they have a conceptual element that cannot be altered without changing one's fundamental conception of the self-other relation. This is what gives the basic norms their curious permanency, despite the fact that human beings have unmistakably invented them rather than discovered them somewhere in a universe of facts.

The concept of property conflicts with the concept of equality because both are directly related to one's concept of 'self': property enhances a self that defines itself as 'equal' to other selves. Conceptually then, it is just as important to democratic theory as equality and individualism. Indeed, any political theory that supposes property can be so distributed that problems are thereby solved cannot be called a democratic theory.

Macpherson's Participatory Model of Democracy

Of the three remaining models of democracy that Macpherson discusses, only the fourth model, participatory democracy, merits any serious consideration. His second model, developmental democracy, is in his own view now only of historical interest. One should notice, though, that the normative element — the encouragement of an individual's potential — seems to have been incorporated into one of the conditions necessary for participatory democracy: 'One is a change in people's consciousness...from seeing themselves and acting as essentially consumers to seeing themselves and acting as exerters and enjoyers of the exertion and development of their own capacities. This is requisite not only to the emergence but also to the operation of participatory democracy.'[24]

We can also dismiss the third model, equilibrium democracy, as not immediately relevant to Macpherson's views on the future of liberal democracy. This model represents an appraisal of the present state of 'capitalism'. Any consideration of its accuracy is likely to become a mere defence of present conditions. Let us, then, turn to participatory democracy.

In Macpherson's view, 'Low participation and social inequity are so bound up with each other that a more equitable and humane society requires a more participatory political system.'[25] The normative emphasis — 'more equitable and humane' — is interesting. Macpherson is not arguing, as the New Left who invented the slogan argued, that 'democracy' is or requires 'rule by the people', or direct rule. Indeed, he maintains that 'We must rely...on indirect democracy.'[26] What he objects to in equilibrium democracy is that it is adapted to and promotes 'an unequal society of conflicting consumers and appropriators';[27] as mentioned before, what he would prefer to promote is the view of men as 'exerters and enjoyers of the exertion'.

What is odd about this is not its Victorian quality but the fact it is so utterly at variance with the strong relativism both implicit and explicit in the concept of participatory democracy. One sees this relativism in Macpherson's own discussion of the possible use of technology: two-way television to promote direct democracy. He observes that it is technically feasible to have yes-no buttons that would allow the public to vote on social and political issues, but he does not raise the obvious normative objection one would expect from a man who has already adopted a normative position. Such a man must surely argue that this kind of participatory democracy is a reflection of pure

[24] *Ibid.*, p. 99. I find this necessary condition indistinguishable from what Macpherson declares John Stuart Mill's emphasis to be: 'his emphasis was...on what democracy could contribute to human development' (*Ibid.*, p. 47). Indeed, Macpherson's own emphasis on 'exerters and enjoyers of the exertion' has a curious Victorian ring to it.
[25] *Ibid.*, p. 94.
[26] *Ibid.*, p. 97.
[27] *Ibid.*, p. 99.

relativism; furthermore, that it could be used only by those who believe that issues such as abortion and capital punishment are matters of private taste to be settled not by debate but by the expression of one's preferences. In other words, the very concept of participatory democracy is a phenomenon induced by the adoption of relativism rather than by the logic of democratic norms. It was unthinkable to those who promoted developmental democracy, for it converts 'self-development' into 'self-expression' and thus totally destroys the very normative concept that Macpherson uses as the basis of his argument for participatory democracy.

This is the problem all relativists face. They can and do have as strong normative positions as non-relativists (e.g. Bertrand Russell on the Vietnam war), but as relativists they are precluded from advancing arguments in support of what they believe (unless they are non-egalitarians who see themselves as modern representatives of Plato's 'guardians'). Though a great many people who began as egalitarians became relativists (the New Left advocates of participatory democracy certainly did) and consequently advocated 'action' — or violence — rather than reformist thought, men like Macpherson are faced with the dilemma of, on the one hand, valuing equality for its normative consequences for society and the individual, while, on the other, being required to regard their norms (including, of course, equality!) as indefensible and basically insupportable by rational analysis. Ironically then, in one way, they can envisage virtually any change in society, provided we can rid ourselves of outmoded prejudices, such as the concept of property; but they cannot advocate the changes or strive to promote them without acknowledging that nothing supports their view but personal predilections — predilections that are not related to the welfare of society. (They could, of course, escape the problem if they were willing to return to some of the classic views of man as by nature motivated by 'good will' and the general good. There is some evidence that Macpherson believes this and that like Rousseau he sees society the way it has existed in history — as a source of corruption and enslavement.)

Is Property a Norm?

According to Macpherson, 'Property...is a man-made device

which establishes certain relations between people.'[28] Although this sounds like an objective definition, it is the beginning of an *argumentum ad hominem*. If one wishes to show that the concept is in some way arbitrary, there is no need to say it is manmade. In fact all our concepts including so-called empirically-based concepts — like colour — can be said to be man-made.[29] The moment we admit that our minds have something to do with the fact of having a concept, we look to the 'needs' of the organism to explain the concept; also, the further we move from empirical data, the more we are tempted to explain concepts in this way. Thus normative concepts can be shown to have no empirical basis whatsoever (no 'ought' can be derived from an 'is'); they are 'explained' with reference to desires, attitudes, tastes, etc.

The peculiarity of the concept of property is that it is *not a norm*. It asserts a relationship between someone and something. (The 'something' need not even be material: in some primitive tribes the most valued property relates to songs which certain people have the exclusive privilege of singing, so that to sing another man's song without his permission becomes an act of theft — an aspect of the concept of property which did not appear in the Western world until the nineteenth century when 'copyright' was incorporated into the legal system.) Macpherson's point that it 'establishes certain relations between people' is but one of the effects of property. His definition is inadequate: it hardly expresses the essence of the concept which is clearly about the relation between someone and something irrespective of the existence or non-existence of others. Robinson Crusoe did not need to await the arrival of Friday to think of his trousers and shoes as his own and hence as something he should take care of. Certainly when Friday arrived, Crusoe's property markedly affected their relationship. Crusoe's superior knowledge, which

---

[28]C.B. Macpherson, *Democratic Theory: Essays in Retrieval* (Oxford, 1973, Reprinted 1977), p. 121.

[29]Colour, as we know, is not a quality of anything. It reflects the fact that humans have evolved receptors sensitive to certain ranges of electro-magnetic spectrum. Human beings cannot 'see' infra-red or ultra-violet — though many insects can — but, within the range of radiation to which we are sensitive, we can make more than a million distinctions we call 'colour', none of them apparent to most other biological organisms. Thus in one sense the concept of colour is man-made, which — to follow Macpherson's line of reasoning — invites the speculation that it is a fiction invented for some purpose.

it is doubtful he would even have considered 'property' — though it clearly was along with its material manifestation in the shape of clothes, weapons and so forth — produced a dominance-submission, master-servant relation that was not imposed but accepted as 'natural' by both of them. Such effects may be inescapable but in no way change the fact that 'property' does not depend on the effect. What it requires is a concept of the self. Precisely because the self would seem incapable of conceiving of itself without the concept of property — I have to think of 'my arms, legs and so forth' in order to conceive of myself as existing — we cannot get rid of the concept. The most we can do is limit the content of the concept — which, of course, all societies have done.

Those societies which place a high value on equality see the ideal as the minimum private property necessary to the concept of self: one's body is one's own but even an extension to what one produces is seen as endangering equality. A number of utopian communes have tried to follow out the logic of equality with regard to property. The result, as in the case of the recent and notorious Walden Two experiment, was that the property each member brought to the community was simply used up. There was no point in even washing one's clothes so long as there were clean clothes around somewhere — formerly someone's property, now a community resource. Until the resources were exhausted, clothes were not washed; for the act of washing turned a member into the communal launderer — a subordinate position in a supposedly egalitarian community. Theoretically, the members would perform the tasks they 'liked' — an attitude that prevailed in the early stage of the commune when people wore clean clothes. But as it was impossible to maintain self-respect by keeping one's clothes clean — someone would take what you had washed — one had the choice of either descending to the general level of slovenliness characteristic of the commune, or of leaving. Everyone or nearly everyone did eventually leave, having been stripped of his property. The exceptions were those in whom the property of the commune was legally vested — the group of members who obviously fitted George Orwell's category of people 'more equal than others' thus providing a new illustration to his classic analysis of the political consequences of utopian egalitarianism.

The fallacy of trying to achieve egalitarianism by abandoning the concept of property lies in the fact that 'equality' cannot mean anything unless there are individuals to be thought of as 'equal'. But individuality requires the concept of self, which in turn is impossible without the notion of property. To limit property to what is necessary to the physical self is to limit the activity and interests of the self to the moment. This contradicts the normal concept of the self's perceiving itself as existing in *time*: 'I' perceive myself as existing not only at this moment but for an indefinite period into the future; hence I will restrain momentary impulses and undertake activities now which are not pleasant or interesting — such as washing clothes or making a tool — so long as my effort will serve me in the future. It is not likely, of course, for this to happen without the notion of property. Locke, then, was quite right when he spoke of property as of something in which one's labour was 'mixed', though wrong when he supposed that such an idea 'explained' the concept. Clearly, the concept must exist before a man can begin to talk of its 'content', as he does when he sees that part of the content arises from the activity of the self.[30]

Macpherson tries to get around the clear evidence of a relation between self and property by speaking of property in terms of 'rights', private property being for him 'an enforceable claim of an individual to some use or benefit of something'. He speaks of such a claim as including also a 'right not to be excluded from the use or benefit...which society or the State has proclaimed to be for common use' such as common lands, parks

---

[30] It is possible, however, to deny that making something creates ownership and even to convince the maker that this is so, but in doing this you cannot prevent him from deciding that it is not worth his while to work — to see the self as extending in time and preparing for the morrow. This is the main reason why we work. Many egalitarians, however, have claimed that work is not meaningless if it results in the accumulation of *communal property*. They point to certain religious sects holding property in common and even to farm families who work to keep the farm going. What they overlook is that the religious communities that have been successful in the accumulation of communal property specifically teach the unimportance of the self in the larger scheme of life. The corporal self is regarded as the 'bone cage' of the soul; life as we know it is but a moment of eternity; private property and materialism are downgraded because the soul is more important than the self. If one does not happen to hold this view, the example is irrelevant. The example of communal effort on the family farm is, of course, different. The sons who contribute their labour to the upkeep of the farm clearly expect to benefit when they inherit the farm. They are making an investment rather than a selfless contribution to a 'community'.

and highways. He admits that this 'common property' does not have the unlimited claim to use that private property has: 'The State may, for instance, ration the use of public lands, or it may limit the kinds of uses anyone may make of the streets or of common waters.'[31] He could have added that 'common property' has *none* of the characteristics of private property — no one, for instance, can sell or bequeath his share in a public park or highway. In other words, the concept of 'public property' is equivalent to the exclusion of what could be property from the concept of property. Indeed, public property can be thought of as property only if the State is regarded as a corporate body asserting a claim vis-à-vis other States.

By denying, in effect, the relation between property and the self and emphasizing both the State's enforcement of private property rights and its capacity to limit what can be private property, Macpherson makes 'property' and its content a legal fiction changeable by *fiat*. Hence we can speak of the emergence of two irreconcilable schools of thought. One asserts that the concept of property is inseparable from that of the self; hence limitations on property are limitations on the individual and therefore on freedom. The other school insists that the concept of property is a legal fiction enforced by the State; that it is the concept of equality that defines 'freedom'; and that 'freedom' requires the modern State to limit property to a greater degree than most Western States do at present. From what has just been said it follows that, if we are to understand democratic theory, we have to come to some decision about the concept of property. Is it a legal fiction or is it an inseparable component of the concept of self?

As has been noted, Macpherson's proposition is that both common property and private property are rights created and enforced by the State. He dismisses the 'popular' view of property in terms of ownership as a mistake, which developed rather late in history. 'In pre-capitalist England,' he maintains, 'property had generally been seen as a right to a revenue.'[32] To make a case for such a bizarre idea, Macpherson limits his discussion to 'land', which from the earliest period could be fitted only with difficulty into the concept of property. Given the concept of

[31] C.B. Macpherson, *Democratic Theory*, p. 124.
[32] *Ibid.*, p. 127.

property, there is no difficulty in understanding such concepts as lending, buying, bequeathing, stealing and damaging with regard to material objects. Yet applying the same concepts to land leads to troublesome questions. (Thus it was necessary to introduce the concept of 'rights' and rely on legal precedent to settle disputes about land tenure.) To attempt to derive our concept of property from an aspect of property that is still by no means clear is like attempting to derive the concepts of black and white from the concept 'grey'. The study of anthropology shows that while all societies have a concept of property, only a limited number — primarily agricultural societies — regard *land* as property. Macpherson's assertion that 'the change in common usage, treating property as the things themselves, came with the spread of the capitalist market economy'[33] is simply false. From the evidence of wills and market transactions — which, incidentally, are among the earliest documents extant — we know that property was from the beginning conceived as the material 'things themselves'; problems in respect of land as property arise precisely because of the difficulty in thinking of land in this way.

There is a certain carelessness in Macpherson's discussion of property. Thus in attempting to argue that private property was a late development while faced with the fact that 'From the beginning of argument about property — which argument is as old as political theory itself — the argument was mainly about private property',[34] Macpherson blandly dismisses the fact by saying 'In any case, the earliest extant theorizing about property was done in societies which did have private property.'[35] The implication is that there are societies that have and some that have not had their views coloured by self-interest. But the anthropological facts are that there is no society that does not have the concept. (This fact would seem to present an insurmountable obstacle to the view that the State creates the rights to property, for some primitive societies do not have a concept of State.) Despite the problems posed by property under certain conditions,[36] the concept exists in all societies — together with

[33] *Ibid.*
[34] *Ibid.*, pp. 124-5.
[35] *Ibid.*, p. 125.
[36] A large number of primitive societies have such strong norms of cooperation and sharing that it seems to the outside observer that few of the characteristics of property

the concomitant concepts of theft, sharing, generosity, etc. It is obvious that Macpherson is mistaken in supposing the State creates property rights. He should have given an example, in his essay, of a society which lacks a concept of property or theft. His failure even to attempt to give such an example suggests that he is blindly following an ideological position (essentially Marxian) rather than attempting to analyse the democratic set of norms.

Macpherson's attempts to reverse known historical developments, his refusal to recognize known facts of anthropology and his utterly improbable derivation of the common man's concept of property from legal wrangling have a clear polemical purpose. He wishes to show that only a legal fiction distinguishes capitalism from socialism and that this fiction is being maintained by the self-interest of the propertied class. Given his view of property, a simple legislative act would establish a classless society.

The fundamental error made by Macpherson and those with similar views lies in their attempt to view property as a norm rather than a concept. By thinking of property as a norm, Macpherson is following the type of analysis that all relativists use today when trying to explain norms: they relate them to desires, tastes and attitudes. But 'property' in itself is not a normative concept. It simply describes a relationship between the self and something that the self regards as in some way a component: 'my' arm and, by extension, my pencil, etc. It becomes normative only when the relation it asserts is ignored by another person. It is then that the normative concept of 'theft' arises — a concept that cannot be accounted for by talking about needs, desires, uses or functions. There concepts cannot be convincingly shown to have any relation to the concept of property. Furthermore, normative concepts like charity, justice and equality are certainly relevant to our behaviour, but — and this point is ignored by Macpherson — they cannot be applied in such a way that the concept of property is thereby negated.

---

are present. Furthermore, among some very primitive nomads property comes close to being an inconvenience rather than a convenience — it is literally a burden that one must carry — and hence is reduced to the bare minimum necessary for food-gathering and hunting, as among the Arunta tribesmen in Australia or the Bushmen in Southern Africa.

Given the self, we necessarily have a concept of property, as the very etymology of the word shows. Deny the concept of property (or treat it as a norm that should be subordinate to other norms) and you inevitably subordinate the self to something that the self as a biological organism must regard as not having such pre-eminence. The common man may not be consciously aware of exactly what it is about socialism and the lofty altruism of the higher religions that makes him suspect they are demanding too much from him, but, so long as biology requires him to be aware of himself, he will find reasoning that runs counter to the conception of self and property unconvincing.

Rawls and His Critics

Freedom, Equality and Reason in Deterministic and Non-deterministic Analysis

Under the deterministic assumption, 'reason' can mean little more than the awareness or summation of one's perceptions and associations. At best it can show only that we have made a mistake in our perceptions, as when 'reason' tells me that a stick does not actually bend in water. But in a deterministic world 'reason' can never be the real basis of choice, for our behaviour has already in effect been chosen for us. Hence under determinism, those who conjecture hypothetic 'contracts' made by reasonable men are really talking about themselves — the factors in their own background and personality that make the hypothesis seem right to them. (People of a similar background will constitute the 'reasonable' men the theorist is talking about.)

Under the non-determinist hypothesis, 'reason' is the faculty which makes freedom meaningful. Indeed, to say that behaviour is 'unreasonable' is to say it has been determined in some way — by immediate circumstances, impulse, mistaken information or another set of factors that in effect make behaviour a mere reflection of deterministic elements in the world. If it were not for the concept of 'reason', free-will would be but an assertion that chance determines human behaviour. In other words, the non-determinist needs the concept of reason to make free-will meaningful.

If both determinists and non-determinists are fully aware that the concepts of freedom and reason put them in opposite camps, this is not true of the concept of equality. It is not so obvious to them that in this case the respective meanings attributed to equality are also fundamentally different. To the determinist, a 'social contract' is a self-evident violation of the principle of equality on which it supposedly rests, for the contract sets up a 'class society' of government and governed — an unequal distribution of at least one good, power — that will almost certainly entail an unequal distribution of other goods. It is not surprising then that determinists denounce social contract theorists as spokesmen for the class in power, even though the evidence for this view which can be gathered from such a theorist as Rawls is conflicting, to say the least.

But if contractual equality seems self-contradictory to a determinist, it nonetheless has a functional place in contract theory as the hypothetic condition which establishes that a contract system is a rational choice: it would be impossible to convince anyone that a contract between unequals establishing inequality could in any way be the result of free-choice. Thus by the nature of his argument the contractualist is required to see equality as an integral part of his system. The meaning given the term must, of course, differ markedly from that given by the determinist.

The determinist is forced by his position to focus on 'facts' and to regard any concept that does not have a factual basis as illusory. We would therefore expect a determinist to reject 'equality', for if any fact is self-evident, it is the fact that men are not literally equal. On the other hand, the determinist today derives his position from a methodology developed by the physical sciences which requires him to believe that its fundamental units for observation are 'equals' in the sense of being interchangeable identities. Hence the scientific study of human behaviour leads to the view that men are literally equal and when this is manifestly not the case, promotes the view that it 'should be' the case. To assert in a deterministic scheme that one believes in 'equality' is to assert that justice — or nature herself — demands that we eliminate all factors promoting inequality and see all demands for equality as 'just', no matter how unreasonable they may otherwise seem. A corollary of this is that class conflict is a natural expression of man's inner sense of justice and that any scheme like the social contract — which not only demands class structure but is designed to eliminate conflict — is unjust and historically false.[37]

The difference between the determinist and non-determinist interpretation of 'human nature' has important consequences with regard to the reception of Rawls's work. Thus Milton Fisk raises what many will consider telling objections to Rawls's views on freedom and contractual reduction of conflict. Rawls's views on freedom of thought are practically identical with those of traditional liberal democratic thought. To Fisk, genuine freedom presupposes restrictions on freedom of expression.[38] He arrives at the repellent view that while a liberal democratic State must be tolerant of its critics, it is virtually a moral duty of the critics to be intolerant.[39]

It is, of course, impossible to defend this view philosophically, but it can be, and obviously is, defended when the premise is that thought is not and cannot be free in the sense that liberal democracy says it is or can be. Then the issue becomes whose thought 'should' be free — the oppressor's or that of the oppressed? If oppression is defined as bad — as it is by both liberal democracy and its critics — the answer is clear and the resultant blend of tolerance and intolerance (with the State on the losing side) is seen as an historical phase on the steady path to the classless society.

---

[37] Because of the manifestly unacceptable meaning given to the term 'equality' by determinists and its ambiguity under a class system, it is a pity that Rawls has not replaced it with a more closely defined term. He has tried 'self-respect' and the dignity of man, but has been rightly criticized for his vagueness. The problem could perhaps be solved if it were recognized that 'equality' for both determinists and non-determinists implies that all individuals regarded as equal are grouped together: the principle of equality might better be termed the '*non-exclusion principle*'. No matter how different a man is, or how unworthy a member of the group, he cannot legitimately be regarded as subject to the treatment we give inferior — or 'superior' — beings; the president is not God, an idiot employee is not a beast, and a criminal is not an enemy. Such a change would at least remove a great deal of confusion.

[38] See: Milton Fisk, 'History and Reason in Rawls' Moral Theory', Norman Daniels (ed.), *Reading Rawls* (Oxford, 1975), p. 60.

[39] Rawls and others holding the traditional liberal democratic view are likely to feel the opposition is insane — that it is a self-evident contradiction to believe in both tolerance and intolerance.

Rawls has not made it clear that his real premise is the indeterminism or freedom of human behaviour. Had he focused on that and frankly stated he was returning to the pre-Darwinian views of 'freedom', he might have seen that there is a way out of the dilemma posed by the determinists. He could have argued that if the 'reason' he is talking about has the characteristics ascribed to it by the determinists — that it is a reflection of conditioning — it would not be biologically advantageous; or rather, it would be identical with the 'instincts' of the lower animals. But reason obviously serves the function of increasing adaptability — as we would expect from Darwinian theory — and cannot possibly be 'conditioned' in any real sense. (A great many people's views merely reflect current ideas on the way they were brought up. Rawls would deny that this is a necessary attribute of reason. Only a determinist is compelled to think so; consequently to him the views of the opposition are likely to seem more free — less conditioned than those of a spokesman for the 'establishment'.) To conclude: it is not likely that the two parties will understand each other until they both recognize that the issue between them is determinism versus 'freedom' and 'reason'.

But if Rawls would find incomprehensible an argument for intolerance put forward as an argument for freedom of speech, what would he make of Fisk's view that the aim of justice under the contract is not to be just? The aim of justice, says Fisk, is the reduction of conflict,[40] but such reduction worsens the position of those whose situation can only be improved by conflict. Are there many? Yes. All those who can think of themselves as or are in fact members of a group other than that in power are by nature not benefited by the contract.

If Fisk sees relativist consequences of the contract, it is this: Any concept of right deriving from human nature which can resolve conflicts of class either justifies the present order or promotes opposition — in fact does not reduce conflict.[41] If Fisk were correct, the contract would work only if it reflected the 'relativist' interests of a governing class who were so able to manipulate freedom of thought or 'reason' that no one would know.

[40] See *ibid.*, p. 70.
[41] See *ibid.*, p. 75.

This is a stunning conclusion but it follows quite logically from a determinist position. If men are not really 'free', if their views of the good 'normally' (under non-manipulated conditions of thought) reflect their conditions and interests in society, it follows that in a society where men are not literally equal, they will normally be in conflict. Furthermore, no matter what the intentions of a contract (setting up at least one class division) may be, it will not produce a 'justice' that anyone other than the establishment could see as such. It must, of course, be emphasized that these conclusions do not follow if you do not begin a determinist view. The central issue, as has been said, between Rawls and his critics is the conflict between determinism and non-determinism. Perhaps the real basis for the interest Rawls had aroused is the fact that he has been bold enough to return to the old free-will norms of freedom, equality, reason, and a justice based on them.

Prudentialism and the Social Contract

The Contract theorist who leans heavily on prudential arguments — as does Rawls (and Hobbes) — inevitably exposes himself to the charge that the contractual system he offers as a minimum of what we can all agree on reflects a petty bourgeois mind. This is not mere name calling. Prudential arguments make many — perhaps most — of us uncomfortable: somehow their proponents seem to miss the essence of social relations — the fellow-feeling which makes us ready to co-operate and is outraged by attitudes of narrow self-interest.

The uncomfortable feeling aroused by the prudential contract has probably played a larger part in the reception of Contract theory than theorists care to admit. What one must look into is whether arguments based on prudence are based on a universal principle. Benjamin Barber maintains they are not.

According to Barber (quoting Rawls), 'The maximin rule "tells us to rank alternatives by their worse possible outcomes".' He subsequently says that 'it is to the maximin rule that the logic of the rules of justice as fairness apparently conforms'.[42] In

---

[42]Benjamin R. Barber, 'Justifying Justice: Problems of Psychology, Politics and Measurement in Rawls', Norman Daniels (ed.), *Reading Rawls*, p. 296. The quotation from Rawls is from his *A Theory of Justice* (Cambridge, Mass., 1971), pp. 152-3.

Barber's view, Rawls 'leaps from the original position, where men are prevented by the veil of ignorance from knowing what their particular statutes will be, to the unwarranted conclusion that this uncertainty will produce in them a rational preference for minimizing risks'.[43] Barber suggests that 'The no-risk predilection for security may be atypical of human choice in the face of uncertainty' and finds it odd that 'a conservative special psychology predisposed towards security has been installed where rationality is supposed to be'.[44]

Now there can be no doubt that gamblers and heroes, among others, do not always follow the maximin strategy. But then Rawls never said they did. As Barber himself says, 'Rawls is at pains to persuade us that while the rule is neither self-evident, nor usual, nor generally applicable, it is uniquely suited to the peculiar conditions of the original position.'[45]

But if Barber is wrong in suggesting that the maximin strategy is not 'natural', he is certainly correct in his appraisal of the 'ambiguity' of Rawls's theory: 'the original position contains two moments, reason and interest, whose thrust tends in contrary directions. It is characterized on the one hand, by rationality and collaboration.... On the other hand...by interest psychology.'[46] Indeed, if the prudential basis of the contract is taken to represent the actual source of our behaviour and notions of the 'Good', the social contract theory would be scarcely distinguishable from Utilitarianism. As Barber observes, 'Although Rawls differs with the utilitarians on the question of aggregating utility, he shares with them...a common ambience in his hedonistic focus on interest, his instrumentalist view of reason, his manipulative approach to political institutions and his pluralist preoccupation with conflict resolution.'[47]

Barber recognizes that these are conclusions Rawls cannot accept, but he sees Rawls's attempt to deal with them as resting 'on rather uncertain foundations in Hobbesian

---

[43]Barber, *op. cit.*, p. 297.
[44]*Ibid.*, p. 298.
[45]*Ibid.*, p. 296. If Rawls did indeed say it was 'not generally applicable', he went too far. In fact, the rule is structured into biological organisms as an 'instinct' — fear.
[46]*Ibid.*, p. 315.
[47]*Ibid.*

ratiocination...shored up by Kantian braces drawn from *a priori matériel* not admissible in the original position.'[48] But if for Rawls (as he puts it himself) 'the principles of justice will be effective only if men have a sense of justice and do therefore respect one another',[49] what is the point of the prudential argument for the contract? Barber himself makes the point, but in terms of an ironic dismissal of Rawls's views: 'In other words, too much altruism would obviate the need for a rationalist theory of justice altogether.'[50]

What Barber does not seem to recognize is that prudential argument is not directed to men in general but essentially to those who appear not to understand why most people respect the law; it is an argument addressed primarily to rebels, and it stands or falls by its power to appeal to them. It is the equivalent of the kind of argument we use in everyday life when confronting those who violate the principles we regard as inviolable. Thus we do not tell an adult thief that it is wrong to steal. We warn him of the imprudence of such behaviour and support legal sanctions which we hope will at least make those who are tempted think twice before violating the norm.

It would also be wrong to suppose that advocates of capital punishment are themselves deterred by fear of punishment. General acceptance of the sanctity of life rests on an entirely different basis, but the prudentialist argument recognizes that — for reasons unknown — we cannot assume that everyone understands non-prudential ethics. Aberrant attitudes do arise and to a large extent can be controlled by making what for most are ethical issues into prudential considerations. There is nothing inconsistent in holding Kantian views and offering Hobbesian arguments. It depends on whom one is talking to.

Justice and Power: Democratic Violence

To Rawls, violence cannot be a 'mode of address'. To Honderich, 'violence may on occasion be...an appeal to the sense of justice of the majority'.[51] This is the essential difference

---

[48]*Ibid.*, p. 317.
[49]Rawls, *A Theory of Justice*, p. 586, quoted by Barber, *op. cit.*, p. 317.
[50]Barber, *ibid.*
[51]Ted Honderich, *Three Essays on Political Violence* (Oxford, 1976), p. 113, footnote.

between Rawls and others writing during the debates on civil disobedience. Indeed, a case can be made for the idea that Rawls's 'contract' was addressed towards such men as Honderich — that it was an argument addressed to 'rebels'. If so, the rebels are clearly convinced they can still make a case. To what extent do they justify their position?

Although Honderich gives considerable attention to the 'rules' of democracy, his fundamental position is that 'The rules of democracy...do not give...the arguments for democracy.... One principal argument...is that, compared to other practices, it gives less autonomy to any individual or minority in determining the policies of a society. Most importantly, it gives less to...the governing representatives.'[52] 'The second argument', he says later, 'is the argument of equality.'[53] Why Honderich should see equality as a 'second' argument is not clear since he also observes that it is 'a necessary truth that if no individual or minority has autonomy with respect to the society's policies, then all have freedom from such autonomy.'[54] The reason for the attention to 'equality' becomes clear as Honderich's argument for violence develops: he wants to give special normative importance to 'equality' in order to detach it from 'freedom' — a position which conflicts with the first and primary argument for democracy.

This seems to be the technique used by all of Rawls's critics: whether arguing for violence, or for equality of property distribution and power. The essential normative difference between their view and Rawls's is the importance given to the construction placed upon 'equality' and the consequence of this difference. Whereas Rawls sees the essential issue as the control of power in order to achieve the just State, his opponents see the issue in terms of equality. To them there can be no justice until the closest possible approximation to literal equality has been achieved; hence Rawls's argument for a contract setting up an 'inequality' as its very basis is unacceptable. The 'reasons' for the unacceptability will differ (as one addresses oneself to different issues), but the normative basis is the egalitarian norm. Let us

[52]*Ibid.*, p. 104.
[53]*Ibid.*, p. 106.
[54]*Ibid.*, p. 107.

now see how Honderich uses it to defend 'violence', the issue that was certainly in the forefront of Rawls's consciousness when he was constructing his argument.

'Can one have a political system that can be said to satisfy the conception of democracy...even though political violence occurs?'[55] asks Honderich. His conclusion is that 'violence does render such systems considerably less democractic than otherwise they might be.'[56] This seems clear enough — and a view Rawls would certainly agree with — but Honderich goes on, surprisingly, to say 'We must not make too much of this conclusion. It would be a mistake to make it decisive.'[57] He will explain later, he tells us. Later he says 'There is...a moral justification for *some but not all...democratic violence...*[if] it serves the ends of freedom, or equality, or both'.[58] He does not explain how this is possible. If (as he said previously on p. 104) democracy is the system which best promotes freedom and if freedom and equality are integrally related (p. 107) and if violence renders the system less democratic (p. 101), it does not seem possible to accept his so-called moral justification. On what principles is the moral system which does the justifying based?

Honderich seems — the line of argument is by no means clear — to proceed as follows: 'democratic practice...excludes coercion' and a 'part of what is excluded...is violence'. There are two kinds of coercion: 'the coercion of force and the coercion of persuasion'.[59] He distinguishes between the two on what seems to be the ground that choice is possible under the coercion of persuasion — choice being absent under force — but he denies that all instances of coercion fall clearly into one category or the other.[60]

He argues that 'governments are not subjected to the coercion of force' by violent acts and that 'the case is similar with electorates and with candidates'; he concludes that 'democratic

---

[55] *Ibid.*, pp. 98-9.
[56] *Ibid.*, p. 101.
[57] *Ibid.*, p. 102.
[58] *Ibid.*, pp. 109-10.
[59] *Ibid.*, p. 110.
[60] *Ibid.*, p. 112.

violence...consists only in the coercion of persuasion'[61] and that it may be 'an attempt to secure *equality* of influence'.[62] Then he reaches the remarkable final conclusion that 'some bombs are like votes.'[63]

How on earth did we move from 'violence does render such a system less democratic' to the idea 'bombs are like votes'? Honderich has manifestly contradicted himself, but how did he convince *himself* that he was following a reasonable argument? The key to his defence of violence in a democracy is the assertion that 'governments are not subjected to the coercion of force.' If this is so, it is difficult to see how what looks like force is in fact 'persuasion'. What 'persuasion' is operating if it is not the threat of harm to those who rely on the government to prevent the 'persuasion' of bombs? One can agree that at no time during even the worst of the civil disorders of the Sixties did anyone doubt that the government had the resources to end the tyranny of the minorities involved; but one of the principal characteristics of democratic systems is that they are systems of justice (persuasion) not of power (force) and that just as a democratic legal system allows thousands of the guilty to escape rather than be unjust towards one innocent man, it will also permit an astounding amount of unjustifiable opposition rather than exercise its power to control it. Advocates of violence argue that minorities have a right to use society as a hostage in 'persuading' the government to accede to their demands; the practice, they say, is not really criminal because the government has the power to solve such problems with bombs and gas chambers.

But democratic governments do not in fact have such power because they are not systems of power but systems of controlling power — systems of justice — as Honderich himself admits. It is his shift from the concept of democracy as a system of justice to democracy as a system of power that enables him to reach his extraordinary conclusion; it is detaching 'equality' from the system of justice and making *it* the criterion of justice that enables him to do this. If you conceive of democracy primarily in terms of 'equality', democracy becomes a system of power with

---

[61] *Ibid.*, p. 113.
[62] *Ibid.*, p. 114.
[63] *Ibid.*, p. 115.

'justice' demanding that the unequal be free to use 'equalizers' like guns and bombs.

Totalitarianism and the Redistribution of Property

In Wolff's view, *A Theory of Justice* is 'before all else, an argument for substantial redistributions of income and wealth' and 'would require very considerable political power to enforce.... The men and women who apply the principle...will be the most powerful persons in the society.'[64] In short, he sees totalitarian implications, which — he argues — are not adequately taken into account by Rawls because his theory 'abstracts from the significant factors determining the nature and development of social reality.'[65] Thus, although Rawls's difference principle 'does not posit a given, once-for-all bundle of goods and services that must be distributed', but only requires that 'any *inequality surplus* be redistributed...the veil of ignorance [the vagueness of the calculations and estimates we are forced to make] has the effect of making all considerations on the production side so thoroughly hypothetical, so *abstract* in the bad sense, that inevitably the difference principle comes to be construed as a pure distribution principle.'[66]

In terms of totalitarianism, Wolff's fundamental objection here is that Rawls 'seems to have no conception of the generation, deployment, limitations, or problems of political power. In a word, he has no theory of the *State*.'[67] This is a very odd remark to make about a contract theory. By definition it is a theory of the State and the distribution of power. It is true that Rawls's theory does not provide a constitution, but — as other critics have pointed out — it is really a defence of existing constitutional arrangements against those who deny they fulfill the requirements of the abstract norms of equality and freedom. If there is anything inadequate in present democratic controls on power, we must not look to Rawls for their correction or suppose he is indifferent to them because he does not understand the

---

[64]Robert Paul Wolff, *Understanding Rawls* (Princeton, 1977), p. 202.
[65]*Ibid.*, p. 204.
[66]*Ibid.*, p. 201.
[67]*Ibid.*, p. 202.

importance of democratic institutional arrangements or for any other reasons. The question is not whether he supports or recognizes their importance — he obviously does — but whether anything he says is incompatible with them. Wolff's argument on redistribution is that such is the case.

If so, as Wolff implies, the 'inequality surplus' which is to be redistributed cannot in fact be distinguished from the kind of redistribution that would occur under the 'from each according to his ability, to each according to his needs' principle, one would be prone to see totalitarian implications, but not for the reasons suggested by Wolff. This kind of redistribution would be so much at odds with our concept of property that it would lead to a resistance which could be met only by an increase of the State's coercive power. But if 'redistribution' takes into account the fact that part of our sense of justice demands private property and that no other element in the concept of justice can override this, then Rawls's formulation — no matter how vague — cannot be mistaken for an argument that 'justice' demands the elimination of private property, or such a major redistribution that resistance and coercion become inevitable. What matters is the sense of justice, not the degree of change. Social change itself does not imply totalitarianism unless it brings about a change in the controls on political power.[68] Wolff's argument about the changes in 'power' produced by changes in legislation does not adequately analyse the precise changes involved under such circumstances.

It is a common argument that certain types of legislation are undemocratic and that the ever-increasing body of legislation is 'totalitarian' in tendency because while increasing regulation of

---

[68]It is true, though, that a drastic social change may bring about a change in the *effective control* on political power. What is the result when a democratic government uses its power to re-distribute income and in doing so largely destroys the well-educated middle class? This has certainly happened in Britain over the past thirty years. In consequence, the influence of the very people who are best qualified to assess what the government is doing, is greatly weakened.

An impoverished intelligentsia is much less able to debate the actions and proposals of government and organize effective opposition to measures that may be against the best interest of the nation. There is, furthermore, no one to replace them and thereby constitute a danger to the rulers. The Communists have for a long time grasped the situation well. Their preference of course lies with more radical measures than taxation. The recent example of Cambodia — where professional classes were wiped out — can attest to this.

the individual by the State it entails a greater degree of restriction on freedom. This is a strange view by those who believe that the fundamental argument for democracy is that it gives less autonomy than any other system to the policy-making group. The argument says nothing at all about the type or quantity of legislation allowable: only that it is a factor violating the fundamental proposition. Legislation that hindered our present controls would certainly be a move away from democracy, but legislation that limited the freedoms or rights we now enjoy would not necessarily be in the direction of totalitarianism in any meaningful sense. It is not true that legislation is the crucial difference between the systems. It is controls on power which are crucial and which define the difference.

The fact that today, through income and estate taxes, democratic governments have the power to make major redistributions of private property in a way that was not possible at the turn of the century has not affected democratic controls on government.[69] Nor have the civil servants responsible for the collection and redistribution of income achieved any special political power: in this sense, those in the income tax branch do not differ from the postal service employees. Wolff's argument, however, is that 'One need not know many of the basic facts of society to recognize that it would require very considerable political power to enforce the sorts of wage rates, tax policies, transfer payments, and job regulation called for by the difference principle. The men and women who apply the principle...will be the most powerful persons in the society.'[70]

Considering the great changes in distribution that have taken place since the turn of the century without such dire results, the facts are clearly against Wolff. The increase in government 'power' has taken place within a system that controls the effects of such an increase. Under non-democratic systems, officials who in recent times implemented policies of this type did indeed

---

[69] One should note, however, a tendency towards a hidden and 'non-accountable' government power. Thus in Britain there has been a considerable increase during recent years in the number of government agencies which have taxing powers but are 'hidden from view'. They send out bills for vaguely specified reasons, but no one seems to know what *legal* authority they have. The man-in-the-street is almost powerless to protect himself against them: a potentially serious breach in democratic control.

[70] Wolff, *op. cit.*, p. 202.

attain the kind of power Wolff foresees under Rawls's redistribution, but this occurred precisely because in each case the system was already undemocratic — there were no adequate controls on the exercise of power. If Wolff is to establish that there are totalitarian implications in Rawls, he will have to demonstrate that the system of justice departs from the system of democratic controls.

Rawls's Norm of Justice and Theory of Justice

In considering anyone's propositions about the 'good', one must first be clear what his fundamental position — or the norm of norms — is. Yet, to my knowledge, commentators on Rawls have not taken up his clearly-stated fundamental principle of justice: 'Each person possesses an inviolability founded on justice that even the welfare of society as a whole cannot override.'[71] 'Therefore', he says, 'the liberties of equal citizenship are taken as settled'.

Rawls's other basic propositions include one that appears designed to cope with relativist objections to those who put forward *any* normative propositions: 'The only thing that permits us to acquiesce in an erroneous theory is the lack of a better one.' He also has a proposition which is essential to our understanding of the difference principle: 'an injustice is tolerable only when it is necessary to avoid an even greater injustice.'[72] But again the fundamental proposition, the norm of norms, the very essence of justice is: 'Each person possesses an inviolability...that even the welfare of the society...cannot override.'

It might be interesting to examine the comments on Rawls in the light of this proposition and the degree to which they either disagree with it or subordinate it to some other norm such as equality or liberty (in some sense other than that given to it by Rawls's fundamental norm). One might also raise the general question of why it has been overlooked despite its primacy in the book, and whether it really expresses 'our intuitive conviction of the primacy of justice.'[73]

[71]Rawls, *op. cit.*, p. 3.
[72]*Ibid.*, p. 4.
[73]*Ibid.*

Rawls's theory of justice speaks of two 'principles' of justice: (1) the principle of greatest equal liberty and (2) (a) the principle of (fair) equality of opportunity and (b) the difference principle.[74] The commentators have naturally accepted these as fundamental norms rather than theoretical propositions derived from a norm (as Rawls makes clear in his initial statement, quoted above). The question, it seems to me, is whether it really follows from the norm that 'the liberties of equal citizenship are taken as settled' or whether the statement about liberty is to be taken as a separate norm — which we also intuitively accept and whose relation to the first norm is now in doubt, unless we also intuitively know their respective ranks.

Rawls's formulation requires us to suppose that the liberty norm is an axiom of the individualist norm: if each of us is inviolable with regard to State or society, we necessarily have by nature equal citizenship. But why should this be, or putting the question another way, what does this mean? Are we looking at an intrinsic good, inviolability, and an extrinsic one, equal liberty? Rawls's book of course, attempts to answer the question of what the 'therefore' means; the real question however is whether any kind of 'therefore' is possible without introducing a number of other 'intuitive' norms. The problem is not that disagreements are likely to increase as we increase the number of intuitively recognized norms — Occam's razor that assumptions must not be multiplied does not seem to apply to ethics — but rather that even one more norm immediately raises an insoluble conflict about their respective positions in a normative hierarchy. There is not much point in agreeing about norms if we cannot agree on what is primary. The critics of Rawls who question the 'justness' of his justice do not in fact reject his intuitive judgements on the norms but the priorities he assigns them; many feel that he gives inadequate attention to equality and the freedoms that follow from assigning it priority. It matters very much, then, whether Rawls's 'therefore' introduces a subsidiary axiomatic statement about 'equality' or a separate intuitively apprehended norm. The crucial question raised by Rawls's book is overlooked: Do we or can we agree that 'inviolability of the individual' is the fundamental norm of

---

[74]See: *ibid.*, pp. 302-3.

'justice'; and further — does this norm contain an axiom about 'equality'?

Rawls's norm, as we may call it, maintains that I cannot justly be compelled to sacrifice my welfare or goods for the sake of some supposedly greater good, though I am free to do so voluntarily. Each of us can presumably make the same statement and in that sense is equal. Inasmuch as we depart from that situation ('you *must* share your goods with others', etc.) we depart from the primary principle of justice. But 'equality' on this level permits major discrepancies in the distribution of goods and declares in effect that the norm of justice has nothing to say about the matter. Other norms may, but the social norm — justice — the one that determines what we can be compelled to do, does not.

Let us suppose that some new philosophic insight enabled us to say that the desired good entailed an equal distribution of goods. Would that alter the concept of 'justice'? No, because the primary concept is that the individual cannot justly be coerced even into being 'good' (compare Rousseau!) without the society becoming unjust.[75]

Suppose, however, that major inequalities could be shown so to alter the relation between individuals (or the relations between individuals and the State) that the individual was no longer inviolable, that he was being coerced — through extreme poverty for instance — to make choice meaningful to him. We would say then that justice requires some measure of interference. In other words, the individual is not absolutely inviolable, as we supposed, but only *relatively* so. (The axiom 'therefore the liberties of equal citizenship' is being invoked.) But what is this relative point? Critics of Rawls's 'maximin' theory (a tendency to minimize risks) object to its vagueness. They want to keep to absolutes such as those possible if you begin with 'equality'. But if you do that, you must abandon the intuitive 'inviolability' and replace it with a kind of equality — literal equality — which is by no means intuitive. It seems that the question to be faced is whether we want or can agree to the inviolability principle and the subordinate very

[75] A proposal to use coercion would sound very odd to law reform commissions because although we have a right to punish criminals — in order to protect ourselves — we have no right to reform them.

qualified axiom about equality, or whether we want and can agree upon some other primary principle. When we have answered this question, we can proceed to the actual theory of justice.

In Defence of Yves R. Simon

The Common Good and Relativism

The importance of Simon's views on the democratic norms of equality and freedom, discussed in his *Philosophy of Democratic Government* (1951), can be attributed to the fact that he analyses them primarily in terms of their capacity to promote the 'common good' or the *entire body of normative principles*. Simon speaks of the 'common good' and 'virtue', whose exact nature is not known to us and hence is not defined (or definable), but is nonetheless acceptable as a meaningful concept: just as 'reality' cannot be defined although it is not only acceptable but necessary to a particular discussion of any of its aspects. Simon pursues this line instead of adopting the relativist view that freedom and equality are the norms defining a democratic society and analysing either the difficulties of maintaining a balance between them or the degree to which particular institutions and practices in democratic society are consistent with, contribute to or detract from the two norms. Instead of attempting to define 'freedom' and 'equality' as the common good, Simon leaves the latter term undefined and discusses both norms in terms of their contribution to it.

Simon's approach raises the following question: if we do not — and perhaps cannot — define all the terms in a proposition (whether ethical or factual), is the proposition still meaningful? Specifically, do we have to be able to define 'common good' in order to assert that 'the common good demands that a problem of united action which cannot be solved by way of unanimity should be solved by way of authority'?[76]

Those who think in purely democratic terms of 'freedom' and 'equality', as if these were the only terms we need consider, will certainly find Simon's view dubious. For them, the 'real' issue is

---

[76]Yves R. Simon, *Philosophy of Democratic Government* [1951] (Chicago, 1961), p. 30.

the relation between the 'authority' (mentioned by Simon) and the equality and freedom under discussion, for in effect they are replacing the term 'common good' with the terms 'freedom' and 'equality' and arriving at a highly dubious proposition.

The difference between the two points of view can be illustrated by drawing an analogy between chemical and ethical analysis. For Simon, the 'common good' appears to be an element in his ethical system, an element which is not further reducible. For others, the 'common good' is a compound whose elements are 'freedom' and 'equality' — just as sugar is a compound of carbon, hydrogen and oxygen — and the task of ethical analysis is to discover the exact proportion of the two elements ('freedom' and 'equality') and their structural interrelation.

Is Simon's discussion of freedom and equality in terms of the common good legitimate? Are we not needlessly mutiplying terms when we reason as if at least one further term is necessary — the common good? Is not this readiness to multiply ethical terms and leave them undefined dangerously close to the essentially relativist view that ethical terms are fundamentally arbitrary and nothing more than reflections of personal attitudes?

In essence, the relativist view is that there is no method of reaching agreement about the 'truth' of ethical propositions. But where there is agreement about the 'good' of particular propositions — as is the case with freedom and equality in societies defining democracy as good — we can at least discuss the relationship between these terms. Furthermore, because the only 'goods' agreed upon are the defining goods of freedom and equality, the 'common good' can only be a body of principles and practices that can be fitted into these concepts. Hence, if it can be established that violence promotes freedom or equality, violence must be accepted as an extrinsic good, despite its further consequences — the consequences it has in terms of other norms. (These other norms are also extrinsic goods which serve freedom and equality.) As Simon observes: 'Not so long ago...it was rather commonly believed that fanaticism was what causes man to feel ruthless toward his fellowmen; it was hoped, accordingly, that the end of dogmas would be a decisive step in the conquest of cruelty. Agnosticism was considered the essence of humanitarianism...[but] in times of social and political convulsions, a skeptical thinker, an agnostic intellectual, may reveal that his sense for the absolute, diverted from being by idealism, rendered acute by culture, and frustrated by doubt, has grown into a destructive frenzy.'[77] Although the passage is rather obscurely phrased, Simon does recognize that it is not a passionate sense of justice that accounts for some of the more horrendous events of modern times but a narrow sense of absolutes, an utter inability to think in terms of the 'common good'. We may be unable to define the common good, but we tend to believe that freedom and equality are to be understood in terms of it — as analysed by Simon — and that the reverse procedure is illegitimate. (Thus few people would agree that the use of violence to achieve equality or freedom is a good.)

Is this intuitive sense of the place of freedom and equality in the scheme of things legitimate, or are we logically compelled to reject Simon's analysis as based on an illusory concept? Can we validly assert that there is a term — the common good — which, although itself not definable, includes something more than 'freedom' and 'equality'?

Logically, of course, if we can legitimize terms by using them in definitions, we can multiply our terms indefinitely and construct wholly artificial systems having no relation to reality. However, if we want to talk about something supposedly real or meaningful — such as democracy — the question is whether the defining terms define anything other than the terms defined. In physics, the two terms 'energy' and 'matter' — which define the whole of 'reality' — are interchangeable forms of the same thing, which remain undefined. This is not true of the terms 'freedom' and 'equality'. There is no formulation showing their interrelationship or any way of arriving at one, nor any way to derive (theoretically) all hypothetic 'goods' from them, as there is — at least in theory — a way of deriving all known forms of matter and energy from atomic structure. We accept the dichotomy of energy and matter because we can show their interrelationship, not because we arbitrarily defined reality in those terms.

The assertion 'There is a common good intuitively felt' is

[77]*Ibid.*, pp. 91-2.

parallel to 'There is a physical reality perceptible to our senses'. From the first proposition, whose real meaning is unknown to us, we can begin to deduce its components. We cannot do it by *fiat*, for this would yield only 'A common good intuitively felt by me', whereas what we need is a generally acceptable good. If we try to take those elements in the hypothetic common good that are generally acceptable and use them to replace the unknown elements, we are confronted by the fact that most people do not accept the substitution: for them, 'freedom' and 'equality' do not and cannot replace the term 'common good', any more than 'energy' and 'matter' can replace the term 'reality'.

Of what use is a discussion of equality and freedom in terms of an unknown quantity, the 'common good'? Does it not make terms already vague even more so? We have to recognize, however, that such an approach is philosophically sounder than the practice of those who seek to keep within the confines of definitions. It is certainly not logically necessary that all terms in a proposition be known. More important, the concept of 'common good' by its very vagueness prevents the kind of logical narrowing of concepts and the resultant fanaticism that we see in totalitarian ideologies or among those who follow the logic of the democratic norms of freedom and equality to arrive at distinctly non-democratic conclusions. The concept of the good remains open.

Simon's Theory in Our Time

Presumably because it is self-evident that one cannot talk about a normative concept such as democracy without assuming that normative concepts are meaningful, Simon marshals his arguments as if the need to use norms was beyond question. He simply dismisses the behavioural sciences as irrelevant. Behaviouralists, on the other hand, dismiss a normative discussion of norms as 'unscientific'. Imagine the reaction of a behaviouralist to Simon's discussion of the pedagogical theory of coercion: 'Aquinas describes with great clarity the pedagogical theory of coercion: by compelling mischievous characters not to commit the bad actions toward which their will is inclined, society creates in them, in spite of their ill will, a system of good habits.... When coercion has succeeded in destroying such inclinations as extreme laziness, intemperance, and violent anger, no element of virtue has been brought into existence, but virtuous acts are much less difficult to elicit.'[78]

If the behaviouralist were tolerant, he might ignore the reference to the authority of Aquinas and the effect of 'will' and say: 'Yes, there is some evidence that coercion — fear — can modify behaviour, but Skinner and others have shown that other forms of behaviour modification are more effective. You talk of laziness, intemperance and violent anger as controllable by coercive methods, but these are vague terms obviously derived from the seven deadly sins. In behavioural analysis the first two do not have any clear referent and the last is as 'natural' a response as 'fear'; hence it is doubtful that it can be modified by some form of coercion — or anything else. Furthermore, you wish to modify them because they are 'obstacles to virtue', but what specific behaviour do you have in mind? If there is one, why not directly modify behaviour so that it is certain that the type you desire will result? Indeed, how can there be such a thing as an obstacle to virtue? There is only desired behaviour and undesired behaviour; the only 'obstacle' is the existence of some type that is undesired.' (Such a response, it should be noted, does not raise the issue of relativism. Anyone who makes any kind of recommendation about behaviour *ipso facto* abandons relativism as a guide to the analysis of behaviour.)

The fundamental difference between Simon and the hypothetical behaviouralist is the issue of free will versus determinism. To Simon, the existence of 'coercion' in a State promoting 'freedom' is a normative problem (for 'coercion' certainly violates the exercise of free will; hence it is necessary to advance an argument which suggests that in practice the object of free will — virtue — is or can be enhanced by State coercion). To the behaviouralist, 'coercion' is a type of determinism which derives its meaning not from the concept of freedom — as it does for Simon — but from the concept of 'violence'. The only problem which the State's coercive machinery poses for the behaviouralist is the purely practical one of whether it is in fact capable of modifying behaviour.

The two points of view are irreconcilable. Simon would feel the behaviouralist had totally misunderstood the main gist of his

[78]*Ibid.*, pp. 110-11.

argument. The behaviouralist would say that Simon had talked about wholly imaginary issues and had dismissed the body of experimentally-based evidence which supports the theory of determinism in human behaviour. It may well be that, if democracy survives, Simon's views will be reconsidered and that his views will receive the acclaim they deserve. But democracy is not likely to survive if most persons of influence in our society (such as politicians, intellectuals and clergymen) come to regard meaningful norms as mere descriptions of types of behaviour and believe that these types are the result of determining factors in our environment. Under the latter assumption, a democratic façade could be preserved for a long period of time. All we have to assume is that democratic institutions and practices are 'goods' to be promoted by the various methods at our disposal, including perhaps coercion, as in the frequently revived recommendations for compulsory voting. Simon, of course, and those who accept his view of norms would feel that the result would not be 'democracy' any more than coerced virtue would be virtue. At any given point of time it might be impossible to distinguish empirically between genuine virtue or genuine democracy and the determined forms.

The concept of determinism implies involuntary change. Determinism requires us to believe that democracy as we understand it today will almost inevitably change one day, quite arbitrarily, into something different. It is hostile to interpretations of human behaviour based on the belief that changes in behaviour are not inevitable but 'chosen' in accordance with norms. Determinists have never been able to explain either the continuities in human behaviour or the sudden changes that empirical evidence clearly reveals. Behaviour can remain the same for centuries or change overnight — as in cases of conversion to some set of normative principles such as Christianity.

The ultimate issue between Simon's approach and that of the behaviouralists is the question of which point of view is more consistent with the facts. Empirical evidence suggests that Simon's view is correct. Modern behavioural sciences have adopted the position that the science of human behaviour must be consistent with the methodology of the physical sciences which is based on determinism; and that if this results in obvious violations of empiricism, we must simply wait until the violations can be explained away as illusions.

Few people realize just how 'unempirical' even modern physical science is, let alone the behavioural sciences. (Thus there was overwhelming evidence at the turn of the century for Alfred Wegener's theory of continental drift — evidence that could not be, and was not, explained in any other way. His theory was rejected on the ground that the continents 'could not' drift, although no theory and no evidence was adduced in support of this contention. The latter was a 'truth' as absolute and unquestioned as any of the assumptions of the Scholastics. It remained 'true' until the 1960s when the theory of plate tectonics enabled geophysicists to acknowledge the empirical evidence.) It is most improbable that Simon's approach will be accepted, no matter how strong the empirical evidence in its favour, until there emerges a normative theory of human behaviour that not only fits the empirical evidence but shows that a deterministic analysis is false.

Behaviouralism, Biosociology and the Perils of Biobehaviouralism

It is generally agreed that such knowledge as we have is derived from evidence supplied by our senses: there is an observer and someone or something observed. Hence came a self-evident truth that we therefore must develop two distinct branches of knowledge — knowledge of the observer and knowledge of the person or thing observed — each based on the evidence of the senses, interdependent, yet each necessarily considered separately. What helped promote the dichotomy was the widespread belief in both the separate creation of man and objective reality. Empirical evidence served the same purpose because the attributes of the inanimate world remained the same (unless influenced by some external factor), whereas man differed from moment to moment. On the one hand, we talked of the 'facts' about things and the 'cause' or 'causes' of any changes; on the other, of the 'behaviour' of man (since he is always 'changing'). We used the concept of norm or value to explain this behaviour just as we used 'causation' to explain the world of the inanimate. If physical science studied the world of things and employed the concept of causation to explain its characteristics, normative science or ethics studied human behaviour, using 'norms' to explain the differences between men. The distinction had — and still has — a solid empirical basis. The theory of evolution, however, implied that we must bring man into the same system as that operating in the inanimate world and, further, that we must disregard the empirical evidence against such a view. In the field of politics, the behaviouralists eagerly accepted the challenge. Political theorists, however, resisted; they did so not because they had less faith in evolution but because, paradoxically, behaviouralism took us too far away from actual human behaviour. The political theorist insists that even if ultimately causation cannot be eliminated as a method of analysis, the immediate situation as regards behaviour has not changed: norms profoundly affect human behaviour, so that ignoring their immediate influence in order to find ultimate causes is a dangerous mistake. It takes us away from a consideration of what we know to be important — for example, concepts of democracy and sovereignty — to focus on hypothetical sources for the norms at particular times and places. The result is always triviality. It is precisely this feature of behaviouralism, triviality, that accounts for the questions raised and the now ten-year old tendency to move to a 'post-behaviouralist' era. But this in itself seems a lopsided approach. The 'post-behaviouralist' era has been with us from the beginning. The immediate and important 'facts' about behaviour are normative facts; what we need is to analyse them appropriately.

How difficult it is for behaviouralists to face this problem emerges clearly from John C. Wahlke's statement[79] in which he deplores the 'preoccupation with attitudes' and 'neglect of behaviour' exhibited by present-day scholars. To Wahlke, 'most

[79]John C. Wahlke's presidential address 'Pre-Behavioralism in Political Science' *(The American Political Science Review*, Vol. LXXIII, No. 1 [March 1979], pp. 9-31) is highly critical of post-behaviouralism: he accuses the post-behavioural era of being too pre-behavioural. The paper, written almost a decade after David Easton's 'post-behavioural manifesto', is an astonishingly retrograde step. To call now for a true behaviouralism is like advocating a return to Stalinism a decade after the condemnation of Stalin's crimes by the 20th Party Congress! But this anachronistic judgement is not Wahlke's only failing. He uncritically assesses the possible role of biology (or biosociology) in the study of politics and by doing so springs a trap for himself. The irony of it all is that the article reveals the bankruptcy of behaviouralism.

of the variables of individual political behaviour investigated by political behaviour research are not conceived in behavioural terms at all, but are defined as entities whose existence and character can only be indirectly inferred, never empirically established.'[80] He is here, at least partly, talking about 'norms', since they are commonly defined as attitudes. Given that he is (at least in part) protesting against the normative element in behaviouralism the basis of the appeal is truly astonishing. Note especially the words 'can only be *inferred*, never *empirically* established' [emphasis added]. The implication is that for him 'empiricism' excludes deduction: what you cannot directly point to is none-empirical. This, incidentally, goes far beyond what Hempel calls the 'narrower thesis of empiricism' — that all 'true' statements can be reduced to empirical statements. Even 'narrow empiricism' allows inference. Nothing that can be called 'science' could exist without it. We would simply have vast assemblages of unrelated observations, which — if they proved anything — would prove solipsism.

To what extent is Wahlke's formulation just an unfortunate lapse, a matter of our catching him out on something he did not intend to say? To answer this we have to keep in mind that the social scientist — while presumably required to agree with the philosopher's views about the nature of norms — cannot, unlike the philosopher, dismiss them as failing to fit the philosophic definition of 'truth'. For the social scientist, norms remain facts about human behaviour; he has to decide whether they are some kind of end product without further effects or whether they are part of a cause-effect sequence. In either case, they are to him an important phenomenon that requires careful consideration; they seem to be unique to human behaviour. If Wahlke admits this (and it is hard to see how he can do otherwise for he accepts the need to use various approaches, including that of the non-behavioural school, in the study of politics), he is not justified in condemning behaviouralism for being 'preoccupied with attitudes' and pre-behaviouralism for corrupting, as it were, the purity of behaviouralism. Nor can he suppose that post-behaviouralism requires an abandonment of the pre-behaviouralist elements; rather it should be more thoroughly

---

[80]*Ibid.*, p. 20.

pre-behaviouralist. The alternative is for the social sciences to abandon inference and become thoroughly solipsistic.

But although Wahlke regards the use of inference (and even analogy) — for the purpose of analysing the nature and effect of norms — as unscientific, he urges its use in the analysis of human nature. We must, he says, overcome our 'behavioural illiteracy' or, in the words of Konrad Lorenz that he quotes, recognize that 'behavioural patterns are just as conservatively and reliably characteristic of species as are the forms of bones, teeth or any other bodily structures' and that 'behaviour patterns have an evolution exactly like that of organs.'[81]

Among biologists, Lorenz is noted for ignoring the very points which his own quotation emphasizes. His study of aggression ignores man's closest living relative — the chimpanzee — and draws instead on the behaviour of unrelated species. (Indeed, Lorenz's interest in behaviour makes him reverse normal biological procedures — as when classifying dogs according to their behavioural characteristics rather than their anatomy). Lorenz's shortcomings do not invalidate the observation quoted by Wahlke. But they help us to realize the major difficulty faced by those who wish to apply knowledge of animal behaviour to the study of human behaviour: not only is man the only member of his species, but also the only member of his genus and — according to some — the only member of his family. Biologists know that man is not closely enough related to other animals to make comparisons between human and animal behaviour convincing. Those biosociologists who are biologists certainly know this and consequently limit speculations about biological patterns to evidence drawn from human behaviour; those among them who are not biologists seem to be unaware of the uniqueness of man. (This may partly account for the tendency among the biosociologically-oriented to revive W. McDougall's instinct school that flourished in the early part of this century.)

Biosociology, so long as it limits its evidence to cross-cultural phenomena and man's history, is worthy of consideration, though perhaps unlikely to produce significant results. Ever since Aristotle, man has tried to explain his behaviour in terms

[81] *Ibid.*, p. 25.

of his 'nature'; we are still seeking for universal biologically-based traits. Nevertheless, the revival of biosociology is understandable as an attempt to expand the set of *drives* that psychoanalysts assume to be the basis of all human behaviour; at present there are not enough known 'drives' to account for all the patterns which this behaviour takes. Two options are open. We can either try to multiply the number of drives behind behavioural patterns or abandon the idea that biology and the concept of 'drive' can explain behaviour. Wahlke seems to think that adoption of the second position by political scientists is 'unscientific'. In fact the reverse is true: this position is the logical alternative to one that empirical evidence has shown to be dubious, to say the least.

Wahlke's type of biobehaviouralism appears to go beyond the current school of biosociology (as represented, for instance, by Edward O. Wilson). 'Most of us are aware,' he says, 'of many examples of..."pre-programmed" behaviour patterns...[such as] the stylized nest-building of Baltimore orioles, the courtship dances of bower birds, the ritualized mate-seeking and domicile-building of beavers.'[82] To Wahlke, the 'pre-programmed' behaviour is a 'principle' that everyone, except those identified with biopolitics, shies away from on the grounds that man is a 'cultural', not an 'instinctual' animal. 'But this argument dodges the main issue', he says, and quotes in support René Dubos's statement that 'Culture is an expression of man's response to the physical and human environment...evolution always involves learning from experience. The learning may take place by storage of genetic information by chromosomes, by accumulation of knowledge and skills in the individual organism, or by transmission...in institutions or in society as a whole.'[83]

Wahlke's article is distinguished by two main points: firstly, he argues for a revival of the instinct school of behaviourism;

---

[82]*Ibid.*

[83]*Ibid.*, p. 26. Dubos's statement does not support Wahlke. At least as quoted by Wahlke, the statements about culture and evolution are logically separate. (Incidentally, the two page numbers given by Wahlke with reference to Dubos's book *So Human an Animal* (1968) are incorrect.) However, whether Wahlke has read something into Dubos that is not there is beside the point. It is Wahlke's position, not Dubos's, that is at issue.

secondly, he favours a (discredited) form of determinism, as revealed by his frequent and obviously-savoured use of the expression 'pre-programmed'.

The analogy between the human brain and computers is peculiarly attractive to determinists, for computers have to be programmed — or to put it another way, their 'behaviour' has to be determined. Hence if it could be shown that computers can even in theory perform any human task, the case for determinism would receive very powerful support. But even in theory, computers can equal human performance only if every possible contingency can be foreseen and programmed for (by human beings): this, of course, is impossible since human beings do not have that much knowledge of the future. On the other hand, we can cope with wholly new experiences, whereas computers are helpless when confronted with anything that is not in their programmes. Unless they already know what 'adjustment' to make, they cannot adjust, for they are quite unable to conceptualize — hence unable to learn.

But if the modishness of computer analogies helps to explain the revival of instinct theory, doubts about the validity of the analogy do not discredit the instinct theory itself. To do this, we need to examine what we 'mean' when we talk of instinct. We speak of 'instinct' with reference to behaviour by the lower animals that resembles rational behaviour although no such thing is possible: Darwin finches use thorns to pry grubs from trees, for their beaks are not adapted to the purpose as are those of woodpeckers; spiders use principles of tension and resultant forces familiar to engineers; bees have incredibly complex dances that indicate the distance, direction, type of flower and quantity of nectar available. The problem is that although the behaviour in each of these cases looks rational, it surely cannot be so, for the rest of the animals' behaviour does not reveal any evidence of superior intellect.

It is the evolutionary theory which offers a fairly satisfactory solution to the problem. Bearing in mind the nature of the problem — that the behaviour in question looks intelligent but cannot be so — the first point is that such behaviour must be biologically advantageous. The premise is that rational behaviour, if biologically possible, is biologically advantageous. The evolution of the human brain is explicable only on the ground that it is biologically advantageous to develop a brain capable of allowing non-determined responses. If the organism followed a determined pattern (as many lower forms of life do) and the physical environment also followed a determined pattern (as we are certain it does), the 'appropriateness' of the biological behaviour to the actual situation would be a matter of chance, and therefore biologically disadvantageous. Thus the more closely we approach determinism in biological response, the closer we come to biological disadvantage, for the two 'sets' of determinism may well be 'out of phase'. If, then, a 'rational' response (in the sense which 'rational' has in non-deterministic philosophy) is made possible by man's brain, we can explain the evolution of the brain. It provides the non-determined behaviour needed to cope with a determined system that is separate from the biological system.

Rational behaviour (such as using tools and constructing shelters) is so advantageous that we find its parallels even where the brain has not evolved sufficiently for the organism to be consciously aware of what it is doing — as with the nest-building of the Baltimore orioles, mentioned by Wahlke. Biology accounts for such behaviour by postulating that genetic changes due to sheer chance may occasionally lead to biologically advantageous behaviour that — because it confers a differential survival rate — becomes characteristic of the species. Although this behaviour may look intelligent, in fact it is not.

There is an empirical difference between intelligent and instinctive behaviour. What we call 'instinctive' behaviour is followed even when it is inappropriate. Thus an army of ants that marches through the jungle is not following the principles of a human army: if its leaders happen to circle to the rear, the ants will march steadily around in a circle until they all perish from inanition. What they are in fact following is a chemical scent left by other ants. Parallels to such blind pursuit of 'instinctive' patterns are not found in humans. (This is one of the reasons why we draw a distinction between 'rational' behaviour and 'instinctive' behaviour.) As compared with rational behaviour, instinctive behaviour can be biologically disadvantageous.

The main objection to the application of instinct theory to man is that instinct and reason are incompatible. The incompatibility arises from the fact that instinctive behaviour is seemingly rational behaviour which in fact is a determined response (biologically advantageous) to stimuli where a rational response is not possible. We find many examples of instinctive behaviour among insects, birds and fish; fewer such patterns among mammals; and fewer still among men. If rational behaviour is possible, it is a far superior alternative, because by definition it is always appropriate to current circumstances; instinctive behaviour, on the other hand, is only generally appropriate to biological requirements. Consequently, the instinctivist school has, strictly speaking, to deny even the possibility of rational behaviour. Empirical evidence strongly supports the view that man's behaviour is 'rational', in the sense of 'appropriate to the circumstances', rather than 'the most prudent imaginable', or expressed in any other terms which imply that we bring to bear our total body of knowledge when making decisions. (Computers evidently do this but humans do not; otherwise we would never have doubts or regrets. It is necessary to insist on this rather limited definition of 'rational' because the determinist school has achieved a certain amount of plausibility by pretending that behaviour is not rational if it can be shown that some other course of action would have been more advantageous.) If we insist on the above (limited) definition, it becomes apparent that instinct cannot explain man's behaviour because it is very seldom 'inappropriate', unlike instinctive animal behaviour. On those occasions when the behaviour is inappropriate, we look towards determinism rather than rationality: we look, for instance, towards the conditioning factors in phobias, or the habit patterns in inappropriate motor responses (compulsive behaviour), or the influence of emotion (as in panic and rage responses). On the whole, however, human behaviour is characteristically rational: we use this fact to define abnormal behaviour.

Instinctive behaviour has still another drawback when compared with rational behaviour: it requires that the organism confine itself to the particular biological niche to which evolution has adapted it. Thus animals adapted to the arctic (desert or forest) cannot survive elsewhere. Man, on the other hand, has been able to cope with any environment where life is possible without adapting biologically. (Various groups of humans have been isolated from each other long enough to be potentially able to evolve different species with different 'instincts', but — since we have not become differentiated into species — one can conclude that we have never adjusted to the environment by biological selection.)

The empirical evidence against the instinctivist school is so overwhelming that we must look elsewhere for explanations of its revival. One of them is rather brazenly foisted upon the discipline by Wahlke as if it were a virtue: 'Instead of arguing about learning or inheritance, nature or nurture, genetics or culture, political scientists can more profitably observe political phenomena carefully, identify and describe accurately whatever widespread patterns of behaviour they detect, and ask to what extent those patterns embody the kind of species-characteristic, preprogrammed behaviour studied by ethologists.'[84]

Wahlke urges us to stop thinking and simply look for evidence of 'instinctive' patterns. But centuries-long experience should by now have convinced all of us that such an enterprise is a waste of time. Why persist in the face of evidence to the contrary? Behaviouralist science — being fundamentally deterministic — may have revived the theory of instinct in the hope of retaining its determinism. This is why we are invited to stop 'arguing', which means 'stop raising questions about what behaviouralists are doing'. The very request to stop arguing is non-rational.

Postscript

Political Theory and Political Freedom: The Problem of Prediction

Theories of behaviour give a useful index of general normative attitudes within the society in which they are held. For instance, although there has been no diminution of aggression in democratic society, there has been a shift in normative attitudes. The notion of 'survival of the fittest' which struck the Victorians as a sound biological theory, because it reflected current social attitudes, has now been replaced by studies of commensalism, ecology and the interdependence of species. Our society may

[84]*Ibid.*

be more violent that that of the nineteenth century, but it disapproves of unrestricted competition and aggression as a way of life.

One expects such parallels between theories of behaviour and norms because the concepts behind them are necessarily subjective interpretations of complex phenomena rather than descriptions of observable regularities, such as are possible in the world of physical phenomena which fit the cause-effect pattern. The only choices open to us in the study of behaviour, as distinct from change in general, are either to verbalize as accurately as possible each situation studied as if it were unique and hope that an accumulation of such studies will reveal regularities (behaviouralism) or to interpret it in terms of the normative-conceptual system which represents man's goal-seeking behaviour, but does not wholly explain even individual behaviour.

If we reject behaviouralism as a misguided attempt to apply the methodology of the physical sciences to phenomena which do not fit the pattern of physics and chemistry, we are nonetheless still working with a conceptual system which evolved, apparently, as a method of controlling and directing individual (rather than the State's) behaviour. That is, even if political theorists are willing to assume that men adopt norms which have for the individual holding them the characteristics of 'natural law' norms rather than relativist ones, we cannot assume that organized political society is capable of holding such norms.

There is, in fact, good reason to suppose that the norms of the sovereign power cannot be the same as those of the society's members. If we allow this possibility, we cannot be assured that the norms of the political power have any of the characteristics of individual norms — which means that predictions possible with regard to the individual's normative behaviour are not necessarily possible in regard to the State. Thus, though we can predict a good deal about an individual's responses to new situations (if we know his norms), we can infer very little about State policy from the State's constitution and profession of principles.

Nonetheless, the norms of an ideologically based State affect its actions: we can distinguish between non-democratic and democratic States if we stop assuming that all the legislation and policy of the democratic State must accord with democratic principles. In so far as the normative behaviour of the State is concerned, we must allow for a greater influence of non-normative, pragmatic factors than in the case of the individual. We define an individual who is only occasionally honest as dishonest, but we define a State which is only sometimes democratic as 'realistic'. To the extent that a democratic State is realistic and pragmatic, its policy is unpredictable.

'Pragmatic' policies are cause and effect policies and are the special field of the behaviouralist. If he can predict at all, it is when a State consciously pursues such a policy. The theorist, on the other hand, is not only incapable of making predictions about pragmatic policy-making but is often hostile to its being exercised. He sees it as an abandonment of direction and a threat to the very existence of the democratic State as an entity distinguishable from other States and worth preserving as an ideal.

The difficulty is that while a 'pragmatic' policy on the part of an individual can be called unprincipled and opportunistic, the same cannot be said about a State. Because of man's sense of time, he is capable of much longer-range goals than the mere satisfaction of innate drives felt by other species and consequently he feels the need for a much greater control over his environment. In order to attain our goals within our sense of a limited time span for doing so, we need to exercise as much control as possible over the environment (which can force us back into cause and effect behaviour). Man has always striven to subdue or coerce 'nature' in order to reach his private goals. (The following can be viewed as a yardstick: when we hear about the necessity of adjusting to nature we know that we are living in a period when norms are losing their importance.)

But if man has had some success in reducing the interference of environment with the attainment of his private goals, the same cannot be said about the State. As regards control over the international environment, the position of modern States has not changed much over the centuries. This is not to say that there has been no change in readiness to co-operate and avoid hostilities. Most States are no longer exclusively or predominantly characterized by expansionist tendencies. Yet although norms of international relations are evolving, their impact is often weak. So long as it is necessary to talk of 'realism' and 'pragmatism' — the need to make an appropriate response to non-normative situations arising in the world of cause and effect — it is unrealistic to talk about the necessity of international law. We can no more expect a nation faced with a serious economic threat from another State to abide by norms of international law than we can expect regular church attendance during a flood.

Normative behaviour — whether of the State or individual — requires control over factors requiring 'adjustment' (cause and effect rather than planned responses) and insofar as there is little control over such factors, political behaviour becomes unpredictable. In this respect, it differs from the type of change occurring in the physical world. There, in order to be able to predict the outcome of interacting factors, man needs no control over the factors involved (except in a purely technical sense). An acid interacts with a base to give a salt plus water. There is no other possibility — no choice in the matter. It is the absence of choice which allows accurate prediction. (We can try to predict where there is a 'choice' factor at work, but our prediction will be subject to error.)

Because the issue of 'prediction' in the social sciences requires a definite stance on the degree of 'choice' open to men, conjectures about prediction strongly affect attitudes to freedom. Thus it is perfectly possible for a social scientist pursuing the goal of 'pure science' to promote anti-democratic attitudes. Indeed, much of the adverse criticism of both Marxism and behaviouralism arises from the recognition that each in its own way is incompatible with democratic ideology, as well as with scientific principles.

Little now need be said about Marxian historical determinism. The view that norms derive from, rather than give rise to, historical situations converts the individual's norms from goals he might choose to attain into descriptions of patterns of behaviour which he is persuaded to uphold. His sense of 'freedom' is an illusion and any determination on his part to hold to the norms in the face of official ideology is evidence (to those in power) of his unenlightened condition. The notion of historical determinism entails anti-individualism, for the capacity of the individual to make right choices is taken from him when the normative bases of choice are exposed as inappropriate to the 'good' society established by revolution. Knowing the nature of norms as supplied by Marxian theory, the good Communist can be 'free', provided he acts in accordance with ideology and does not allow norms derived from earlier historical conditions to influence his decisions; he cannot allow 'private conscience' to influence his decision-making in the way it not only can, but must, do under the democratic conception of society. It is not the private conscience and its norms that must direct social and political policy in the communist world but knowledge derived from dialectical materialism. No one but the initiated has the necessary 'freedom'; hence the 'good' society — or the truly 'free' society — must encourage ideological purity among its members and insist on it during the process of decision-making.

Behaviouralists begin with a different notion of 'prediction'; consequently their notion of 'freedom' differs from that of the communist world. Their 'science' is peculiarly well adapted to current democratic views about the nature of choice and hence that of 'freedom'. The behaviouralist is necessarily a relativist to whom the relationship between norms and past, present or future behaviour is so uncertain that he prefers to ignore these norms and seek the real springs of behaviour in an 'objective' study of the latter — that is, uninfluenced by any conception of norms and their significance.

Whether this is possible is not the issue here. What matters is that behaviouralism encourages the view that men are 'free' only to the extent that their behaviour is unpredictable and that, at those points where prediction becomes possible, men are not 'free' but have their behaviour determined for them by factors of which they are not aware (until behaviouralism later reveals them).[85]

The defect of both the Marxian and behaviouralist viewpoints as 'scientific' approaches to the study of political behaviour is that they embody self-fulfilling prophecies. They become the

---

[85] It may turn out that there are no such factors. Behaviouralists are not convinced that their studies will ever be more than particular descriptions of the way men have behaved at particular points in time. The 'freedom' which they promote is consistent only with relativistic views according to which norms represent impulses of unknown origin and unknown influence on behaviour. This view ignores that freedom requires the possibility of a rational choice between alternatives.

foundation of normative attitudes: those who begin merely with the hope of studying political behaviour in a scholarly and 'scientific' manner end by promoting an attitude to freedom which is incompatible with democratic conceptions.

'Frontiers' of Democratic Theory

The issue which has long faced democratic theory is the division between those thinkers who wish to reorder 'classical theory' to fit the fact that men are not in fact equal and those who hold the view that democratic theory requires some kind of actual equality. It seems strange, however, that the issue should remain at the forefront of the theorists' preoccupation.[86] True, new evidence of inequality keeps accumulating and new attempts to explain it away become necessary to those who feel that some kind of 'factual' equality represents the necessary basis of a democratic society. But why is the issue of factual equality or inequality still at the 'frontier' of theory? Recurrent discussions of 'normative equality' would be perfectly understandable. Normative equality is part of the normative system we call 'democracy and as such requires reconsideration as new situations arise. But the persistence of discussions of 'factual' equality and inequality as if they were essential to the concept of democracy requires some comment.

In the first place, empirically-centred research — almost universal today — is capable of dealing only with 'factual' equality. Although discussions of modern empirical research represent the issue as a conflict between 'classical theorists' and some kind of 'revisionists', the factorization necessary in sociological studies of groups — distinctions based on income, housing, occupational class, etc. — necessarily focuses attention on kinds of inequality that have little to do with classical theory. It is quite true that if it were not for the theory of sovereignty, factual inequality would be a serious embarrassment to democratic theory. If 'democracy' had to mean, or could mean, government of the people by the people, the factual inequalities would raise serious doubts about its normative assumptions and even its

[86]Which is, for instance, suggested by the contents of Henry S. Kariel's anthology *Frontiers of Democratic Theory* (New York, 1970).

viability as a form of government and society. But classical democratic theory arose within the framework of a concept of sovereignty which excludes the possibility of literal government of the people by themselves. The issue of factual inequality is a modern one, but that does not really make it a new frontier.

However, the methodology and assumptions used in empirical social science have tended to make the issue of factual equality a major problem in democratic societies. The demands being pressed by many groups today are not for 'equality' of treatment, but for such treatment that the *result* will be 'equality', which can be equated to proportionate representation in the standard categories social scientists apply when investigating society. Thus some insist that so long as there are fewer professionals among the blacks, so long as income levels do not parallel those of the whites and so long as there are distinctive black and white residential areas, there must be some sort of discrimination at work; furthermore, that it is the role of government so to legislate that the social scientists' categories no longer reveal a racial pattern.

Now this notion of 'equality' and these demands for equalitarian treatment bear little resemblance to traditional notions. But the consequences for a democratic society faced by such demands can be quite serious. Factual equality is not attainable by a complex industrial society and, indeed, is hardly desirable so long as there are many different notions of the good life. Yet the demand exists and it is the task of political theory to face it. At present, social scientists in general are creating the very problems they are seeking to solve, but political theorists offer few comments.

In attempting an answer, the problem that the theorist must tackle is that 'environment' is the 'cause' and that the solution is to alter circumstances so that they disappear. From his point of view, so long as our society supposes that the manipulation of society will solve problems, it will not be able to do so regardless of its technical resources, since the problem does not lie in the environment. For him, the problem of what limits should be set to equalization in society has been posed by those who look at men and society in a certain way; that is, in order to raise the question of the limits to equality, he must first deny that the problem is primary. For him the primary problem is that our democratic society must first alter its view of what constitutes a social problem.

Attention needs to be given to certain other aspects of the division of theorists into 'classicists' and 'revisionists', and to the attendant issue of the state of democratic theory. What is rather striking is the parallel between the present situation in democracies and the historical response of the Roman Catholic Church to heresy. For centuries the Church was able to allow divergent teachings and practices without losing its essential unity. Despite what Protestant polemicists have since said, the Church historically was a remarkably tolerant institution embracing a wide range of views. As a general proposition, we might say that 'tolerance' is necessary to successful government, whether the government relates to spiritual welfare or secular well-being. But the Catholic Church reached a point in its history where the policies that had worked for centuries seemed only to increase its problems and strengthen opposition to it. The argument that the forms and practices of the Church were those of the 'true' church and that it had the right to coerce heretics did not strengthen its position. Ultimately, the Church ceased to be the most powerful spiritual organization. Was it undermined by its opponents who demanded reform, or by something else?

To say, as adverse critics have since done, that the Church responded to demands for reform simply — and belatedly — by attempting to repress its detractors is not quite true. What can be described as the Catholic Reformation had its roots in the period antecedent to Protestantism; furthermore, the techniques now employed by democratic governments faced with demands for 'reform' were employed by the Church, as one would expect of an institution which has survived to the present day. The problem the Church faced, however, was that much of the criticism was a symptom, rather than a cause, of the disaffection; hence, it was impossible to carry out the 'reforms' demanded. The trifling theological issues raised by critics could hardly have been the real issues, for they differed from community to community and from time to time, exactly like modern demonstrations for and against particular issues and policies do. Indeed, it is easier to see what the real issues were by examining the different directions taken by Catholic and

Protestant communities than by studying theological debates. (Broadly, it is not true that the opposition had (and has) a clearer conception of what was wrong than the authority it opposed). But political theory cannot await the judgement of history on society's current difficulties. What we need to recognize is that the very mutliplicity of different issues raised demonstrates that the issues are not 'real' and that an attempt to deal with them by 'reforms' based on the objections made will solve little.

What such an attempt does achieve is to split theorists into two camps — the classicists and the revisionists. Their respective positions resemble the positions adopted by the Protestants and Catholics in the past. The classicists, like the Puritans, argue for a return to purity of principle, though it is by no means clear what the pure principles of democracy are. The revisionists argue that we should retain faith in democracy as it is — a system which has inherited and upheld the original conception — but adapt it to practical realities. To them much of democracy is ritualistic (they speak, for instance, of 'legitimation devices') but the ritual has significance in terms of democratic traditions. What this orientation towards the ritualistic side of democracy entails is the attitude that democratic institutions, practices and policies are the 'right' ones because 'democracy' is the best form of government. Just what 'democracy' is, and how well its institutions and policies reflect the ideal, are questions that ought not to be asked: they are treated not as genuine questions but as evidence of disaffection or heresy.

The revisionist development in theory tends to dissolve into behaviouralism, which derives its premises about society from similar conceptions of democracy. Consequently the division in political science is not between two branches of theory, but between theorists and behaviouralists. The split between the two gives every sign of being permanent, unless a conscious effort is made to resolve it. The task of reconciling the two is a major problem facing political theory. But a political theory capable of achieving this aim will be different from the theory we know now. It will not be able, for instance, to commit itself to notions of democratic 'purity' and ignore the facts about life in a modern democracy. This does not mean that the theorist must become more of a pragmatist. What is required is a recognition that however different theory and behaviouralism may seem, they both represent attempts to understand, and respond appropriately to, conditions within society which are based on assumptions about norms they hold in common. There are serious obstacles standing in the way of a reconciliation: the behaviouralists tend to appeal to scientism and relativism in support of their position, whereas the theorists reject both modes of thought. Furthermore, the split between them reflects a division in society which cannot be resolved in the same way as the former divergence of religious viewpoints. It has proved quite possible to have one secular State and two or more religious organizations, but it is not easy to conceive of one State and two or more warring social ideologies operating within its bounds over the long run.[87]

Can Democratic Theory Re-order Society?

The strength of political theory is that it has always rested on the 'commonsense' view — suggested by introspection and empirical evidence — that we have a conception of a self extending in time; that we can choose to act in different ways; that we try to choose in accordance with self-interest; and that we use norms as statements about our self-interest. This attitude is general. No matter what philosophy has to say about the 'commonsense' view, philosophers themselves act upon it. (No determinist in truth *acts* as if he were a determinist, or a relativist as if he were one.) Given these facts about human behaviour, democratic theory is the only approach to the analysis of political behaviour capable of offering guidance that makes sense to the public. For this reason, unless their language is too abstruse, books on theory can influence public consciousness — an influence which behavioural studies can never achieve.

[87] One particular aspect which almost rules out reconciliation is connected with the consequences of belonging to one of the two groups into which society is divided. Malcolm Muggeridge has drawn attention to the fact of 'how difficult it is, in an ideologically polarized society like ours, to take up any position without being automatically assumed to hold all the views and attitudes associated with it.' *Chronicles of Wasted Time Part I: The Green Stick* (London, 1972, p. 273). Professionally, a political scientist is labelled as either a behaviouralist or a theorist and the fact of being so classified makes it difficult for him to gain acceptance of views which do not conform with the category into which he has been placed.

What exactly is it that democratic theory can convey? We can define democratic theory as the bringing to bear upon prospective human political and social behaviour of the experience and analytical power derived from man's past. It would be untrue to say that we do not need such information or that behavioural studies show better what men actually do. It is not just 'what we do' that matters. What matters is the making of decisions; and to make them on a basis other than that of trial and error we must have political theory. Its importance is not likely to disappear unless we suppose that the norms upon which democratic theory is based will cease to operate.

Can democratic theory re-order society? The best that a theory of determinist-based social science can offer is an explanation of what we are doing and a prediction of what we will do. Insofar as the prediction proves false, the theory is false. It cannot possibly serve as a guide to the re-ordering of society because, like everything else, under determinism society simply changes and cannot be 'ordered'.

In asking whether normative political theory can precede social change and serve as a tool to re-order society, we are making a non-determinist assumption. At the same time we are making some kind of 'determinist' assumption: unless human behaviour is determined by something, neither prediction nor re-ordering is possible. (A wholly non-determinist viewpoint differs from that of the determinist in that it makes 'knowledge' of social change impossible [because in a non-determinist's view, which is based on free will, such knowledge does not apply to the future]. Both make knowledge 'functionless'. [Knowledge is functional if man can make choices.])

To escape this difficulty, normative political theory makes the 'commonsense' assumption that there are certain principles of behaviour — norms — of whose ultimate origin and nature we are not sure, but which in a way provide some general descriptions of behaviour. They not only make statements about things as they are, but also offer 'explanations' of men's behaviour and can serve as tools for making predictions.

The problem, however, is that there is a good deal of uncertainty about the scope — not to speak of the hierarchy — of norms. Democratic theory can hardly hope to serve as a reliable guide to the re-ordering of society so long as we do not know what position its norms (such as liberty and equality) occupy in the normative hierarchy. Furthermore, there are other factors which limit the application of political theory to political decision-making: political philosophers have not made it clear how the theory can be applied without reflecting the subjective preferences of the theorist. On the other hand, empirical studies — showing, for instance, that the voting public does or does not want 'school busing' — may seem more pertinent and trustworthy guides to decision-making than theoretical analyses choosing between the requirements of democracy and specific programmes.

Despite these uncertainties and difficulties, policy decisions have to be made. As they cannot be based on trial and error (or trial and error methodology disguised under the cloak of 'social experiments'), it is theory that ultimately prevails.[88] Considering the widespread hostility to theory — any theory — and the conviction that what we need are 'facts' about our society, this would be inexplicable if norms were simply subjective judgements — something we say about other men's behaviour. But they are not: they are principles for making choices. Without them, the only behaviour possible would be one directly related to the fulfilment of biological drives. In a democracy, then, political decision-making requires some kind of democratic theory, or an analysis of the interaction between democratic norms. If this is not supplied by specialists in the field, then those concerned with decision-making as well as those concerned with the results (primarily the public) must develop their own theories. Indeed, much of the unreasonable opposition to government by political activists in recent years has clearly been based on naïve theorizing about what democratic governments ought to do. (This, at any rate, is how they themselves have justified their position. We can dismiss these justifications as irrelevant only if we are determinists who deny that norms and the logic of norms *can* affect behaviour). Both the public and policy-makers have made serious errors of judgement as a result of naïve

[88] In democratic countries a large part of what we call the 'constitution' is clearly democratic theory. Democratic government represents not so much 'the wishes of the governed' as the requirements of democratic theory: the actual working constitution appears to embody the views of the upholders of the 'constitution' as to what democratic theory requires.

pseudo-theorizing that political theorists could easily expose as such. It is interesting to note, however, that the expert's opinion has not so much been rejected as not offered. Too may political theorists seem to see their discipline as parallel to the traditional view of theory in the physical sciences: as something that has no immediate practical application. Yet norms, unlike the ultimate particles and forces of physicists, are the *immediate* 'causes' of behaviour, the principles behind men's actions. Unlike the interaction of energy and matter in the physicist's conception of reality, the norms of the theorist do not order themselves. They are only as orderly in their interaction as the mind which orders them. If the theorist does not do this and fails to offer advice on the above basis, both the policy-maker and the public are left to their own devices. What often follows is unnecessary conflict, confusion and muddling through.

The Impact of Relativism

Once we admit that our society is inherently relativistic because of its present institutional forms, we must face squarely the central issue posed: that of decadence. A society is decadent when its government can no longer depend on the loyalty of its members: that is, on their conviction that the government and its policies are legitimate. When a society is capable of recognizing problems — for example, its potentiality to become overpopulated — but is prevented from solving them by the nature of its assumptions (egalitarianism in the above case) and has no way of resolving the issue because the normative order necessary to reaching a decision has disintegrated, it is decadent. When a society is incapable of solving problems except through coercion and is not expected to act in any other way, it is also decadent.

Use of the word 'decadent' here does not, of course, imply mere disapproval, but mainly that the society is not viable. There are limits to the degree of government coercion and failure to adjust that are open to a society when there are narrow limits to the loyalty of its members. At one time most people felt that these limits were set by the extent to which the practices of the government accorded with the wishes of the people — the consent theory — and the analysis of democracy has long been coloured by this supposition, if not predicated upon. Whether it ever had any substance is doubtful. It does not make much sense to speak of 'consenting' to be born into a particular form of social organization, or 'consenting' to a government one has voted against. But whatever the merits of the idea may have been, it is clearly not applicable when relativism is inculcated. Under relativism 'consent' is reduced to its elemental meaning of individual acceptance or rejection of particular proposals, of their according or not according with private wishes. No argument can convince a relativist that on general principles he should consent to the majority view, or consent to the policy of a democratically constituted government. There are no general principles. There can be no loyalties. Under relativism, loyalty is limited to issues entailing self-interest, and self-interest is determined by the self (in a narrow sense) — not by reason, normative considerations, or authority. This attitude is not a 'natural' one to which society has to accommodate itself. The evidence is convincing that we must be socialized into the extraordinarily limited concept of the self and self-interest that it entails. But under relativism it is inescapable. If theorists do not take this fact into account, and they do not even touch on this kind of consequence of relativism, they are not offering a relevant analysis of our society.

It is not easy to decide what place relativism will hold in future philosophic speculation. What we should keep in mind is that when relativism excludes its alternatives, men become ideologists, as they have today. They may not admit it, indeed cannot admit it, for relativism and ideological commitment are logically incompatible, but the necessity for taking action and having goals is a more binding requirement on man than living in accord with his world view. As a philosophic principle, relativism forces one into expediency, which in the modern ideologically-based State means an uncritical acceptance of life as it comes. The modern relativist philosopher has opted out of society while submitting to its aimlessness.

It is for philosophy to say whether the disappearance of the philosopher-gadfly is 'good' or not. In the modern megalopolitan State it would hardly seem to matter whether there are any: the modern State is designed to minimize the influence of the individual thinker.

The case is different when we consider society as a whole and the relativism of the 'influence' groups — principally the social scientists who supply information to the decision-makers. Here relativism is having disastrous consequences.

The great majority of social scientists, who are apparently acquiring more and more influence, are relativists in the sense in which most philosophers are. They may have come to their relativism, from a different approach — through the influence of scientism, anthropological and sociological findings or psychological assumptions — but they resemble the philosophers in denying the binding power of norms in a way which is not followed by the common man. This puts them in the philosophically untenable position of supplying the sovereign power with information that must lead to binding decisions while they themselves believe that such decisions can be defended only as 'rules of the game'. The role of the sovereign is to command, of the people to obey, and of the information-gatherers to reduce the coercive element as much as possible: outright coercion being an inefficient mode of conducting a game. This attitude ensures that no really useful information will reach the sovereign power, which needs a good knowledge of norms within the society if it is to be other than arbitrary. Modern relativism has thus created an unbridgeable gap between sovereign and society and helped to make modern democracy a great deal more coercive than its underlying principles will tolerate. Authorities today are not receiving the kind of normative information they need in what is, and must be, a normative-based society.[89]

A social science that is increasingly serving the interest of the social scientist by giving him an occupation is hardly defensible as a science. Too many sociologists and political scientists are like priests who have lost their faith and seek to defend their continuance in office on the grounds that they do no harm. It is

---

[89] David Easton has suggested a possible solution to the problem: the social scientist should become as committed as most other members of society; but he has not suggested a technique by which the social scientist can remain a social scientist while adopting a 'non-scientific' position. Nor has he proposed a technique by which the social scientist can select from the normative hodge-podge of society the norms to which he can commit himself. The social scientist's arbitrary commitment would render him useless — even dangerous — to the sovereign authority, who could well see him as a rival. Hence the social scientist is quite right to be 'conservative' in Easton's sense and avoid 'rocking the boat', even though he is not serving the public interest by doing so. At least he is serving his own interest.

hard to feel anything but indignation at the time-servers who advise government on its policies. As David Easton says, commitment is necessary, but if social scientists are to be both committed and scientists, they will have to review their relativism. It is logically impossible for the sovereign power to be relativist in the way modern social science thinks of him. It is improbable that the entire society will be relativist in the way that social scientists are relativist. Between the normativism of sovereignty and the normativism of society we cannot much longer have the kind of relativism we have. Whether we can have some other kind, it is hard to say.

Bibliography

Gabriel A. Almond and Sidney Verba, *The Civic Culture* (Little Brown, Boston, 1965).
Hannah Arendt, *Crises of the Republic* (Harcourt Brace Jovanovich, New York, 1972).
Robert Ardrey, *The Social Contract* (Atheneum, New York, 1970).
―――, *The Territorial Imperative* (Atheneum, New York, 1966).

Henry Bienen, *Violence and Social Change* (The University of Chicago Press, Chicago & London, 1968).
Pierre Birnbaum, Jack Lively and Geraint Parry (eds.), *Democracy, Consensus and Social Contract* (Sage Publications, London & Beverly Hills, 1978).
David Braybrooke, *Three Tests for Democracy: Personal Rights, Human Welfare, Collective Preference* (Random House, NewYork,1968).

Robert Claiborne, *God or Beast: Evolution and Human Nature* (W. W. Norton, New York, 1974).
Carl Cohen, *Democracy* (The Free Press, New York, 1971).
Charles F. Cnudde and Deane E. Neubauer (eds.), *Empirical Democratic Theory* (Markham, Chicago, 1969).

Robert A. Dahl, *A Preface to Democratic Theory* (The University of Chicago Press, Chicago, 1956).
Norman Daniels (ed.), *Reading Rawls* (Basil Blackwell, Oxford, 1975).
Lane Davis, 'The Cost of Realism: Contemporary Restatements of Democracy', *The Western Political Quarterly*, Vol. XVII, no: 1 (March 1964). Reprinted in Charles A. McCoy and John Playford (eds), *Apolitical Politics: A Critique of Behavioralism* (Thomas Y. Crowell, New York, 1967).
René Dubos, *So Human an Animal* (Charles Scribner's Sons, New York, 1968).

Bibliography

David Easton, *A Systems Analysis of Political Life* (John Wiley & Sons, New York, 1965).
Jacques Ellul, *The Political Illusion* (Alfred A. Knopf, New York, 1967).
Abe Fortas, *Concerning Dissent and Civil Disobedience* (The New American Library, New York, 1968).

G. David Garson, *Group Theories of Politics* (Sage Publications, Beverly Hills & London, 1978).
Hugh Davis Graham and Ted Robert Gurr, *Violence in America* (The New American Library, New York, 1969).
Kenneth W. Grundy and Michael A. Weinstein, *The Ideologies of Violence* (Charles E. Merrill, Columbus, Ohio, 1974).

H. Hirsch & D. C. Perry (eds.), *Violence as Politics* (Harper & Row, New York, 1973).
Barry Holden, *The Nature of Democracy* (Thomas Nelson, London, 1974).
Ted Honderich, *Three Essays on Political Violence* (Basil Blackwell, Oxford, 1976).

Karl Jaspers, *The Future of Mankind* [1958] (The University of Chicago Press, Chicago & London, 1963).

Henry S. Kariel (ed.), *Frontiers of Democratic Theory* (Random House, New York, 1970).
Hans Kelsen, 'Foundations of Democracy', *Ethics*, Vol. LXVI, no: 1, Part II (October 1955). Reprinted in W. J. Stankiewicz (ed.), *Political Thought Since World War II* (The Free Press of Glencoe, New York, 1964).
William Alton Kelso, *American Democratic Theory: Pluralism and Its Critics* (Greenwood Press, Westport, Conn., 1978).
Kathleen Kinkade, *A Walden Two Experiment* (William Morrow, New York, 1973).

Konrad Lorenz, *On Aggression* (Methuen, London, 1966).

Charles A. McCoy and John Playford (eds.), *Apolitical Politics: A Critique of Behavioralism* (Thomas Y. Crowell, New York, 1967).
Leslie Macfarlane, *Violence and the State* (Thomas Nelson, London, 1974).
W. J. M. Mackenzie, *Power, Violence, Decision* (Penguin, Harmondsworth, 1975).

C. B. Macpherson, *Democratic Theory: Essays in Retrieval* (Clarendon Press, Oxford, 1973).
——, *The Life and Times of Liberal Democracy* (Oxford University Press, Oxford, 1977).
——, *The Real World of Democracy* (CBC, Toronto, 1965).
Herbert Marcuse, *One-Dimensional Man* (Beacon Press, Boston, 1966).
H. B. Mayo, *An Introduction to Democratic Theory* (Oxford University Press, New York, 1960).
Kenneth A. Megill, *The New Democratic Theory* (The Free Press, New York, 1970).
Fred R. von der Mehden, *Comparative Political Violence* (Prentice-Hall, Englewood Cliffs, N.J., 1973).
Desmond Morris, *The Naked Ape* (Constable, London, 1967).

Reinhold Niebuhr, *The Children of Light and the Children of Darkness* [1944] (Charles Scribner's Sons, New York, 1960).
Reinhold Niebuhr and Paul E. Sigmund, *The Democratic Experience: Past and Prospects* (Frederic A. Praeger, New York, 1969).
H. L. Nieburg, *Political Violence* (St. Martin's Press, New York, 1969).

Carole Pateman, *Participation and Democratic Theory* (Cambridge University Press, Cambridge, 1970).
J. Roland Pennock and John W. Chapman (eds.), *NOMOS XVI: Participation in Politics* (Lieber-Atherton, New York, 1975).
John Plamenatz, *Democracy and Illusion* (Longman, London, 1973).
Nelson W. Polsby, *Community Power and Political Theory* (Yale University Press, New Haven, 1963).
Kenneth Prewitt and Alan Stone, *The Ruling Elites: Elite Theory, Power, and American Democracy* (Harper & Row, New York, 1973).

David Ricci, *Community Power and Democratic Theory: The Logic of Political Analysis* (Random House, New York, 1971).
John Rawls, *A Theory of Justice* (Harvard University Press, Cambridge, Mass., 1971).
Neal Riemer, *The Revival of Democratic Theory* (Appleton-Century-Crofts, New York, 1962).

Giovanni Sartori, *Democratic Theory* (Wayne State University Press, Detroit, 1962).

Joseph A. Schumpeter, *Capitalism, Socialism and Democracy* [1942] (Harper & Row, New York,1962).

Yves R. Simon, *Philosophy of Democratic Government* [1951] (The University of Chicago Press, Chicago, 1961. Midway reprint 1977).

B. F. Skinner, *Walden Two* [1948] (Macmillan, New York, 1962).

———, *Beyond Freedom and Dignity* (Alfred A. Knopf, New York, 1971).

David Spitz, *Patterns of Anti-Democratic Thought* (The Free Press, New York, 1965).

W. J. Stankiewicz, *Aspects of Political Theory: Classical Concepts in an Age of Relativism* (Collier Macmillan, London, 1976).

———, (ed.), *In Defense of Sovereignty* (Oxford University Press, New York, 1969).

———, (ed.), *Political Thought Since World War II: Critical & Interpretive Essays* (The Free Press of Glencoe, New York, 1964).

———, 'Sovereignty', *Encyclopaedia Britannica*, 15th Edition, 1974, Macropaedia, vol. 17.

Herbert Tingsten, *The Problem of Democracy* [1945] (The Bedminister Press, Totowa, N.J., 1965).

Thomas Landon Thorson, *Biopolitics* (Holt, Rinehart and Winston, New York, 1970).

———, *The Logic of Democracy* (Holt, Rinehart and Winston, New York, 1962).

John C. Wahlke, 'Pre-Behavioralism in Political Science', *The American Political Science Review*, Vol. LXXIII, No. 1 (March 1979).

Eugene Victor Walter, *Terror and Resistance: A Study of Political Violence* (Oxford University Press, New York, 1969).

Edward O. Wilson, *On Human Nature* (Harvard University Press, Cambridge, Mass., 1978).

Robert Paul Wolff, *In Defense of Anarchism* (Harper & Row, New York, 1970).

———, *Understanding Rawls* (Princeton University Press, Princeton, 1977).

Robert Paul Wolff, Barrington Moore Jr. and Herbert Marcuse, *A Critique of Pure Tolerance* (Beacon Press, Boston, 1965).

Oran R. Young, *Systems of Political Science* (Prentice-Hall, Englewood Cliffs, N.J., 1968).

Howard Zinn, *Disobedience and Democracy: Nine Fallacies on Law and Order* (Vintage Books, New York, 1968).

Index

Acton, Lord, 114
Aggression, 111
Aggressiveness, 24-6, 45, 62
Almond, Gabriel A., 154, 154n; on democracy, 153-5; and democratic opinion, 155n; on types of political culture, 155n
Anarchism, 94, 97-8
Anti-rationalism, 5-7, 20, 21, 26; and relativism, 20-1.
Apolitical Politics: A Critique of Behavioralism (Charles A. McCoy and John Playford, eds.), 179n
Aquinas, Thomas: on coercion, 231-2
Ardrey, Robert, 42, 42n
Arendt, Hannah, 54n, 62; and determinism, 58-9; on human nature, 55-7; on power, 55-60; on violence, 54-9
Aristotle, 237
Arunta, 211n
Aspects of Political Theory (W. J. Stankiewicz), 5n, 17n
Authority, 255; and democracy, 94-7; and group theory, 184; and 'instinct' school, 173; and participation, 162-3; and relativism, 94-7; Yves R. Simon on, 229
Ayer, A.J., 63

Bachrach, Peter, 199n
Baratz, Morton, 199n
Barber, Benjamin R., 216n; and prudentialism, 216-7; on Rawls, 217-8
Bay, Christian, 19n, 199n
Behaviouralism: and democracy, 150-7, 158-9; and democratic ideology, 245; and determinism, 113; and empiricism, 233-4; and freedom, 246-7, 246n; limitations of, 151-9; and methodology, 158; and norms, 231-3; and political realism, 181; and political theory, 158-9, 235; and reason, 174, 240-2; and relativism, 20, 246-7, 251; and scientism, 41n, 251; and Yves R. Simon, 232-3; and social scientists, 182; and violence, 41-2, 57-8, 60-1
Behaviouralists: and freedom, 246; versus political theorists, 250
Behaviourism: Watson's, 115
Bentham, Jeremy, 92, 200
Berlin, Isaiah, 86
Bienen, Henry, 19n
Biobehaviouralism: and evolutionary theory, 239-40; and 'instinct' theory, 239-42; perils of, 237-42

263

Biopolitics (Thomas Landon Thorson), 133, 133n, 137
Biosociology, 237-8; and Wahlke, 235n
Birnbaum, Pierre, 167n
Brave New World (Aldous Huxley), 114, 114n, 115
Braybrooke, David, 87n; on democracy, 87-93; on freedom, 87; and relativism, 87-93; on rights, 87-91
Braybrooke's 'Paradigm', 93
Bronowski, J., 199n; on scientific theory, 199
Bushmen, 211n

Capital Punishment, 189n, 205, 218
Capitalism, Socialism and Democracy (Joseph A. Schumpeter), 65n
Catholic Church: tolerance of, 249
Chapman, John W., 176n
Children of Light and the Children of Darkness, The (Reinhold Niebuhr), 71n 73
Chronicles of Wasted Time Part I: The Green Stick (Malcolm Muggeridge), 251n
Church: and democracy, 98-9; and natural law, 2; and reform, 249-50; and the State, 98-100, 126; and tolerance, 104-6
Citizenship: and democracy, 177; and group theory, 185; Kateb on, 167; and minorities, 185; and participation, 167-70; 177; Rawls on, 225-6; and rights, 184-5; van Gunsteren on, 167-9
Civic Culture, The (Gabriel A. Almond and Sidney Verba), 153, 154n, 155
Claiborne, Robert, 42, 42n
Cnudde, Charles F., 151n 159n; and empirical democratic theory, 157-8; and empirical theory, 153
Coercion, 23, 25, 26, 29, 30, 34-6, 39, 59, 60, 61, 106, 110, 111, 220, 221, 254; and government versus the individual, 110; and ideology, 36; and political obedience, 34-6; Yves R. Simon on, 231-3; and the State, 23, 29, 34-6, 59, 61-2, 84, 106, 110; and violence, 29, 30, 31, 39
Cohen, Carl: on democracy, 12-4
Cole, G. D. H., 160
Community Power and Democratic Theory: The Logic of Political Analysis (David Ricci), 186n, 190n
Comparative Political Violence (Fred R. von der Mehden), 52n
Concerning Dissent and Civil Disobedience (Abe Fortas), 36n
Connolly, W. E., 199n
Consent, 60, 61, 83, 254-5; and determinism, 60; and power, 152; and relativism, 255
Contract Theory: and participation, 175-6; and sovereignty, 176
Cooke, Alistair, 90n
Copernican Theory, 199
Coser, Lewis A., 44
Cram, Ralph A., 129, 130
Crisis of the Republic (Hannah Arendt), 54n
Critique of Pure Tolerance, A (Robert Paul Wolff, Barrington Moore, Jr and Herbert Marcuse), 103n

Index

Dahl, Robert A., 24n., 154n.; on democracy, 153-4; on human nature, 24; on power, 186
Daniels, Norman, 214n, 216n
Darwin, Charles, 61
Davis, Lane, 179n.: on democracy, 179-80; on political realism, 179-80
Democracy: Almond on, 153-5; and anarchism, 97-8; and authority, 94-7, 99; and behaviouralism, 15, 150-7, 158-9; Braybrooke on, 87-93; and capitalism, 84-5; and citizenship, 177; classical theory, 65-70, 160, 162, 179; and coercion, 30-1, 106; Carl Cohen on, 12-4; Dahl on, 153-4; Davis on, 179-80; defence of, 22, 117; and determinism, 233; and egalitarianism, 15, 18; and electoral system, 117-33; and eligibility for office, 120-1; and empirical theory, 153-5; and equality and individualism, 33; and ethical behaviour, 106; and franchise, 119-29; and freedom, 15; and games theory, 139-40; and government, 8, 154; Holden on, 17; Honderich on, 219-22; and individualism, 18; Jaspers on, 100-1; and justice, 221; Kelsen on, 99; and legislated morality, 106; and legislation, 224; and liberty, 108; Lippmann on, 131-2; C. B. Macpherson on, 82-7, 120-1, 200-12; and majority rule, 33; and Marxism, 245-7; H. B. Mayo on, 118-27; Megill on, 164-6; Niebuhr on, 71-7; and norms, 11, 101-2, 104, 106-8, 117, 192; and obligations, 195-200; and participation, 13, 13n, 97-8, 154-5, 192; Plamenatz on, 195-200; and pluralism, 193; and political theory, 10; and power, 82, 83, 221; and private conscience, 33; and procedures, 195-200; and property, 84-5; and protestantism, 68-9, 73-4; and reason, 1; and relativism, 2, 4-5, 11, 16-7, 19, 20-1, 64-93, 132; without relativism, 74; and rights, 195-200; and rule of law, 109-13; Schumpeter on, 65-71; Yves R. Simon on, 228-34; and social contract, 172; Spitz on, 129-33; and the State, 243-4; as superideology, 80-2; and systems theories, 143-50; theory of, 9-12, 18; theory and norms, 9-12; Tingsten on, 77-82; and tolerance, 98-108; and totalitarianism, 83, 224; Verba on, 153-5; and violence, 19-63, 19n, 218-22
Democracy (Carl Cohen), 12, 13n
Democracy and Illusion (John Plamenatz), 195, 195n
Democracy, Consensus and Social Contract (Pierre Birnbaum, Jack Lively and Geraint Parry, eds.), 167n
Democratic Experience: Past and Prospects, The (Reinhold Neibuhr and Paul E. Sigmund), 75, 76n
Democratic Order: and ideological tolerance, 108
Democratic Society: and behavioural engineering, 114-5
Democratic Theory: and anarchism, 94, 95; approaches to,

18; and behaviouralism, 182; and decision-making, 253-4; defined, 252; and equality, 247ff; and equality and liberty, 19; and human nature, 61-3; and participation, 160ff; and political realism, 178-81; and property, 203, 209; and 'pure politics', 181-3; and relativism, 64-93, 254-7; and sovereignty, 63; and violence, 61-3

Democratic Theory: Essays in Retrieval (C. B. Macpherson), 206n, 209n

D'Entrèves, A. P.: and natural law, 4

Determinism, 169; and behaviouralism, 113; and consent, 60; and democracy, 233; and equality, 212ff, 214n; and freedom, 111, 212ff; and human behaviour, 111, 233; and human nature, 214; and justice, 111; in C. B. Macpherson, 86-7; and power, 58-9; and punishment, 112, 112n; and reason, 174, 212-6, 240-2; and rule of law, 111-3; and social contract, 213; and society, 252-7

Determinism, Historical, 181

Difference Principle (Rawls's), 222, 224, 225, 226

Disobedience and Democracy: Nine Fallacies on Law and Order (Howard Zinn), 37n

Divine Right of Kings, 16

Dred Scott Case (1857), 198

Dubos, René, 238n, on culture, 238

Duties: and participation, 161; and rights, 121-2, 197

Easton, David, 134n-135n, 147n, 235n, 256n; on input-output system, 147-50

Egalitarian Norms, 27

Egalitarian Society, 26; doctrinaire nature of, 35

Egalitarianism, 21, 25, 33, 81, 83, 114-6, 197, 202; and democracy, 18; and electoral system, 119; institutionalized forms of, 25; and property, 207-8; and relativism, 14-7, 205; and restricted eligibility for office, 129; and universal franchise, 124, 127; in Walden Two, 207

Electoral System: and democracy, 117-33; and egalitarianism, 119; and eligibility for office, 127-9; and equality, 118ff; and freedom of choice, 124; as fundamental norm, 121; and justice, 121-2; Lippmann on, 131-2; H. B. Mayo on, 118-27; and party system, 127-8; and relativism, 119

Eligibility for Office: and democracy, 120-1; restrictions in, 128-9

Ellul, Jacques, 163n; on participation, 163-4

Empirical Democratic Theory (Charles F. Cnudde and Deane E. Neubauer, eds.), 151, 151n

Empirical Research: and equality, 247-8

Empirical Theory: Cnudde on, 153; and democracy, 153-5; Neubauer on, 153

Empiricism: and behaviouralism, 233-4; and group theory, 184; limitations of, 138ff, 157-9; and political theory, 157-9; and power, 152-3; and

self-other propositions, 188-9; and solipsism, 188
Equality, 6, 10n, 33, 71, 85, 101, 102, 116, 117, 131, 143, 160, 170, 205, 207, 209, 221, 222, 225, 253; as conceptual framework, 11, 12; and democratic theory, 247ff; and 'democratic violence', 220; and determinism, 212ff, 214n; and electoral system, 118ff; and empirical research, 247-8; and empiricism, 158-9; framework of, 12; Honderich on, 219-22; literal, 15, 126, 213, 219, 227; as norm, 10, 94-6; and participation, 161; of power, 63; and property, 202-3; Rawls on, 226-8; and rights and duties, 161; Yves R. Simon on, 228-34
Equality of Opportunity: and Rawls, 226
Essays in the Public Philosophy (W. Lippmann), 3
Ethics: and political science, 191n; and relativism, 176-8
Evolution: theory of, 42

Fisk, Milton, 214n; on freedom, 214; on Rawls, 214
Fortas, Abe, 36n; on dissent and political obligation, 36-9
Franchise, 6; and democracy, 119-29; restricted, 120-1, 124-5; and self-interest, 122-3; universal, 119, 121-7, 161; arguments for universal, 121ff
Fraternity, 10n, 170
Frazer, James G., 46
Freedom, 10n, 73, 87, 101, 103, 117, 131, 160, 209, 219, 222, 224; and behaviouralism, 246-7, 246n; as conceptual framework, 11, 12; and democratic violence, 220; and determinism, 111, 212ff; Fisk on, 214; and Marxian historical determinism, 245-7; as norm, 10, 94-6, 102; and political theory, 62-3; Rawls on, 214, 215, 216; religious, 98; Yves R. Simon on, 228-34; and violation of law, 110; and violence, 29, 43
Freedom of Assembly, 10
Freedom of Choice: and electoral system, 124
Freedom of Speech, 10, 89, 91, 126, 214, 215
Freedom of Thought, 103
Free-will, 115
Freud, Sigmund, 5, 56, 111n, 115, 194; his theory, 61, 64
Freudian Determinism: and science, 116n; and the State, 171
Freudian Theory: and the individual, 171
Fromm, Erich, 59
Frontiers of Democratic Theory (Henry S. Kariel), 247n
Functional Analysis: limitations of, 46-9
Functionalism: limitations of, 144-7; as systems approach, 144-7; Oran R. Young on, 145-7
Future of Mankind, The (Karl Jaspers), 101n

Games Theory: limitations of, 138-9
Garson, G. David, 183n, 184n; on group theory, 183-4
General Will, 5, 32
God or Beast: Evolution and Human Nature (Robert Claiborne), 42, 42n

Golden Bough, The (James G. Frazer), 46
Government: and democracy, 8, 154; and laws, 110; and participation, 154-5; and power, 55; and rights and duties, 122; and sovereignty, 44; as system of justice, 221; and transfer of power, 117ff; influence of voters on, 125
Graham, Hugh Davis, 19n, 127n, 60
Group Theories of Politics (G. David Garson), 183n
Group Theory: and authority, 184; and citizenship, 185; and empiricism, 184; Garson on, 183-4; and legitimacy, 185; and minorities, 185; and neopluralism, 183-95; and power, 184; and rights, 184-5; and sovereignty, 185ff; and the State, 185
Grundy, Kenneth W., 40n, 42, 43, 44; on violence, 40-6
Gulliver's Travels (Jonathan Swift), 141
Gurr, Ted Robert, 19n, 27n, 60

Hayek, F. A., 80
Hegel, Friedrich, 180
Hempel, Carl G.: and empiricism, 236
Hereditary Rule, 117-8, 119, 126-7
Hirsch, H., 19n, 26n
Hobbes, Thomas, 29, 42, 48, 49, 57, 73, 74, 86, 217, 218; and authority, 163; and human behaviour, 7, 123; on human nature, 123, 194; and natural law, 2; and prudentialism, 216; and reason, 2; and relativism, 3; and social contract, 171, 174, 194; and state of nature, 174, 195; and violence, 44-6
Holden, Barry, 17n; on relativism and democracy, 17
Holmes, Justice: on freedom of speech, 89
Honderich, Ted, 218n; and democracy, 219-22; and equality, 219-22; on violence, 218-22
Human Nature, 55-7, 58, 61-3, 75, 123, 214; and participation, 170-2; and violence, 41-3, 45
Human Rights, 172
Hume, David, 5
Huxley, Aldous, 114, 115, 142

Ideologies of Violence, The (Kenneth W. Grundy and Michael A. Weinstein), 40, 40n, 41n, 44, 45
Ideology, 22; and coercion, 36; and normative inter-relationships, 83; and norms, 83; and relativism, 65; and sociological relativisim, 80-1; and the State, 71; and tolerance, 100
In Defense of Anarchism (Robert Paul Wolff), 96, 96n
In Defense of Sovereignty (W. J. Stankiewicz, ed.), 5n
Individual: and norms, 243-7; and the State, 255
Individualism, 117, 132, 143; and democracy, 18, 33; and determinism, 111; and Marxian historical determinism, 245-7; in modern society, 22-3; as norm, 94, 95; and property, 208-12; and relativism, 197; and social contract, 174-5; and welfare, 93

Index

Input-Output System: Easton on, 147-50
Instrumentalism: and relativism, 113
Introduction to Democratic Theory, An (H. B. Mayo), 118n

Jaspers, Karl, 101n; on democracy, 100-1; on tolerance, 101
Joad, C. E. M.: on empiricism, 188
Justice, 216, 223; and democracy, 221; and 'democratic violence', 218-22; and determinism, 112n; and electoral system, 121-2; Fisk on, 215; and interest groups, 168; Niebuhr on, 74; and policymaking norms, 140; and power, 218-22; Rawls on, 218, 225-8; and rights and duties, 121-2; and rule of law, 111

Kant, Immanuel, 218
Kariel, Henry S., 247n
Kateb, George, 167n; on citizenship, 167
Kelsen, Hans, 78n; on democracy, 99; and philosophic relativism, 78; and relativism, 79, 99
Kelso, William Alton: on pluralism, 191-5
Kinkade, Kathleen, 114-6, 115n

Ladd, John, 176n; on participation, 176-7
Laski, H. J.: on pluralism, 169
Law and Order, 3n, 21, 23, 26, 172; and majority rule, 108; and relativism, 108
Legitimacy: and group theory, 185; and relativism, 58; and violence, 53-4

Liberty, 22, 132, 253; Rawls on, 226; and tolerance, 108
Life and Times of Liberal Democracy, The (C. B. Macpherson), 169n, 200, 200n
Lindsay, A. D.: on norms, 72
Lippmann, Walter, 129, 130; and democracy, 131-2; and electoral system, 131-2; and natural law, 4; and relativism, 3, 3n-4n
Lively, Jack, 167n
Locke, John: on property, 84, 208; and social contract, 174
Logic of Democracy, The (Thomas Landon Thorson), 133
Lorenz, Konrad, 42, 42n, 237
Luther, Martin, 73, 74
Luttbeg, N. R., 184n

McCloskey, H., 184n
McCoy, Charles A., 179n
McDougall, W.: instinct theory, 237
Macfarlane, Leslie, 59n; on Arendt, 59; on power, 59-61
Mackenzie, W. J. M., 49n; on violence and decision-making, 49-52
McLuhan, Marshall, 137
Macpherson, C. B., 15n, 169n, 200n, 204n, 206n, 209n; on democracy, 82-7, 120-1, 200-12; and deterministic relativism, 82-7; and developmental democracy, 203; and equilibrium democracy, 204; on norms, 72; and participatory democracy, 169-70, 203-5; and property, 200-3, 205-12; and protective democracy, 200ff; and relativism, 204-5

Machiavelli, Niccolo, 48
Majority Rule, 15, 64, 95, 117, 119, 131, 132, 162, 172, 182; and conformity, 23; and democracy, 33; and egalitarianism, 197; and minority rights, 6; as norm, 11; and private conscience, 32; and reason, 6-7; and referendum, 93; and relativism, 20-1, 108, 197; as a technical device, 64; and violence, 51
Marcuse, Herbert, 11n, 12, 62, 103n; on 'the free society', 11n; on participation, 170-1; on tolerance, 103-6
Marx, Karl, 54, 56, 85, 169, 180; and democracy, 83
Marxism: and democratic ideology, 245; and C. B. Macpherson, 200, 201, 211; and the State, 171; and study of political behaviour, 246
Mayo, H. B., 118n; on democracy, 118-27; and electoral system, 118-27; and transfer of power, 118-27
Maximin Rule (Rawls's), 216-7, 227
Megill, Kenneth A., 164-6, 164n
Mencken, H. L., 90n
Michels, Robert, 199n
Milbrath, L. W., 184n
Mill, John Stuart, 160, 204n
Minogue, Kenneth, 172n; on social contract, 172-3
Moore, Barrington, Jr, 103n
Morris, Desmond, 42, 42n
Mosca, Gaetano, 199n
Mount, Ferdinand: on freedom, equality and fraternity, 10n
Muggeridge, Malcolm, 251n

Naked Ape, The (Desmond Morris), 42n
National Commission on the Causes and Prevention of Violence: report of, 27-8
Natural Law, 74, 96, 135, 243; and the Church, 2; Hobbes on, 2
Natural Rights, 117
Nature of Democracy, The (Barry Holden), 17n
Neo-pluralism, 183-95; and Dahl, 186-7; and group theory, 183-95; and power, 186-91; and relativism, 188-91; and sovereignty, 186-7
Neubauer, Deane E., 151n, 159n; and empirical theory, 153, 157-8
New Democratic Theory, The (Kenneth A. Megill), 164, 164n
Niebuhr, Reinhold, 71n, 73, 76n; on democracy, 71-7; and determinism, 76-7; on justice, 74; and relativism, 71-7
Nieburg, H. L., 19n; on violence, 26n, 44-5
1984 (George Orwell), 114, 114n, 115
NOMOS XVI: Participation in Politics (J. Roland Pennock and John W. Chapman, eds.), 167n
Normativism, 97; and historical determinism, 86-7
Norms, 168, 169, 176-8, 180, 181, 182, 183, 185, 196, 197, 198, 199, 201, 202, 203, 205, 206, 211, 212, 216, 218, 222, 225, 226, 227, 228, 229, 231, 233, 234, 244, 252, 253, 254; and absolutism, 101, 102; and democracy, 101-2, 106-8, 114, 192; democratic, 71; and facts,

7; and freedom of speech, 89; and the individual, 2; Lindsay on, 72; and C. B. Macpherson, 72, 83, 86-7; and Marxian historical determinism, 245-7; nature of, 104; and political science, 191n; and positive law, 3n; and post-behaviouralism, 235; and reason, 3, 8; and relativism, 2, 5, 28, 75-82, 192; relativistic, 188, 191; and social conditions, 79-80; and social scientists, 236; and the State, 135, 135n; in Tingsten, 78-82; and theories of behaviour, 242ff; and tolerance, 106; verification of, 41; and 'welfare', 92

Obligations: and democracy, 195-200
Occam's Razor, 226
Olson, M., 184
On Aggression (Konrad Lorenz), 42n
One-Dimensional Man (Herbert Marcuse), 11n
One Man-One Vote, 123-7; alternatives to, 9; relativist conception of, 9
Orwell, George, 115-6, 207; on power, 114

Pareto, Vilfredo, 92, 199n
Parry, Geraint, 167n
Partial Theory, 138-41; and decision-making, 140
Participation: and authority, 162-3; and citizenship, 167-70, 177; and classical theories of democracy, 160-1; and contract theory, 175-6; defined in terms of democracy, 192; and democratic process, 166-7; and democratic theory, 97, 160ff; and 'duty' 161; Ellul on, 163-4; interchangeable with equality, 161; and human nature, 170-2; Ladd on, 176-7; C. B. Macpherson on 169-70; Pateman on, 160-2; and radicalization, 164-6; and reason, 178; requiring relativism, 163; as protest against relativism, 176-8; and rights and duties, 161; and social contract, 172-6; and sovereignty, 161-3, 176; and the State, 161
Participation and Democratic Theory (Carole Pateman), 98n, 160n
Participation in Politics (J. Roland Pennock and John W. Chapman, eds.), 176n
Participatory Democracy, 143; C. B. Macpherson on, 203-5; and trade unions, 13n-14n
Pateman, Carole, 98n, 160n; on participation, 98, 160-2
Patterns of Anti-Democratic Thought (David Spitz), 129n
Pavlov, Ivan, 115
Pennock, J. Roland, 176n
Perry, D. C., 19n, 26n
Philosophy of Democratic Government (Yves R. Simon), 228, 228n
Plamenatz, John, 195n, 199n; on democracy, 195-200
Planning Debate, 80
Plato, 134, 205
Playford, John, 179n
Pluralism, 51, 152; and corporate theory, 194; and democracy, 193; Kelso on, 191-5; and laissez-faire theory, 194; Laski on, 169; and Marxism, 193; and participation, 168;

and participatory democracy, 192; and power, 193; Ricci on, 186; and sovereignty, 192, 193; and theory of State, 195
Political Illusion, The (Jacques Ellul), 163n
Political Obligation: and coercion, 34-6; and ideology, 100; and obedience, 34-6; and relativism, 37-9
Political Realism: and behaviouralism, 181
Political Theorists: and behaviouralists, 250; and equality, 159
Political Theory: and authority, 134; and behavioural analysis, 155; and behaviouralism, 158-9, 235; and behaviouralist determinism, 173; and democracy, 9, 10; when not democratic, 203; and empiricism, 157-9; and freedom, 62-3; and group theory, 183-5; and human behaviour, 251; misleading conception of, 200; and political freedom, 242-7; and relativism, 64-93; 192, 254-7; and re-ordering of society, 252-7; task of, 5; Thorson on, 133-7; 'traditional' theory, 15
Political Thought Since World War II (W. J. Stankiewicz, ed.), 78n
Political Violence (H. L. Nieburg), 19n, 26n
Polsby, Nelson W.: rule of pluralist theory, 186-7; on stratified power, 152
Positive Law: and norms, 3n; and reason, 3
Post-behaviouralism: and norms, 235

Power: actual and potential, 190n; Arendt on, 55-60; and consent, 152; controls on, 222; Dahl on, 186; and democracy, 82, 221; and 'democratic violence', 218-22; and determinism, 58-9; and empiricism, 152-3; as essence of government, 55; and group theory, 184; and justice, 218-22; indefinite limits of, 70; Macfarlane on, 59-61; and minorities, 185; and neo-pluralism, 186-91; and pluralism, 193; and property, 202; and redistribution of wealth, 222; influence of relativism on the limits of, 70; Ricci on, 186; and social change, 223n, 224-5; and sovereignty, 47-8, 152-3; systems of, 83-4; transfer of, 22
Power, Violence, Decision (W. J. M. Mackenzie), 49n
Prediction: and attitudes to freedom, 245
Preface to Democratic Theory, A (Robert A. Dahl), 24n, 154n
Prisoner's Dilemma, 174
Problem of Democracy, The (Herbert Tingsten), 77, 77n, 79
Property, 91; in C. B. Macpherson, 84-5; and totalitarianism, 222-5; in Wolff, 222-5
Prudentialism: and Hobbes, 216; and Rawls, 216ff; and social contract, 216-22; and utilitarianism, 217
Ptolemaic Theory, 199
Public Philosophy, 3, 4, 131; and reason, 9
Pye, L. W., 184n

Rawls, John, 62, 217n, 218n; on

citizenship, 225-6; critics of, 212-28; and difference principle, 222; on equality, 216, 225-8; Fisk on, 214; and freedom, 214, 215, 216; on justice, 218, 225-8; on liberty, 226; and maximin rule, 216-7; and prudentialism, 216ff; on reason, 215, 216; and theory of State, 222; and utilitarianism, 217; and violence, 218-21
Reading Rawls (Norman Daniels, ed.), 214n, 216n
Real World of Democracy, The (C. B. Macpherson), 120
Realism, 9; and relativism, 181
Reason, 135n.; and behaviouralism, 174, 240-2; and communication, 8; and determinism, 174, 212-6, 240-2; and freewill, 212; Hobbes on, 2; and human behaviour, 174; and instinct theory, 240-2; and majority rule, 6-7; as methodology, 8; and non-rational behaviour, 7-9; as norm, 116; and norms, 3, 8; and participation, 178; and positive law, 3; and rational normative behaviour, 4; and rationalization, 7, 115; Rawls on, 215, 216; application of under relativism, 2; excluded under relativism, 107; 'illegitimate' under relativism, 132; and tolerance, 6, 107
Reason, Age of, 8-9
Referendum, 93
Relativism: and absolutism, 80-1; and anti-rationalism, 20-1; and authority, 94-7; and behaviouralism, 20, 246-7, 251; and Braybrooke, 87-93; and consent, 254-5; and decision-making, 177-8; and democracy, 2, 4-5, 11, 16-7, 19, 20-1, 132; and democratic theory, 64-93, 254-7; and egalitarianism, 14-7, 205; and electoral system, 119; and ethics, 1, 176-8; future of, 255-7; and government power, 70; and simplification of Hobbesian scheme, 2-3; influence of, 2; and instrumentalism, 113; and legitimacy, 58; in C. B. Macpherson, 82-7, 204-5; and natural law, 3; and neopluralism, 188-91; and norms, 1, 5, 15, 21, 28, 134, 192; and participation, 163, 176-8; and participatory democracy, 204ff; and political obligation, 37-9; and political theory, 64-93, 192, 254-7; influence of on power, 70; and realism, 181; and reason, 2, 107, 132; and rights, 89-91; in Schumpeter, 65-71; and Yves R. Simon, 229; and social scientists, 256; and decadent society, 254-5; and sovereign power, 256-7; in Spitz, 130-1; in Tingsten, 77-82; and tolerance, 64-5, 104-6, 107; and violence, 28; and voting, 2
Ricci, David, 186n, 190n; on neo-pluralism, 190n; on pluralism, 186; on power, 186
Right of Free Assembly, 90
Right to Vote, 161
Right to Work, 12
Rights: Braybrooke on, 87-91; and citizenship, 184-5; defined as norms, 88; and democracy, 195-200; and duties, 197; and equality, 161; and group theory, 184-5; and property,

208, 210, 211; and relativism, 89-91; and Thrasymachus, 185
Rights and Duties, 121-2; and voting, 9
Roucek, Joseph S., 44
Rousseau, Jean Jacques, 160, 205, 227; and common good, 169; and General Will, 32; and social contract, 174
Rule of Law: and coercion, 109-11; and democracy, 109-13; and determinism, 111-3; and enforcement, 110; erosion of, 108-13; and free choice, 111; and justice, 111; nature of, 109-10, 113; and prudentialism, 111-2; and rational choice, 108-13; and responsibility, 111; and self-interest, 110-1; and violence, 110
Russell, Bertrand, 205

St Francis of Assisi, 5-6
Schumpeter, Joseph A., 65n, 69n, 160, 199n; on democracy, 65-71; and relativism, 65-71
Science: and Freudian determinism, 116n; and solipsism, 189
Scientism, 64; and behaviouralism, 41n, 251; and human behaviour, 136; and systems theory, 143-4
Self, 84-5, 174-6, 188, 189, 189n, 191, 202, 207, 208, 208n, 209, 211-2, 255; and rule of law, 111; versus society, 109-13, 111n
Shaka, 45-8; and functional violence, 48-9
Sigmund, Paul E., 76n
Simon, Yves R., 228n; on authority, 229; and behaviouralism, 232-3; and coercion, 231-3; on 'common good', 228-34; on democracy, 228-34; and 'free will', 232; and relativism, 229
Skinner, B. F., 114n, 232; and instrumentalism, 113-4
So Human an Animal (René Dubos), 238n
Social Contract, 171-2, 183, 214; and determinism, 213; and Fisk, 215-6; Hobbes on, 174, 194; and individualism, 172, 174-5; Locke on, 174; and Minogue, 172-3; and participation, 172-6; and prudentialism, 216-22; Rawls on, 62; Rousseau on, 174; and the State, 172-3
Social Contract, The (Robert Ardrey), 42
Social Sciences: prediction in, 242-7; and relativism, 15; and violence, 42-6
Social Scientists: and anti-democratic attitudes, 245; and behaviouralism, 182; and norms, 196, 236; and relativism, 256
Sovereign Power: Easton on, 150
Sovereignty, 69-70, 195, 235; and classical democratic theory, 248; and democratic policy, 33; and democratic theory, 63; and government, 44; and group theory, 185ff; Hobbesian, 62; and law and order, 29; neo-classical definition of (W. J. Stankiewicz), 5n; and neo-pluralism, 186-7; and participation, 161-3, 176; and pluralism, 192, 193; and power, 47-8, 152-3; and relativism, 256-7; and tolerance, 107
Sovereignty, Theory of, 247; and

Index 275

democratic theory, 97
Spitz, David, 129n; on the 'average man', 129-30; on democracy, 129-33; and relativism, 130-1
Stankiewicz, W. J., 5n, 17n, 78n; neo-classical definition of sovereignty, 5n
State: and behaviour control, 7-8; and the Church, 126; and coercion, 23, 29, 56, 61-2, 84, 106; State's coercion and political obligation, 34-6; and community, 167; and democracy, 243-4; and democratic norms, 7-8; and dissent, 71; and Freudian determinism, 171; and group theory, 185; and ideology, 71; and the individual, 172-3, 174, 175-6, 255; and justice, 106n; and law and order, 108; and legislated morality, 106; and normative order, 31; and norms, 135, 135n, 243-5; and opposition, 135n; and participation, 161; and property, 85, 209-12; and social contract, 172; theory of, 222; and tolerance, 105, 108; and violence, 29-31, 40, 55
State, Theory of: and pluralism, 195
Swift, Jonathan, 141, 142
Systems Analysis of Political Life, A (David Easton), 147n
Systems of Political Science (Oran R. Young), 145n
Systems Theories: and democracy, 143-50; limitations of, 141-4

Teilhard de Chardin, Pierre, 136
Teleology, 14, 145n
Territorial Imperative, The (Robert Ardrey), 42n
Terror and Resistance: A Study of Political Violence (E. V. Walter), 46, 46n
Theory of Justice, A (John Rawls), 216n, 218n, 222
Thorson, Thomas Landon, 133n; on communication, 136-7; on political systems, 134n-135n; and political theory, 133-7
Three Essays on Political Violence (Ted Honderich), 218n
Three Tests for Democracy: Personal Rights, Human Welfare, Collective Preference (David Braybrooke), 87n
Tingsten, Herbert, 77n; on democracy, 77-82; and sociological relativism, 77-82
Tolerance, 64, 249; and democracy, 98-108; and democratic society, 107; and ideology, 100; Marcuse on, 103-6; as norm, 104-6, 197-8; and relativism, 64-5, 104-6, 107; and sovereignty, 107; and theory of knowledge, 106; and toleration, 105
Totalitarianism, 172; and democracy, 224; and power, 83; and property, 222-5; and social change, 223, 223n; and tolerance, 104
Trade Unions, 182; and participatory democracy, 13n-14n

Understanding Rawls (Robert Paul Wolff), 222n
Unreason, 4
Utilitarianism: and prudentialism, 217; and Rawls, 217

Van Gunsteren, Herman, 167n;

on citizenship, 167-9
Verba, Sidney, 154, 154n, 184n; on democracy, 153-5; and democratic opinion, 155n; on types of political culture, 155n
Vintage Mencken, The (Alistair Cooke, ed.), 90n
Violence, 108, 135n, 183, 205; in American society, 24ff; Arendt on, 54-9; and behaviouralism, 41-2; and coercion, 29, 30, 31, 39; as confrontation of two relativisms, 32; and democracy, 19-63, 19n, 218-22; and democratic theory, 18, 19ff, 61-3; and determinism, 112, 112n; and evolution theory, 42; and freedom, 29, 43; functional, 48-9; Grundy on, 40-6; Hobbes on, 44-6; Honderich on, 218-22; and human nature, 41-3, 45; justification of, 31, 39ff; and legitimacy, 53-4; Mackenzie on, 49-52; and majority rule, 51; Nieburg on, 26n, 44-5; and normative order, 22, 23; Rawls on, 218-21; and relativism, 28; and rule of law, 110; and social science, 42-6; and the State, 29-31, 40, 55; Weinstein on, 40-6
Violence and Social Change (Henry Bienen), 19n
Violence and the State (Leslie Macfarlane), 59n
Violence as Politics (H. Hirsch and D. C. Perry, eds.), 19n, 26n

Violence in America (H. D. Graham and T. R. Gurr), 19n, 27n
Vom Wesen und Wert der Demokratie (Hans Kelsen), 78n
Von der Mehden, Fred R., 52n; on comparative political violence, 52-4
Voting, 182; and normative system, 132

Wahlke, John C., 235n, 238n; and behaviouralism, 235-42; and biosociology, 235n, 238, 242; and post-behaviouralism, 235n, 236-7
Walden Two (B. F. Skinner), 114
Walden Two Experiment, A (Kathleen Kinkade), 115n
Walker, J. L., 184n
Walter, Eugene Victor, 46n, 48; on violence in non-European societies, 46-9
Watson, John, 115
Wegener, Alfred, 234
Weinstein, Michael A., 40n, 42, 43, 44; on violence, 40-6
Wilson, Edward O., 238
Wolff, Robert Paul, 19n, 96n, 103n, 222n; on anarchism, 96; on property, 222-5; on Rawls, 222-5; and relativism, 96

Young, Oran R., 145-7, 145n

Ziegler, H. 184n
Zinn, Howard, 37n; on dissent and political obligation, 36-9